CAREER SERVICES TODAY

A DYNAMIC COLLEGE PROFESSION

CAREER SERVICES TODAY

A DYNAMIC COLLEGE PROFESSION

By C. Randall Powell
and Donald K. Kirts

THE COLLEGE PLACEMENT COUNCIL, INC.

ACKNOWLEDGEMENTS

THIS BOOK IS NOT the work of two authors writing behind cloistered doors. *Career Services Today* is an open book for which the authors sought advice and input from hundreds of people and publications.

We wish to thank the people behind the scenes who laid the groundwork for much of what is in the book—the members of the College Placement Council's Committee on Career Services Book, a special committee appointed to oversee the project. The committee was chaired with great skill by Alfred R. Looman (Valparaiso University). In addition to the authors, it also included Glenda F. Lentz (University of South Florida), Donaleah Fields (Houston Community College), Richard A. Stewart (Purdue University), Robert D. Safford (Arthur Young & Company), and Warren E. Kauffman (College Placement Council staff).

The committee met with, and without, the authors several times and gave us continued guidance, but at no point did we feel that they attempted to unduly influence our approach. It takes many hours to read, review, comment, and reread a manuscript this size, and the book is much the better for the committee's efforts.

Our mentor and editor was Warren Kauffman. Although most people recognize the hours that a project of this magnitude demands from authors, few realize the enormous work of an editor. His work was compounded because he had to merge sections written independently as well as jointly by two different authors. Warren Kauffman has done a remarkable job in integrating our styles, organization, and format. Certain parts of the book were affected by developments which occurred after the sections were written. The editor and Lynne Davis Battle, CPC's Manager of Governmental and Legal Affairs, drew the task of updating these sections just before the book went to press.

Before writing any one section, both authors sought the advice of several colleagues in and out of our institutions. We hope that readers do not assume that the concepts and practices presented are solely the ideas of the authors. There was so much input from literally hundreds of professionals in our field that we decided that naming each of them would be impossible. Rather than risk omitting a major contributor in this Acknowledgement section, we decided to offer each our personal thanks and a written acknowledgement for their input. The encouragement that we received from everyone we approached was inspirational.

Almost two years passed from the time we started writing to when the book went to press. The ones who feel the time pressures the most are family members. Don's wife, Suzanne, and their two daughters, and Randy's wife, Kathy, and their two sons surely felt our commitment to this project. We sincerely owe them a deep gratitude for their understanding and encouragement.

We are indebted also to two very special people. Frieda Robertson, the Office Manager of the Indiana University Business Placement Office, deserves our heartfelt appreciation for typing the majority of the manuscript no less than two times, editing, reviewing, critiquing, and inspiring our work. We want to express similar appreciation to Paulette McKenna, the Secretary in the Lafayette College Counseling Center, who filled a similar role for co-author Don.

We also want to thank the CPC leadership in 1977–78 for having confidence in our ability to start and finish this project. It was truly an honor for both of us to be asked to write *Career Services Today*. We only hope that we have lived up to everyone's expectations.

In conclusion, we want to officially state that we accept any and all limitations found in this book. It could never be all inclusive, but we do hope that we have properly distilled the gist of available data. We would like to invite all readers to submit their criticisms and suggestions to us. CPC will undoubtedly revise or rewrite this book as the profession grows and matures. Your suggestions will enhance future revisions.

C. R. P.
D. K. K.

FOREWORD

THE SUB-TITLE OF THIS book refers to the placement profession as "dynamic," which it is, and that explains why the book is being published at this time. The career counseling and placement field is undergoing continual change and growth in order to meet the changing needs of students and the other publics which the profession serves.

The original text on placement, published by the College Placement Council in 1962, was *The Fundamentals of College Placement*. By the end of the 1960s this book needed updating, so a CPC committee, after reviewing the needs of the profession at that time and noting the areas not covered in the first book, asked Everett W. Stephens of Babson College to bring *Fundamentals* up-to-date, and also to include more on principles and practices and career planning. The result was Stephens' *Career Counseling and Placement in Higher Education*, published in 1970.

Intentionally, Stephens' book did not dwell on the "nuts and bolts" aspects of placement, but the demand for information of this type prompted CPC to publish, in 1975, an operational handbook, *Career Planning and Placement Handbook*, written by James W. Souther of the University of Washington.

In an emerging profession no book on the subject remains current for long. Aware of the many changes taking place, CPC formed a committee to determine the nature of a book which would be more than an update of the previous books. What was needed, the committee decided, was more on career counseling, not just the theory but also the practice of counseling. The members agreed the book should also bring together, in one text, most of what is known about the principles and practices of placement, including the legal and financial aspects and information pertaining to professional development.

On the matter of authors, the committee decided the book would require two, one to write on counseling and the other on placement. Further, they were to be professionals who could write on the basis of their own extensive experience. Fortunately, the two whom the committee approached, Dr. C. Randall Powell and Dr. Donald K. Kirts, accepted the committee's invitation. Both have approached their assignment with enthusiasm and imagination. They immediately captured the intent of the book, as outlined by the committee, with the result that their final manuscript required almost no revision. Not only did each author cover his area in a thorough manner, but both recognized and provided for the differences in office operations and organizational structures.

Because it provides a detailed background on career counseling and placement, this book should be extremely useful for those just starting in the profession. It is not, however, intended solely for the inexperienced, for practitioners with many years in the profession will find a review of the book very helpful.

A. R. L.

College Placement Council Committee
on New Career Services Book

Alfred R. Looman, Chairperson
  Valparaiso University
Donald K. Kirts
  Lafayette College
Glenda F. Lentz
  University of South Florida
C. Randall Powell
  Indiana University
Donaleah Fields
  Houston Community College
Richard A. Stewart
  Purdue University
Robert D. Safford
  Arthur Young & Company
Warren E. Kauffman
  College Placement Council

CONTENTS

CHAPTER 2

Foundations for Effective Career Services 21

CHAPTER 3

Overview of Services 43

PART II

CHAPTER 4

Career Counseling   73

PART III

CHAPTER 5

Career Planning Resources 121

PART IV

CHAPTER 6

The Job Search Process 155

CHAPTER 7

Campus Interviewing Service   197

CHAPTER 8

Management of Career Services   217

CHAPTER 9

The Legal and Financial Environment   245

CHAPTER 10

Professional Development 277

CHAPTER 11

Role of Employers in Placement 299

CHAPTER 12

External Relations

APPENDIX

PREFACE

THE GOAL OF THIS book is to focus attention on the ideas, concepts, philosophies, principles, and practices followed by professionals in career planning and placement. A framework is presented that may be used by practitioners as a foundation upon which to construct a sound program. Although suggestions are offered to assist in technique and method, the detail is left to the practitioner. The techniques suggested are for illustration purposes and only suggest some of the approaches that have been used successfully by others. The methods represent a sharing of ideas with colleagues that the authors have gleaned from professional publications and personal experience.

Primary Audiences

The primary audience for this publication is the career planning and placement professional, both experienced and inexperienced personnel. An attempt is made to organize, define, and explain the many ideas and concepts accepted by most professionals in a manner that can be communicated to others. No claim is made for presenting fresh, profession-shattering concepts. The work represents a gathering of many loose ends, tried and proven practices, accepted principles, and abiding philosophy, which are molded together in a meaningful structure that may be useful to others.

A second important audience is counselors. Individuals involved in a wide array of different types of counseling such as academic, personal, or vocational may find the material helpful. Counseling of any type is rarely successful working in a narrow niche because clients frequently need help for several aspects of their personalities, not just a tiny portion of life planning. Life planning involves a total dimension.

The individual contemplating a career in the student personnel field should also find the book helpful. Individuals wishing to make a career in student personnel functions such as residence life, financial aid, registration, admissions, student services, or placement need an understanding of the career planning and placement functions since they are related to the total student personnel service.

As discussed later, the placement function impacts significantly upon the reputation of an institution, just as the reputation of the institution affects placement. Leaders in higher education may enhance their basic understanding of the potentially positive role of placement in the institution through a review of the material in this book.

The membership of the College Placement Council and its affiliated regional associations includes both private and government employers. Professionalism is equally as important for college relations staff personnel as it is for college personnel. Since the central focus of the material in this book is student-oriented, some might translate this to mean that it is "college-only" material. This generalization is false. Effective college relations for employing organizations begins with an understanding of college concerns, problems, and principles. Mutual sharing and common learning experiences will enhance professionalism for all personnel.

PART I

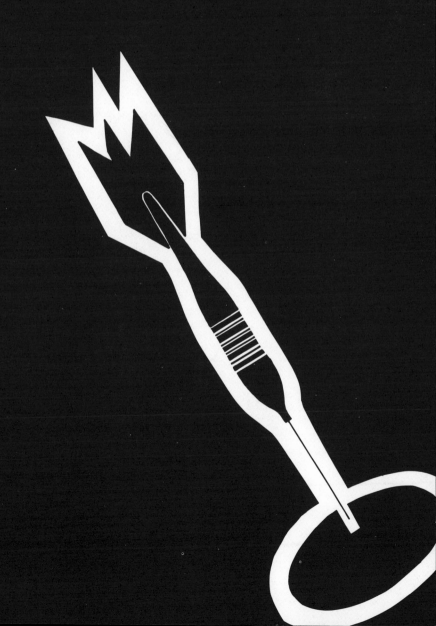

CHAPTER 1

CAREER PLANNING AND PLACEMENT

THE CAREER PLANNING AND placement profession stands at a crossroads. Changing economic and demographic environments dictate a reevaluation of future directions within the field.

Before the midfifties, a placement office on the college campus played an entirely different role than the placement office of the 1955–75 era. The next era promises still another approach. This ability to change directions demonstrates the dynamic and healthy position that the profession commands.

Where has the profession been? Where is it now? Where is it heading? This book provides some of the answers. More importantly, this book presents a definitive statement of the guiding philosophies and principles that form the foundation of the profession. Although everything in this book is not accepted by every professional in the field as the complete and sole truth, consultations with large numbers of leaders in the profession suggest acceptance in broad terms.

Placement is a profession. The placement function exists within the academic and administrative structure of nearly every institution of higher education. A profession may be defined as an occupation requiring advanced training in an accepted body of knowledge. A profession provides a service to a specific clientele, based upon special skills administered through an accepted code of ethics and standards. A set of practices, reflecting the philosophy, ethics, and standards, forms the common bond among practitioners. Some professions require initial and periodic examinations to insure adherence to the high standards established for the profession.

Placement professionals strive to meet all of the criteria typically found in a true profession. The foundation rests upon a strong vocational theory base and an extensive body of knowledge that continues to grow. The primary clientele consists of college students in varying levels of career development. The services offered to students impact greatly upon faculty, alumni, university leaders, and employers of college graduates. The total constituency, however, is much broader than the student body. A set of principles, ethics, and standards guides practitioners through a network of professional organizations which form the national College Placement Council, Inc. Regular training is provided through the regional placement associations and CPC to assist professionals in their desire to stay abreast of developments and maintain high levels of excellence.

New generations of leaders replaced the founding fathers years ago, and yet the placement profession continues to prosper. Change came but philosophy and principles remain. The strength of the profession and its associations comes from a constant sharing and renewing of common goals. Methods to achieve the common goals change slowly and differ only slightly, depending on an institution's unique qualities. Within the profession, the process of change has been more evolutionary than revolutionary but still readily attuned to current conditions.

Placement—Its Broadest Meaning

The term "placement" is a misnomer. The word is vague, misleading, restrictive, and implies selection of a job for a graduate. No placement office gets or gives graduates jobs. To get around this stigma, many offices have adopted other names. These new names include Career Counseling and Placement Office, Career Center, Career Services, Career Planning and Placement Office, or Office of Career Planning.

On the positive side, the term "placement" has national, almost universal, recognition. Employers use the term frequently, as do students, university leaders, and faculty members. Although the initial connotation leaves one frustrated and with a negative feeling, over the years the word has come to imply some extremely positive impressions.

Our dynamic marketing-oriented society wants brevity. Many acronyms contain expansive meanings that burst into multi-dimensional images when used. If the general population insists on using the word "placement," professionals in the field may just have to expand people's impression by promoting the true meaning of the term.

For brevity, placement is used throughout this book, but in its broadest meaning.

Definitions

Like the word "placement," there are other words that are bantered about within and outside the profession that have much broader meanings than each word standing alone implies. Several of these words need to be defined initially.

Job. Employment or work situation taken for the purpose of earning wages for completing a task, series of tasks, or a definitive piece of work. A job is often temporary in nature and rarely implies a long-term commitment to a given type of work. A job seldom requires a long training period before mastering the work assigned although this could happen in skilled trades and crafts.

Career. A work or vocational experience that an individual selects to pursue through life. The word implies a long-time commitment to a certain profession or occupation. It indicates advancement and achievement in a field that requires significant training before entering the profession. A career assignment normally requires completion of a college degree.

Planning. Represents devising a scheme for doing, making, or arranging a project, program, or schedule. Planning is a process that occurs over time. The plan may be revised as new information becomes available.

Counseling. A process by which an individual is assisted in assessing personal status and stimulated to evaluate alternatives, make a feasible choice consistent with personal circumstances, accept the choice, and initiate appropriate action.

Advising. The giving of information or instruction to help an individual direct judgment or conduct.

Placement. Part of the process of career planning that teaches individuals how to translate career goals into a plan of action designed to satisfy predefined objectives with a realistic view of the world of work. Placement involves an integration of an individual's self-concept and existing career options.

Placement is often viewed as a series of job-search-related activities such as resume preparation, contacting employers, interviewing, etc. Job search activities become extremely important in the career planning process because they provide one of the first real-life exposures to the career field. The placement activity often represents the first step in reality testing. If the placement activity begins early in the final academic year, sufficient time remains to compromise fantasies and realities and to revise a placement approach that is in keeping with the career objective and marketplace.

A key ingredient in the placement step is the employer. Employers usually accept the obligation to become part of the career exploration process. The placement function has the unique ability to bring together employers and students in roles other than interviewing. The employer's motive in hiring the most talented individuals is so strong that the firm wants to participate in the educational process.

Placement is often defined as a series of activities that are related to the employment process. The result is much broader. As noted earlier, placement is just one part of the career planning process.

Career Planning. An activity that occurs over a person's working lifetime. Career planning is distinct from life/work planning which attempts to integrate a much wider array of planning variables, such as family, religion, personal values, leisure, etc. in addition to work-related variables. For many individuals, not all, the process of separating work and non-work variables and then attempting to bring them together in a total life/work plan is essential. Career planning relates and focuses specifically on the working phase of an individual's life. If a proper approach is taken to career planning, particularly in self-assessment, the variables should fall into place.

Career Planning Process. A process involving three major activities: self-assessment, career exploration, and placement. Each activity may be completed initially as an independent project, but the career planning process cannot be optimally successful without viewing each activity as part of an integrated system. Important feedback loops in each activity tend to reinforce or modify earlier preliminary career decisions.

As the career planning process continues, compromises emerge. The self concept becomes better defined as new career information is processed. The job search activity adds significantly to the new career information bases. Specification, clarification, and compromise begin to firm up the overall career plan.

The initial phase of career planning is completed upon acceptance of an entry-level, career-related assignment with a specific employer. Another phase sets in as individuals replay the process as new work-related experiences add new information to the process. The reevaluation phases continue throughout life on a periodic, although unpredictable, basis. The figure below gives a graphical view of this concept.

Basic Philosophy

A philosophy consists of a framework of thinking about a body of knowledge that can be used to develop general principles governing the conduct of operating guidelines and prac-

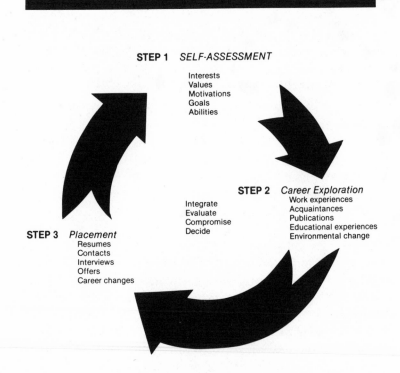

CAREER PLANNING CONCEPT

"Life-long Periodical Process"

STEP 1 *SELF-ASSESSMENT*

Interests
Values
Motivations
Goals
Abilities

STEP 2 *Career Exploration*

Work experiences
Acquaintances
Publications
Educational experiences
Environmental change

Integrate
Evaluate
Compromise
Decide

STEP 3 *Placement*

Resumes
Contacts
Interviews
Offers
Career changes

tices. Philosophy is the genesis of development of a system of principles designed to put concepts into operation.

The career planning, placement, and recruitment process—particularly as it relates to college students and college-trained individuals—is built upon a body of knowledge accumulated over a number of years and supported by a strong theory base. Professionals in the field regularly train others by sharing the concepts, philosophy, principles, and operational techniques.

The career planning and placement profession rests on a philosophical foundation consistent with the basic developmental theories of vocational choice and the free enterprise system. All constituencies being serviced by the profession operate in an environment where freedom of choice is imperative. The moderating influence among various constituencies is the concept of competition which generates the moderate degree of pressure needed to maintain progress.

The central philosophy of career planning is to teach students how to help themselves in the establishment of career objectives and in the implementation of procedures designed to satisfy career goals. The effectiveness of the career planning and placement function can best be measured by the educational value for students.

Career planning and placement strives for full employment of all graduating college students in career assignments that will best utilize the individual's talents and be consistent with previous educational training and life experiences. Career planning is a developmental process that occurs over the lifetime of an individual. The process is an on-going activity that continues to feed on self-assessment, career exploration, and placement activities. Successful career choices are based on a decision-making process that draws upon the exploration and placement processes to fulfill an individual's self-concept.

The decision-making process that leads to a free career choice can be aided by professional counseling which offers help in understanding the self-concept, presents career alternatives, and provides a medium to reality-test and revise career choices. Placement is an integral part of this counseling process.

The career planning and placement function is part of the educational role of development of the whole individual, a process that is not restricted solely to the employment function. The placement role in career planning serves as a laboratory to test, evaluate, and refine career choices. Placement operates within the instructional, research, and service modes common to all college environments. Career planning relies on the traditional methods of learning, including teaching, counseling, and research.

The career planning function on a college campus is service oriented. The primary constituency is students. To effectively serve the primary group, however, a number of other important constituencies must be served, including faculty, employers of college graduates, alumni, and university administrators.

The primary function of education is not to match college graduates to society's need for trained personnel. The most frequent reason given by college graduates for going to college is for upward mobility. These two statements appear to be incongruent. The moderator is not some bureaucratic dictator fiddling with people's lives, but is the individual college student who must make decisions affecting career choice with a high level of career awareness.

The proper role of a career counselor is to assist the student in acquiring a high level of career awareness. Students should recognize that a college degree does not guarantee a job upon graduation. What they do not know is how to translate interests, abilities, and aspirations into meaningful career decisions. The counselor's role is to assist in transferring a self-assessment into a career placement plan and to relate career goals to life goals.

Evolution of a Profession

Clearly, the placement function is not a new concept. The idea is as old as the universities. Prior to the dramatic increase in enrollments, most placement activity, including career counseling, was handled by college faculty members. Most faculty members developed a close working relationship with their students and, as the need for employment arose, referrals were made directly to potential employers. The "old boy" system functioned well until the number of students surpassed the ability of individual mentors to get to know graduates.

In the very early years, placement of graduates was not always a problem because many of the students came from upper-class backgrounds. Prominent families often placed their children in some aspect of the family business. A high percentage of other graduates went into the professions of medicine, law, ministry, and education. Many of the early U.S. schools were agrarian oriented and graduates often returned to the family farm to utilize many of the new technologies they had learned. Because of the small number of students, family ties, professional orientation, and concern by individual faculty, placement rarely presented major national concerns.

Early History

In the early years, the placement profession stressed on-campus recruitment for several reasons. During the Thirties and part of the Forties, the number of college graduates was small and yet few jobs were available. Given the attitudes of the times, faculty members and administrators literally beat the bushes to find employers to hire graduates. The placement professional, often a faculty member, made an effort to "polish" the graduates, many of whom came from agrarian backgrounds, to insure acceptability by potential employers.

As more graduates emerged after World War II into a prospering economy, a reversal occurred. Employers eagerly accepted invitations to visit campus. Placement offices took on the "appointment bureau" image and sometimes the name. Given the employer's desire to get more involved on campus, the membership rolls of the regional placement associations grew and conferences flourished. Although lean employment years were experienced in major recessions, most college graduates found employment quite readily.

The postwar baby boom brought ever-increasing numbers of children into elementary and secondary schools. Graduates not wishing to work in business or government easily found pleasant and secure, if not well paid, jobs in education.

Egalitarianism created the need for a system to deal with a major national problem. As the availability of higher education opened to the masses of the new, middle-class Americans, the faculty-student ratio dropped sharply. No longer could the "old boy" system be relied upon to assist in finding appropriate, career-related employment for graduates. A few of the better students found aid, but the large class sizes prevented individualized concern.

The children of blue-collar workers were graduating and relatively few of the families could provide jobs for their children. The industrial expansion, however, created greater needs for engineers, managers, educators, and professional personnel. Opportunities were available, but no organized way existed to bring college graduates and employers together. A need existed and placement, as we know it today, took its initial roots. The boom started by World War II and its aftermath fostered the birth of the profession. Although the profession is not new, the pattern that is used today is a rather recent phenomenon.

The moderating factor that held what could have been a chaotic situation together was the existence of professional organizations. Pioneers in the profession, from both colleges and employers, recognized the critical need for establishing a base built upon mutual trust and understanding. Communication between the parties created the trust and understanding.

The early leaders hammered out, both implicitly and explicitly, a set of guidelines to be used by employers, colleges, and students. Although a strong enforcement club in a free society is not possible, an honest and sincere effort by all three parties made the system function smoothly. Many of the earlier guidelines were accepted practices rather than philosophy or principles. The concepts were implicit in the way the practices were developed and used.

Contrasting Developments Worldwide

An interesting note is that many of the developing countries of the world today are just emerging to the point where America was 25 to 35 years ago. One important difference is that their educational systems have grown much faster than their industrial output. When governments encourage education without having a strong technological base to utilize highly trained talent, unhappiness and unrest may result. We are fortunate that in the U.S. economic growth, technological change, and educational advancement grew simultaneously with only a few imbalances caused by unusual cyclical patterns.

Several countries of the world view our placement system with a high degree of interest. Several U.S. placement professionals have, in fact, consulted with other countries that are trying to learn more about the career planning and placement programs. Ironically, the U.S. placement system grew within a free enterprise society without government support or intervention. The free interchange of ideas among private enterprise, education, and government built the backbone of the profession.

Evolving Changes

Until the mid-to-late-Sixties, the majority of placement offices stressed on-campus recruitment programs. When children of the postwar baby boom reached college age, enrollments mushroomed and the number of graduates began to exceed the demand for their services. The Vietnam war efforts absorbed huge numbers of graduating males for both the military and the booming economy. It became clear that, as the war died down, large numbers of college graduates returning from the military would need to enter the job market along with thousands of currently graduating students. During the 1967–77 decade, the supply/demand balance gradually shifted.

The placement profession changed tactics. Employers adopted different recruiting methods. When the baby boom passed, teachers no longer were in demand. Federal government employment plateaued. A higher percentage of high school graduates opted for college. Private-sector employment increased but not at previous rates. The result forced placement offices to take on more of a role of teaching students about career alternatives within the framework of supply and demand. The change meant teaching graduates about the world of work and how to objectively approach the initial employment situation.

The teaching and educational role for placement offices was not new. The emphasis just shifted from two-thirds of the activity being centered on campus interviewing to two-thirds being centered on the function of teaching graduates how to help themselves.

Some placement offices have courses for credit in career planning that date back over twenty years. Many placement offices always have held regular workshops in career planning and placement. These concepts really never gained much exposure or national concern until the shift in supply and demand. One of the early textbooks written by placement directors was *Planning Your Career* (1963) by John Steele and Robert Calvert.

The on-campus college recruiting concept is not dead. It is not going to die either. Employers need it and the profession has traditionally responded positively to the needs of members. The focus in the next decade may be on recruiting at universities with large enrollments, and recruiting graduates with specialties in engineering, science, accounting, business, and other select academic fields in which graduates are in short supply. This group of students constitutes a growing 30 percent or more of college graduates and needs to be served as effectively as possible by placement professionals.

Students affected most by the shift in the supply/demand balance are liberal arts and education majors at all degree levels. This group makes up about 50–60 percent of all college graduates and impacts greatly upon the small liberal arts colleges whose entire student bodies often fall into this group. Graduates going into professions in health-related fields seem largely unaffected.

Future Trends

The dramatic demand shift literally woke up the profession. For years, a few visionaries preached the importance of working with the whole individual. Learning is not confined to the classroom. The career planning and placement function is an integral part of the total education process.

Placement involves teaching and counseling, either individually or in groups, on each phase of the career planning process. The professional must find new methods and techniques to help clients evaluate themselves, new instructional ways to teach them to obtain career information, and new approaches to the actual employment process.

The placement professional of the future must be a concerned educator, a trained counselor, and a professional manager. Employers have an equal voice in matters impacting upon their concerns. Employers demand recruitment service from the colleges and students need the type of exposure the employer can offer the academic community.

Providing the high level of service needed implies that placement officials must be prepared to manage a significant recruitment program. Of course, the energies that any one school places in the recruitment function clearly must be related to the type of student body. Business, engineering, and technical schools must place a higher percentage of resources into the placement function than the liberal arts institution. An efficiently managed program should still leave more than half of placement resources available for the career planning function.

In summary, the early roots of the profession grew out of the close rapport of faculty and students. As graduating classes grew larger, the placement function became a shared relationship among faculty members, placement personnel, and students. On-campus recruiting consumed a significant amount of the placement office resources. The shift in the supply/demand ratio in the late Sixties and early Seventies swung the pendulum back toward more career counseling. The immediate goal is to strike some balance between the three components of the career planning process—assessment, exploration, and placement. All three activities represent integral and integrated parts of the activities of all placement operations.

The Regional Associations

The first cooperative association between employers and colleges began in 1926 as the Eastern College Personnel Officers. The stated objective by the five dedicated founders was "to promote professional improvement for the members through an interchange of information on common problems." The other six regional placement associations were organized in the 1947–52 era. Since employment in the U.S. is largely geographically oriented, the regional associations are organized according to state boundaries.

Prior to World War II only a limited number of colleges had placement offices, and very few employers had well-defined programs of college recruiting. Since World War II college placement and employer recruitment activities have had phenomenal growth. Although regional association constitutions differ in some respects, their common purpose is to sponsor conferences, workshops, committee activity, and research that will increase the professionalization of the various placement-recruitment functions.

There are seven placement associations, each self-governing and independent, in the United States:

ECPO—Eastern College Personnel Officers
MAPA—Middle Atlantic Placement Association
MCPA—Midwest College Placement Association
RMCPA—Rocky Mountain College Placement Association

SCPA—Southern College Placement Association
SWPA—Southwest Placement Association
WCPA—Western College Placement Association

While the criteria for membership vary, the associations generally admit placement educators representing two-, three-, and four-year colleges and universities and employer representatives actively engaged in the recruitment of college graduates.

The College Placement Council

In 1956, the seven regional associations formed a national confederation of placement associations, the College Placement Council, Inc. (CPC). The regional associations operate largely on a volunteer basis although a few have a paid executive secretary. Membership in a regional association is a prerequisite for membership in CPC, which represents approximately 6,000 employer and college constituents.

The Council is governed by the Board of Regional Governors, which is made up of two representatives from each of the associations—one college and one employer—and six officers.

A charter associate is the University and College Placement Association of Canada, which over the years has evolved into the CPC of that country. In addition, affiliate status is held by the National Association for Law Placement. At this writing, two other organizations were considering application for affiliate status: the Employment Management Association and the Association for School, College and University Staffing.

The non-profit Council maintains a staff in Bethlehem, Pennsylvania, to provide various services to the career planning, placement, and recruitment field. In its early years, CPC was primarily a publishing house, and it still produces the major publications in the field—the *College Placement Annual, Journal of College Placement, Salary Survey,* and twenty-some other directories, books, booklets, and audio and video cassettes.

Today, however, CPC is much more. It serves the field as its national voice and liaison with legislators and government agencies; it has instituted a growing professional development program involving institutes, seminars and workshops; it collects and interprets statistical data; and it maintains a Research Information Center which has the largest collection of information on college-trained men and women in the country.

Because legislation and governmental regulations have impacted placement and recruitment so dramatically in recent years, the Council opened a Washington office in 1978 in order to maintain a stronger presence in the Capital. The legal aspects of placement and recruitment have become so pervasive that a separate chapter is being devoted to the subject.

The CPC Foundation

The CPC Foundation is the research arm of the College Placement Council. The Foundation was organized in 1967 to obtain funding to underwrite special programs which, because of their magnitude, cannot be financed through the normal CPC operational budget.

A number of significant research reports have been produced on the career plans and realizations of college graduates. A new Foundation thrust is the generation of grants to underwrite special projects designed to promote professional development of practitioners and the career planning, placement, and recruitment function itself.

Proposals seeking grants are regularly made to corporations and foundations as part of a continuing fund-raising campaign. Regular proposals are also submitted to government agencies.

College Placement Services

College Placement Services, Inc., (CPS) was formed in 1964 as an outgrowth of the interests and activities of several persons who were members of the College Placement Council. The initial thrust of the CPS program was to establish and upgrade career counseling and placement services at the traditionally black colleges.

The program became fully active when it received a $310,000 grant from the Ford Foundation in 1965. This grant was followed by five additional Ford Foundation grants of varying amounts, some for general support of CPS and some for special projects. Since 1971, CPS financial support has come from over 180 corporations and corporate foundations and from assisting agency fees derived from grants made by the U.S. Office of Education under Title III of the Higher Education Act of 1965.

In 1969, CPS expanded its operations to provide services to all minority groups and to all two- and four-year colleges having substantial enrollments of minority students.

Since its inception, CPS has provided direct services to 124 colleges and universities. These have included 83 historically black four-year institutions, 28 four-year institutions with large enrollments of minority students, and 13 two-year colleges with large or predominant minority enrollments. At least 25 additional four-year colleges with large minority student enrollments have received limited services from CPS.

CPS' direct services to colleges include consultation, analysis, and evaluation of existing organization and procedures, and planning of future development or expansion of activities in the field of career counseling and placement. These CPS services are provided through on-campus visits of consulting teams.

To complement these direct services, CPS has been heavily involved in the training of personnel to operate career counseling and placement programs. More than 34 workshops and institutes of various types have been sponsored by CPS. These include: a graduate degree program in career counseling and placement which is offered at a university; two-week institutes that award academic credit at the graduate level; and one- and two-day workshops. Over 240 placement officers, counselors, and faculty members have participated in these various training programs. CPS also sponsors an annual conference for career counseling and placement officers of minority students.

CPS is also active in publications. Two most notable are *A Model Career Counseling and Placement Program*, which provides specific examples and guidance in implementing a comprehensive program (a third edition will be published in 1979), and *Handbook for Recruiting at Minority Colleges*, which is published biennially and provides much data about four-year minority colleges, including enrollments and graduating seniors by academic major and sex.

CHAPTER 2

FOUNDATIONS FOR EFFECTIVE CAREER SERVICES

THE EFFECTIVE DELIVERY of career services is a primary objective of career planning and placement professionals. The following discussion aims to explore certain aspects of successful career planning operations. The more specific procedural elements of placement are discussed later. The variety of activities and programs outlined are not applicable on all campuses but are intended to add to the resources from which the career counselor may draw in devising a tailored plan for a particular situation.

Organizational Setting

Institutions employing career counselors usually have stated educational missions which they are attempting to accomplish through various programs and services. Career counselors have the responsibility to help fulfill the educational mission, to assist in establishing priorities, and to reach the stated objectives of the organization. Career counseling is an integral part of the total organization, not standing apart as an adjunctive function, but remaining involved in the main stream of the educational enterprise.

Career counselors involved in the educational mission will be as active as possible in the total life of the institution. Serving on committees, assisting with other departmental programs, contributing where possible to curriculum development, and being involved in the extra-curricular life of the campus is typical. If career counselors wish to be considered full professionals on an equal footing with other professionals in the educational institution, they must behave as professionals in the life of the organization they serve. Counselors also must feel they are adequately supported by institutional priorities in order to work from a position of strength in assisting the individual student with career plans. This attitude and status of the career counselor will affect the quality of direct service.

The essential raw material of good counseling is the quality of the counselor's personality. Insofar as one feels relatively comfortable, fully functioning as a person and a professional, the counselor is in a position of relative strength and better able to provide a wide range of services dictated by the varied needs of the student. As career counseling personnel become more widely accepted by peers in the institution, greater credibility is developed for proposed programs and services. Career counseling, well conceived, is not offered in a vacuum but is centered fully in the life of the institution. Although this may appear idealistic, the goal is possible to achieve insofar as the service is needed by the student body.

Foundations for Program

The preparation of foundations for program development is essential in the educational institution experiencing tight budget controls. A mood of student consumerism is apparent today and it may be a powerful factor in favor of well planned programs in career services. The political strategy in developing this foundation must include student leaders who represent the largest segment of the college community and that segment on which the institution is primarily dependent for its very survival.

Regardless of the established roles and patterns of interaction of the professional personnel on campus, no one can deny the importance of persistent student need and demand for assistance in legitimate educational endeavors. At a time when many departments are threatened by low enrollments and when most service elements, including career counseling, are being held much more accountable for their existence, the importance of careful assessment of student need is underscored. Attention is to be given to those programs and services which attract students to the institution and continue to meet their wide-ranging educational needs.

One of the most frequent questions directed toward admissions personnel is, "What happens to your graduates?", or "What career services are available to students?" These matters are particularly crucial to liberal arts institutions but are also of vital concern to all responsible individuals in higher education. The career counselor who is charged with the responsibility of assessing needs and providing programs will profit by involving students on advisory councils, study groups, or planning committees to help provide the necessary data in the assessment of needs. Students and faculty interested in exploring the career development dimensions of campus life can be a powerful force in establishing priorities that affect budgets and provide for necessary facilities and service programs.

The counselor is known to be knowledgeable and proficient in the area of human relations. These skills may also be applied to assist institutions in developing valid programs that reflect the leadership's sensitivity to responsibility for meeting the needs of campus constituents. A program that is likely to be accepted by many segments of the organization will be one in which these various constituents have had some input to allow for a sense of "owning" the program. Using the best known skills of communication and group interaction, the career counselor is in a unique position to involve the various campus constituents in discussions of needs and proposed activities. Any career service program will be ahead if it is perceived as belonging to the campus, not simply fulfilling the needs of the career counselor.

Network of Resources

Career planning programs need to be recognizably systematic in organization and operation. Not only must each program element "fit" into the whole, but the entire network of campus resources for career planning should demonstrate an interagency cooperation that is harmonious and effective. An appropriate responsibility of career planning personnel is to identify, mobilize, train, and coordinate the various personnel in the college community. Providing for comprehensive programs calls for the consideration of all pertinent campus resources.

The career counselor should view the total "college experience" from the vantage point of a new student who is probably unaware of the well defined departmental organizations with their subdivisions and established interrelationships. It is helpful for the student to sense some logical ordering of activities for career planning assistance. From the counselor's perspective, there needs to be a sensitized network of "career assistants" who may, of course, have other primary roles to play in the college.

Ideally, the student can enter the career planning system at any point and activate the entire system. When all resource personnel, such as faculty advisors and residence staff, are adequately prepared to deliver direct service or refer the student to the appropriate resource, then the campus network approaches the goal of efficient delivery of career services. This has the effect, beyond the primary goal of assisting the individual student, of sensitizing or educating larger elements of the college community to career concerns and services.

The responsibility for initiating and maintaining high levels of understanding and training among the "career assistants" usually rests with career planning and placement directors. The career counseling professional orchestrates the system by providing for the various components, maintaining quality service throughout the system, and evaluating outcomes in relation to institutional and student goals.

Accountability

As career service professionals assume responsibility for ever larger and more vital functions, accountability must be kept in the forefront to develop a firm base for initial support and further development. Career planning programs need high visibility among all constituents to foster understanding and continued support. Misconceptions are to be expected and must be corrected by effective communication with professional colleagues and students.

The career counselor is accountable to the students who have needs in the area of career development. The counselor is also accountable to the institution as a client and to the educational mission of the institution. In planning for career development programs, cost effectiveness may become important in view of budgetary concerns. Attention to the development of external relations, as discussed in a later chapter, and carefully prepared data-based reports should assist in matters of financial support.

Proactive Approaches

Career counseling approaches need to be proactive, reaching out with activities to increase awareness of needs and services. The thrust is essentially preventive and developmental in an attempt to meet students early in the college experience at points of their perceived needs. The quality of pre-counseling contacts offered in awareness programs is paramount, for this is the point at which the prospective counselee begins to make decisions regarding the usefulness of the service and the nature of the staff.

The availability of assistance with career planning activities is announced initially through publications and contacts made by admissions personnel as they meet with prospective students. In order to develop and maintain high awareness of services available, the career counselor initiates contacts with persons on the admissions staff. Occasional joint staff meetings may be productive in the sharing of concerns and the development of better awareness of services.

It is important that professional counselors define their activities and educate their peers in the benefits and limitations of their offerings. If the professional role is not defined by the counselor, others will be forced to do so, often with inadequate information. The practitioner who knows the field and the particular staff competencies will best be able to define services available and promote the development of areas needing attention. The tactful initiative of career counseling personnel begins the awareness program for colleagues by providing information regarding career service activities.

New Student Orientation

Another important method of developing awareness is through orientation programs regularly offered entering students by the office of student personnel or related division. Frequently, student leaders are employed to assist with the orientation of new students. These student leaders are often very perceptive of what is acceptable to the entering student in terms of desired media-format and timing of information packages. It would be helpful to gain the assistance of these student leaders in designing any particular program element presented during orientation.

The imaginative and innovative approach that meets students where they are is more likely to capture their attention and facilitate early awareness of career planning services. The ingenuity of the career counseling staff will be tested at this point. The counselor must guard against unrealistic expectations of wide acceptance of programming by new students since there are many competing needs which must also be satisfied in the total adjustment to campus life. The careful planting of information may lead to later acceptability of career service assistance in making decisions about courses, choosing a major, and other career related matters.

A well-planned program offered during orientation may highlight how students use career services. Approaches designed to increase awareness should provide high impact and enhance the marketability of the service. The use of visual aids and student participation in the program tend to make it more real and alive for the new student.

Many students hesitate to use campus services for a variety of reasons. Thus, career awareness programming is designed to decrease the resistances and increase the acceptance of these services as an integral part of their educational program. The program package should be as brief and action oriented as possible. A fifteen-minute presentation on how a student would use the career service could be well received. Slides or a locally produced film add an important dimension to any large group presentation. Some orientation programs may provide for small group gatherings using faculty or student advisors.

Well prepared items relating to career planning can be interjected, using this cadre of advisors as an extension of the career counseling service. An attractive pamphlet can assist in reminding the new student after the meeting what has been said about the services being offered.

An ideal goal for awareness programming would be that no new students would be able to say after one semester on campus that they had never heard of the career planning service. Whether they choose to use it or not is another matter. It is the responsibility of professional counselors to make their service known and to assist students in finding how they might use the service.

Student-Faculty Advisory Groups

Career services resting squarely in the main stream of campus activity deserve and require adequate representation on official college boards and committees. On many campuses this represents a long established tradition. Career service personnel have had regular input to curricular offerings and have influenced student life in extra-curricular areas. In institutions where there is no immediate provision for student and faculty involvement in career service policy and planning matters, the career services director may wish to initiate a student-faculty advisory group. This group would draw on interested faculty from a variety of departments and student leaders representing the main constituents of the student body.

Planned Communication. The advisory group serves many important functions. It primarily allows for the free interchange of ideas among career personnel, students, and faculty. It appears that adequate communication will not occur unless it is well planned. All members of the college community perceive their lives as being rushed, if not hectic. It would be a mistake to expect spontaneous and casual communication to suffice for input in this vital area. These communication functions will be best served by structuring a group that is as diverse and widely representative as possible, but also representative of members who are interested in career service programming.

Needs Assessment. The assessment of needs of different student and faculty groups is one area for advisory group involvement. This helps avoid expenditures of energies and resources on programs designed to answer questions no one is asking. By careful assessment, gathering data by a variety of means, getting expert opinion or interviewing the target group, an advisory group can collect and evaluate data relative to particular campus needs. This also facilitates the generation of a general plan for possible new programs and development of some idea of the population at whom they are to be directed.

The advisory group also assists the career service personnel in developing specific objectives of new programs and their relative importance. The career staff may enjoy advisory group support in reaching objectives by proposing programs to meet identified needs. This would allow the staff to determine needs of the population being served as well as the amount of staff and facilities required to design the needed program.

A consideration of funding may be crucial. At this point, the advisory committee may be of great value to the career planning staff. Members of the group represent a number of consumers and persons with political influence from a variety of departments. The carefully assessed needs and stated objectives which have led to the design of a program now need the attention of the wider community for the support required to carry out the program. This is particularly true if additional staff and funds are required. Many good and worthwhile program proposals must compete for very scarce dollars on most campuses. It is the documented assessment of student needs which will be met by the proposed program that must ultimately speak for itself.

Outcome Evaluation. The program design must include a plan for the evaluation of outcome. It should identify as many measures of the specific objectives as possible, including changes or developments that would be expected from program efforts. The proposed design might also specify plans for the evaluation of the program at the process level as well as its outcome. The advisory group may wish to oversee a pilot run of the program and then evaluate the results.

When these activities are completed and the results assimilated, the advisory group can be helpful in adopting, amending, or discarding the pilot program. In this fashion, an advisory group can continue to cycle program elements through its planning functions to clarify direction and add support, both directly by participation with the career service and indirectly by the communication patterns activated when the students and faculty members return to their own area of activity on campus.

The advisory group can be a very supportive, informative group that helps bring career services into the mainstream of the educational enterprise. It need not be overly formal but the career services director should pay careful attention to the details of the process. The career director is a group facilitator as well as participant in the advisory group. The group does not necessarily get involved with administrative policy and decision-making, but is more concerned with ideas and program considerations. A selected group of students and faculty on any campus can be an influential ally when these persons are interested and willing to participate in the development of career planning services.

A SYSTEMS APPROACH

Putting it together in a systems approach is a challenge for any career service staff. The following is an example of a program using many of the elements identified earlier with an emphasis on process orientation. It is not intended to be all inclusive and certainly not applicable on every campus. The setting for the example is a small college with limited professional staff. The components should have transferability to the larger university through its various departments or colleges.

Coordination of Resources

The program is sponsored jointly by the professional counseling and placement personnel and comes into being through the use of planning and advisory committees in discussion with key administrators. The program planning is initiated out of student need as this has been determined by the advisory group in conjunction with specific proposals from the professional staff. The organization of services to provide for the program calls on the close coordination of placement and counseling operations. It is immediately apparent that a good political base must exist for this to occur.

If the career service is to be treated as an important department within the institution, it needs to demonstrate how the department is essential to the operation of the college. The staff and advisory group prepare proposals and meet with departmental and student representatives to promote understanding and gain support. These activities help provide the way for adequate budgeting within the institution and also set up the base for requesting additional outside funding. All this assumes the prior completion of a thorough needs assessment. After sufficient support for staff and facilities has been secured, the program is announced through awareness-raising activities as detailed earlier.

One of the main purposes of this systems approach is to orchestrate the various resources of the campus. This requires gaining the support of the college's various constituencies: students, faculty, administration, alumni, and community resource persons. The program needs to be generally announced by articles in the college newspaper, alumni magazine, and other media. These announcements may illustrate how the activities are interrelated and lead to the desired outcome or objective of the program.

The ancient proverb "Give me a fish, and I will eat today, teach me to fish and I will eat for the rest of my life," summarizes the process orientation of such a systematic program. The program is intended to be comprehensive and span a four-year period for the undergraduate. Flexibility is a key characteristic of the program, allowing participants to easily move in or out at any particular point in the process.

As mentioned in an earlier section concerning announcement of services, the professional staff takes an assertive stance in the orientation programming of the college. At the beginning of the academic year, special assemblies are provided for the freshmen and seniors in separate meetings to encourage participation by demonstrating how this approach may work for them. The four-year program highlighting some of the activities available is explained.

The freshmen are introduced to specific awareness programs during the orientation period prior to the beginning of classes in the fall. This is a program which all freshmen are expected to attend and is infused into other academic informational systems. The career counselor is directly involved, assisting in the coordination of advising systems during this orientation period. From the point of view of the new student, the career and academic concerns are not clearly separate at this time. Frequently there is a rather simple approach to the selection of courses and a tentative major in line with early, perhaps unexplored, career goals.

Peer counselors are recruited, organized, and trained during the preceeding semester prior to the arrival of the new student on campus. The peer counselor or career assistant is prepared to assist in the orientation programs and to continue to offer services throughout the academic year. Peer counselors do not take the place of professional counselors but do add dimensions of outreach not possible through professionals alone.

The peer counselor is prepared by training to perform certain limited and carefully supervised functions in the career counseling arena. Activities may include seminars for other students to explore decision-making involving course selection and, on occasion in cooperation with faculty advisors, to provide informational sessions on academic and career planning activities. The peer counselor role stays within the limits of competence of the particular counselor and is under the regular supervision of the professional career counselor.

Awareness Programming

The awareness programming for freshmen follows a funneling design. All freshmen are informed in large assemblies about the resources available to them and are specifically invited by word, and later by written notice, to attend a smaller group session within the first four weeks of classes. At this time, the career counselor, with the assistance of peer counselors, explains the program available to the interested student. The medium used is a slide presentation that details the steps in the process and is augumented by the comments of counselors. The entire briefing session lasts no longer than twenty minutes. It includes a brief response questionnaire which is completed by all those attending. The questionnaire asks the students to indicate the kind of information and/or services they believe might be helpful. A final question allows them to indicate if they would prefer an individual interview to begin their career planning. A positive response on the questionnaire, indicating a desire for additional help, allows the career counselor to establish an interview time for that individual student in the career counseling center.

The first orientation session may include nearly the entire new class of students since full attendance is expected. The second round of smaller group meetings to which about thirty students are invited on a voluntary basis will, of course, meet the needs of fewer students. Of the small groups about half in attendance may desire further interviews and activities during the first semester of their college career. Based on their questionnaire responses, these people are then scheduled directly into specific groups of four or five students for a further detailed examination of career resources. Some prefer an individual session to any further group activity.

The peer counselors assist the professional career counselor in these small group meetings by describing materials to which the new student is being introduced and explaining the use and availability of library and other resources in the career center. The presence of the peer counselor adds credibility to the program and tends to encourage attendance at other meetings and activities being provided.

Self-Assessment

The self-assessment activities offered by the career program are open to all students who have indicated the desire for further consultation. Options are available to them. They may participate in a small group session with a career counselor where the specifics of self and career exploration are reviewed. Brief video-taped recordings are useful in conveying the experience of upperclassmen with some of the career planning activities. New students are assisted in determining which activities might be most profitable for them. The audiovisual presentation also increases interest since the material is locally produced and shows their campus and perhaps upperclass students whom they recognize.

During the small group meeting, the counselor introduces occupational information sources available in the career library. The methods for using the material are demonstrated. The availability of various tests and inventories and further individual consultation is also announced.

Another option available to students is to schedule an individual interview with a career counselor. Experience suggests that most often students prefer the individual session with the professional counselor to begin their career planning. Although costly, this is perhaps the method of choice at this point since the counselor is able to explore the immediate concerns of the student. These may include social, academic, and personal aspects as well as explicit career questions. It is possible then to focus on career dimensions as a goal-centered part of the counseling process.

If it seems advisable and timely, the counselor and student may agree that a vocational interest inventory or other career exercise would be helpful. The testing session or the career exercise group is then conducted with other new students and a later individual session is scheduled to synthesize or interpret the activities completed. Additional activities tailored to the students' specific needs are then planned.

Occasionally, particular students will need additional personal counseling which may be handled by the career counselor or referred to other counseling personnel with the understanding that the student will return to career-oriented activities at the appropriate time. Through the small group orientation sessions, the student has been alerted to the variety of campus resources and is better prepared to take advantage of the total system of referrals.

It is at this stage of the self-assessment process that the blending of traditional counseling and the newer approach of career planning becomes apparent. Depending upon the student's position on the continuum of personal adjustment, the stage is set for the appropriate counseling behavior to meet the needs of the student at the present time. If personal counseling is called for, it is given priority to better prepare the student for career planning activities.

Career Exploration

In the career exploration phase of the program, traditional placement and counseling functions are in close collaboration. The two main components of this phase are pertinent, accurate occupational information and the experiential elements of career planning. This combination permits assimilation of information into the personal plan of the student.

The use of career courses is most appropriate at this phase, for they incorporate some of the self-assessment, career exploration, and job training activities into a single course. In many cases they provide for an adventure in retailing, industry, teaching, or other chosen fields of inquiry. Such a course may be offered during an interim period, as a noncredit course, or on an independent study basis for students in a particular curriculum.

Alumni are usually most willing to contribute time to students. The request of a serious undergraduate for assistance with career planning may come as a refreshing change from the usual requests for dollars. The experience further informs the alumni of programmatic activities at their alma mater and enhances their relation with the institution. Frequently, particular departments sponsor career events that bring to campus their own graduates to mingle with current or prospective majors in that department.

In some colleges the alumni office assists in surveying all alumni regarding their willingness to participate in career activities. The publication of an alumni career directory is most helpful. This lists alumni by occupation, undergraduate major, and geographic location. Students may then contact alumni in their home areas during vacation times or devise a more systematic scheme for informational interviews.

Students involved actively in the exploration phase of the program are put in contact with local business and industrial leaders. Some may be in college relations work but others will represent a variety of occupational and professional roles. Through contact with the placement office, representatives in college relations work are frequently prepared to conduct seminars on particular aspects of the employment scene and on the meaning of work in their organization. These seminars are potent learning devices and add a refreshing dimension to the approach of many courses in subjects and fields chosen by the student.

The model program offers a unique feature in that academic credit is available for field study. This is a helpful tool in the career planning and vocational development of the student. The field study allows full course credit for several hours a week spent in industry, business, social service, or other fields related to the student's interests. This is formalized and regulated by the preparation of a proposal outlining the educational objectives of the field study and involving the concurrence of a faculty advisor on campus and a field supervisor on location.

Each individually tailored field study must specify the objective of the program and the method of evaluation. Upon successful completion of the field study course, the student is assigned an academic grade. When carefully designed and properly supervised, this experience may provide the most powerful of all career exploration experiences in the program. It also has valuable spinoff benefits for later career contacts and the accumulation of work experience.

Job Search Training

As the program progresses, upperclass students become active in more specific job-acquisition skill training. The career counselor offers a senior convocation early in the fall semester. Most seniors participate since the convocation also provides for the registration in placement activities of the year. Following a pattern similar to that used in the freshman year, the program moves from the more general to the more specific. The seniors are called into conference with a career counselor in groups of five or six according to major. By using this approach much of the pertinent information can be related to groups with common interests. This is another example of the use of groups in counseling.

These sessions get down to specifics about necessary information and procedures in a "no-nonsense, sleeves-rolled-up" environment. Videotapes and other innovative devices are used to communicate messages, attitudes, and information from recent seniors back to this beginning senior group.

This is a reality-oriented session. Materials are introduced and the various forms for tests and applications, such as for government positions, are provided. In further sessions of this group, specific instruction is given for the construction of a personal resume that reflects unique personality and interest patterns. Individuals are then encouraged to schedule individual interviews with the career counselor to critique the resume and sort through job strategy factors.

One of the more interesting and productive resources for instruction in skill development is the training interview. The videotaping of a mock interview can be most instructive. Many individuals take advantage of this training program to prepare for interviews with business and industrial representatives on campus or on location. The device is also frequently used by students applying to professional schools where the interview is a crucial step in the application process.

Professional career counseling at this stage supports and assists the senior in the decisions that must be made concerning a variety of job offers or the situation when no offers are received. Opportunities often arise for referral to other agencies to augment the work done by the career counselor. The program is intended to be chronologically coherent and integrated while maintaining maximum flexibility. A graphic illustration of this process is shown on page 39. It is designed to be systematic and capable of energizing the campus-wide network of resources. As institutional resources are available, this career planning service may also be used by alumni in making job or career changes. For many graduates the career planning and placement office is thought of as an important resource for assistance in matters of career and life planning.

Interagency Cooperation

The coordination of student personnel services is of major concern to most college administrations. The wide range of services frequently dispersed throughout the campus presents a challenge for the development of adequate communication and cooperation. Career counselors may wish to identify the departments or agencies more directly related to their work and deliberately plan for the exchange of ideas relative to better cooperation. The offices of admissions, alumni relations, and psychological services represent persons who may be very directly involved with the career planning and placement operation.

Increasingly, admissions staffs need to know the outcome of college preparation. Particularly in demand are the data which are frequently generated by the placement office concerning the progress of graduates of the various programs of the university or college. Furthermore, the admissions staff encounters the early questions of prospective students and thus may be

**SELECTED ELEMENTS OF A SYSTEMS APPROACH
TO CAREER PLANNING**

STUDENTS	CAREER PLANNING ACTIVITIES		RESOURCE PERSONNEL
F R E S H M A N	AWARENESS	Admissions Events	
		Registration	
		Orientation	
		Announcement of Career Planning Resources	
S O P H O M O R E	ASSESSMENT	Individual Interview	Administrative Staff
		Vocational Inventories	
		Small Group Exercises	Career Planning Staff
		Evaluation Session	
			Faculty Advisers
J U N I O R	EXPOSURE	Career Planning Course	
		Part-time Work Experiences	Alumni and Community Resources
		Career Information Seminars	
		Specific Career Field Data	
S E N I O R	TRAINING	Field Study Co-ordination	
		Job-search Techniques	
		Interview Training	
		Job Interviews	

able to provide valuable information for awareness programming conducted by the career service.

The alumni relations staff in many institutions is able to provide valuable resources of alumni who have agreed to meet with students in their place of work to discuss career opportunities in their particular profession or occupational setting. These on-site visits add a vital link in the career exploration process. They are enhanced by support and encouragement from the career planning staff.

The mutual referral network established between counseling services and career planning services is a must if an effective campus-wide program is the objective. This will require effort on the part of both agencies to provide staff time for the planning of mutual programs and the establishment of clear referral procedures. Particularly helpful is personal acquaintance among staff members provided through the exchange of information regarding professional practice distinctive to each office.

Referral to a professional colleague is facilitated by an accurate knowledge of what the other professional might provide to complement the counseling objective. Lack of knowledge of what other counselors may do to assist students in conjunction with one's own service detracts from a sense of trust in the referral process. Regular work together on common programs or projects enhances this understanding and facilitates the movement of the student within the network of helpers.

Where the number of staff members in a career planning service is limited, an alliance with psychological counselors may provide for certain testing programs and assistance with the total self-assessment process students need. The cooperative arrangement is particularly helpful if certain counselors within the psychological counseling service are designated as career assistants and are related to the career planning and placement services.

The special expertise required in assisting with career planning programs where self-assessment and career exploration are involved requires a close working relationship with all members of the team. In some cases, the career planning staff is prepared in numbers and by training to conduct the testing and self-assessment program on their own. Where this is not the case, interagency cooperation is essential.

The career counselor may be in the best position to initiate this liaison and establish arrangements with designated counselors in other services. These arrangements may remain informal or be formalized within the administrative staff. In either case, the effective functioning of co-workers will depend primarily upon the sense of personal trust and understanding of operational objectives, not merely on formal flow charts of administrative personnel.

Many campus agencies are well established and have been entrenched for years, whereas the career planning component of placement services may be a more recent arrival on the scene. Therefore, in the establishment of effective interagency cooperation, the career counselor may have to take the initiative to patiently and persistently develop the contacts and work out the cooperative channels with other agencies. The overall benefit for student programming is worth the effort.

Establishment of the model for interdepartmental cooperation also provides for cooperative ventures with particular departmental advisors or other student service officers who more readily will see how to participate, given the visibility of the cooperative model between career planning and certain other counseling agencies.

In career planning operations, assistance provided through the academic advising system may be helpful for certain classes of students. This may involve training for academic advisors who routinely see all students perhaps once each semester for registration purposes. This can be an opportune time for assistance with career planning questions.

These academic advisors represent an extension of the career planning staff to the extent that they are willing and prepared to do so. This assistance may take the form of information dissemination or limited counseling, depending upon the setting, time, and skill available on the part of the advisor. Many institutions also involve selected student counselors to assist with the academic advising process. This provides an avenue for the use of the peer counselor in conjunction with the academic advisor in a multi-dimensional assistance program related to career planning.

CHAPTER 3

OVERVIEW OF SERVICES

THE BASIC SERVICES typically found in career planning and placement offices are identified and defined in operational terms in this chapter. The primary constituencies are students and employers. There are also important ramifications for faculty, administrators, and the general public. Most of the services offered significantly influence more than one of the constituencies. The discussion first focuses on the student-oriented services and then considers services directed toward employers.

The underlying philosophy is that each of the services, whether directed toward student or employer, should become an integral part of the educational mission of the college. Career planning and placement activities take place in an atmosphere rich with educational opportunities. For every service offered the following question must be answered: how does this service further the educational purposes of the institution?

Each career service has elements of teaching, counseling, and research functions intertwined. The career professional uses a variety of tools and resources to bring the elements together. Synthesizing the elements may involve the use of special techniques, career development exercises, and resource persons such as employers. The emphasis here is more on methods than educational theory or philosophy. When appropriately designed and managed, however, the specific services, methods, and procedures build upon and contribute to educational philosophy.

STUDENT SERVICES

Student-centered services focus attention on relationships between career professionals and students. These services share information which a career specialist has gained through years of academic study and work experience. Sharing career information is the theme of each student-centered service. Because of space limitations not every possible service can be identified and discussed. The goal is merely to provide the direction and tone upon which enterprising career professionals can build a program unique to their institution's characteristics.

Resume Service

For college students the resume service is the basic introduction to an employer. The resume is the most important placement-related document that students prepare because it is circulated widely and seen by many potential employers. A good resume makes the difference between obtaining an interview or not. Assistance in preparation of the resume is a central service offered by nearly every placement office.

Many campuses utilize the College Placement Council's standardized College Interview Data Form. Nearly every employer accepts this standardized resume form in lieu of a complete application form before the initial campus interview. If there is further interest after the campus visit, most employers then will request students to complete the firm's application blank.

An improperly or carelessly prepared resume, whether free-form or the college interview form, reflects negatively upon both the individual and the college. Recognizing this, most colleges go over each students's resume before it is finally submitted for distribution to potential employers and make suggestions for improvement. This 20-to-30-minute investment in time by students and staff members is well worth the effort. Every resume has room for improvement.

Encouraging students to come into the career service for advice on the resume has some important secondary benefits. Few students recognize the need for career counseling. As a result, many fail to schedule an appointment with a staff member to discuss their career objectives. Most students, however, see the value in having a professional review their resume. This "excuse" is one of the most effective ways to encourage students to make use of the career center.

Student Files

Most placement services maintain files on graduating students. Few people truly realize the cost factor associated with this student service. In many offices it represents more than one full-time clerical position. Most files contain the following information.

Resume. This summary of the applicant's background may be a free form or pre-printed form. Most placement offices receive a broad approval from registrants to refer copies of the resume to any interested employer or graduate school.

Faculty Recommendations. The Family Educational Rights and Privacy Act of 1974 (FERPA) has changed policies of many placement offices, but most still maintain references in student files. FERPA gives candidates the right to view evaluations where they have not waived the right to review them. Registrants may also request that poor references be destroyed, but this involves a special appeal process. Since the law is in a constant state of change, placement offices should rely on current publications from CPC and other sources to stay abreast of regulations.

Faculty references are used much less frequently today than in the past, especially by business and industry employers. References have become a minor part of the final selection process for several reasons. Many employers feel that evaluations are not good predictors of job-related success because they measure qualities in a setting highly distinct from the work climate. Some employers complain that references all look alike because fewer faculty are now willing to give anything less than positive comments since students may read them. As a result, many employers feel that references lack objectivity. Another complaint is that faculty simply do not know the students as well as they did in the days of smaller enrollments.

These complaints are not new to placement officials, but they are changing some employment strategies. One value beyond the use for employment purposes is encouragement of student-faculty relationships. Many students feel that they need a reason to talk to faculty, and since they need the faculty input into the employment process, the required reference provides the vehicle for making the contact. The need for references also motivates students to gain closer working relationships with faculty.

Transcripts. A few placement offices maintain the official grade and course transcripts of registrants and send them to specific employers upon the request of the student or employer if a signed transcript release has been obtained. Some offices request unofficial transcripts from students and these are mailed upon request. Most business firms prefer the official transcripts which most frequently are sent by the registrar at the request of the student or through a transcript release.

Interview Evaluations. Some placement services request employers to complete a candid evaluation of each student interviewed on campus. This evaluation often goes into the student file. The purpose is to provide professional counseling to students about the interview process. The feedback is designed to improve performance in future interviews.

Other Information. Files occasionally contain some type of record on the interviews taken on campus. They may also include a career counselor's notes. Many employers send copies of all correspondence with students to the placement office, and these letters frequently are placed in the registrant's file. This correspondence is extremely valuable because it contains salary information which is shared with the College Placement Council for the *Salary Survey*, a reporting service widely used by both employers and placement offices to keep abreast of average beginning salaries. As final placement data become available, most offices file the information in the registrant's file.

For placement services with large campus interviewing and student referral programs, student files require much time, money, and space. Maintaining student files is an essential activity but one for which little credit or acknowledgement is given.

Career Counseling

Career counseling and job placement are combined as an integrated function in every career planning and placement service. Career counseling provides the foundation upon which successful job placement into a given career field is built. Placement is only a part of career planning. Career counseling without the reality testing that placement provides cannot stand alone. The two areas may be viewed as separate functions for teaching purposes, but in practice each component is a part of a total career planning process.

Both career counseling and placement consist of separate identifiable sub-components that come together to create the process. The placement function covers a series of elements which, if taken together, form a program in effective career search. Career counseling also consists of a series of elements each of which is essential in developing meaningful and realistic career goals. Each placement service offers variations of these basic components of the career planning process.

Career counseling begins long before college and continues long after college. This lifelong process is picked up and assisted by the career planning and placement service when the student enrolls in college. Although the service is a voluntary election on the part of the entering student, the process continues whether or not the student seeks professional aid. It is not uncommon for students to wait until the senior year to request assistance, but that does not mean that they received no career counseling during the first years of college. There are many sources of career assistance. Career planning is almost an instinctive phenomenon.

Self-Assessment. Who am I? Where am I going? Why am I here? How did I get here? Identity questions pose one of the greatest challenges to young minds and placement counselors. Answers seldom flow easily. Many students need help in assessing where they have been, where they are, and where they are going. The career planning and placement service must have a competent staff that is qualified and eager to deal with these inquiries.

A number of aids can assist both counselors and counselees. A trained professional listens, responds, confronts, and draws information from the students which can be used to build a realistic view of self and assist in devising appropriate action plans. The professional serves as a catalyst. The self-concept is an evolving picture puzzle that the individual fits together as information is collected, analyzed, and processed. This process may occur in either an individual counseling session or small group setting. A more detailed discussion of basic counseling skills follows in a later chapter.

Counselors also have access to psychological tests to aid the student in the refinement of the self-concept. About one-third of placement services offer vocational testing, but a higher percentage have access to services and facilities to which applicants may be referred. Vocational testing with the placement service appears to be more common at smaller colleges.

Another important aid designed to assist in the self-evaluation process is career workbooks which contain inventories, exercises, and projects designed to elicit further information. Even resume preparation has an important input into the self-assessment. All of these methods give the student a better understanding of background, interests, qualifications, skills, aptitudes, personality, attitudes, etc. Equipped with this information, an individual is better prepared to cope with the next phase of career planning.

Career Exploration. Students want to know what types of career fields and entry-level jobs are open to them. In fact, students often appear less eager to undertake the self-evaluation than the career exploration phase of career planning. Career information comes from reading, talking, and doing.

The importance of career information resources is emphasized throughout this book. Many placement services maintain their own career library, or at least a bibliography of publications available in the main library of the college. No individual counselor could ever suggest all of the possible career avenues open to students. Ascertaining what is available for someone with a given set of qualifications is a major library research project. This research is an individual project but one which can be simplified by proper direction from a trained career counselor.

Many students are in a position to observe individuals working in a wide range of occupations. One of the most realistic sources of career knowledge comes from talking to professionals already in the occupation.

A few students have an opportunity to participate in cooperative education and professional internship learning experiences. By actually doing the job at a paraprofessional level, a wide array of career information may be collected. The experience may reinforce earlier expectations and confirm the career choice or destroy past expectations and move career exploration on to another occupation.

Integration. The role of the career specialist is to assist in the integration of the self-assessment with the career exploration. How does the collected career information match the self-concept? Are compromises necessary?

Career counseling and advising comprise one of the most time-consuming activities within the placement service. Many hours are spent with each person. Computer-assisted counseling and self-counseling guides may lessen the time spent with each candidate in the future, but the career counseling function will continue to require large amounts of staff time. Career counseling is one of the essential services offered by career planning and placement services, and its cost must be calculated into the overall budget of the program.

Placement Counseling

Placement counseling turns career counseling into job action. Placement is one element of the planning process that provides a reality test. It provides a feedback loop that permits refinements, modifications, and specifications in the total career choice decision.

Placement counseling starts with a broad definition of an occupation or career field decision already made. The broad decision is next narrowed to a specific job objective based upon an awareness of the current job market and specific job descriptions. Starting at point A, what is the path needed to reach point Z? The more general career goals are translated into specific job objectives.

Like career counseling, placement counseling consists of sub-processes that form a feedback loop. This loop allows for immediate clarification and compromises if necessary. The sequence begins with resume preparation, cover letter design, and development of a contact network. The sequence continues with primary interviews, communications, secondary interviews, job offers, and evaluation, and culminates in a specific job acceptance decision. Throughout this sequential process the career counselor serves as a sounding board, teacher, advisor, feedback counselor, and motivator.

In addition to the direct role with the student, the professional must manage the system so that it can accommodate large numbers of individuals. The placement counseling role is as time-consuming as the career counseling role because there are many points in the sequence of events that require individual student attention.

Group Counseling

The number of students and alumni desiring career counseling has grown rapidly, while staff size has not grown proportionately larger. This situation has forced many career planning and placement services to move to group counseling. In many situations group counseling may be just as effective as one-to-one counseling if it is supplemented with appropriate personal counseling.

Some elements of career planning demand individual counseling, but other elements lend themselves well to large and small group instruction. Tutorial instruction may be the ideal teaching method, but experience suggests that learning a subject area in a classroom setting may be equally effective for many people. Some career planning instruction is even well suited for large group lectures.

To optimally utilize the limited college resources, methods need to be developed to evaluate which components of career planning require individual counseling sessions and which can be effectively taught in groups. The luxury of one-to-one counseling for all elements is probably a thing of the past. More group instruction is inevitable.

Some of the early pioneers in group counseling learned that there are benefits other than lower costs. Individual counseling for certain placement functions frequently results in repetitive interviews with the same essential points covered in each session. When individuals come into a counseling session with the essentials understood and completed, the session can focus on the individual's unique situation. Group counseling can make personal counseling much more productive. Group counseling frees a considerable amount of the counselor's time and permits a more productive use of that time, particularly as it relates to dealing with unique situations and circumstances.

Academic Counseling

No fine line exists between academic and career counseling because the two must be highly interrelated. As a result, more than a few placement counselors find themselves involved in academic counseling, particularly if the college is small or the service is decentralized. The centralized service that makes academic course recommendations and advises students on academic programs to follow, based upon the student's career objectives, must be careful. College faculty traditionally are very sensitive to recommendations that suggest one course over another.

Design of curricula and specific academic programs is a faculty responsibility. If the career planning and placement service has done a proper job in preparing information for faculty about the world of work as it relates to various disciplines, faculty members can make curricular decisions that will enhance the career potential of students. If the faculty has not been consulted prior to curriculum design and counselors influence students directly, an important relationship may be seriously damaged.

Direct academic counseling may not be the direction taken by the majority of career planning and placement services in the future. In many colleges, however, the placement function may well provide meaningful input into curriculum alternatives for faculty to evaluate. The job market, particularly in the short run, is not likely to influence the subjects students elect but, in the long run, evidence suggests that students will be attracted to academic programs that are vocationally sound as well as educationally fruitful.

The career planning and placement service of the future will likely play an important role in the development of academic programs. As with students, the role will be that of provider of a wide range of information to consider in making important curriculum decisions.

Career Planning Courses

A growing number of career planning and placement services are developing courses in career planning. The trend is toward offering one to three hours of academic credit, depending upon the length and scope of the course. The instructor is frequently a career professional, but many colleges offer the course in an academic department as part of the discipline's curriculum. A few academic departments even require the course before graduation. Even in the academic department, the liaison with the career planning and placement staff is common.

Content. The length and content of the courses vary considerably. In the early Seventies, the Research Committee of the Midwest College Placement Association took on the project of collecting course syllabi from many different colleges. The topics most frequently covered appear in the chart on pages 54–55. Some topics were covered in great depth at some colleges while others were very superficially discussed.

Most of the key word topics in the chart are self-explanatory, but there is considerable overlap and duplication. All of these topics cannot be adequately covered in one semester; therefore, emphasis is frequently placed on a few topics most pertinent to the group being taught. To a great extent, the decision depends upon the class standing of participants and academic interests. For example, seniors desire more placement readiness emphasis, while freshmen may need more self-evaluation and exploratory emphasis. Students with declared interests in engineering, business, journalism, and other vocationally oriented subject areas may require less emphasis on occupational alternatives than liberal arts majors. Any career planning course has to be specifically designed for its audience.

Goals. The objectives of career planning courses relate to the fundamental concepts of the career planning process. The central theme is to aid individuals in determining specific personal career and life goals. The methods and techniques used to accomplish this are remarkably similar. Many of the pro-

CAREER   PLANNING

Adjustment Problems	Communications
Advancement Techniques	Competitive Situation
American Work Economy	Contact Networks
Career Alternatives	Continuing Education
Career Clusters	Cost of Living Comparisons
Career Counseling	Cover Letter Preparation
Career/Course Relationships	Curriculum Philosophy
Career Decision Making	Educational Philosophy
Career Education	Employment Contacts
Career Exploration	Employment Process
Career Fields	Evaluative Tools/ Techniques
Career Group Process	Free Enterprise
Career Information	Goal Setting
Career Objectives	Government Employment
Career Paths	Graduate Schools
Career Patterns	Industries
Career Planning Techniques	Internship Programs
Career Simulation	Interpersonal Relations
Career Skills	Interview Elements
Careers and College Majors	Interview Preparation

grams go a step forward and propose to help the individual develop a job search plan for achieving career goals. A few programs continue the process by offering guidance in selection of a career field.

Methods. Many colleges use similar methods in presenting the materials and topics to be covered. The lecture-discussion approach is most common, but it is supplemented greatly with other methods of instruction. Employer involvement appears to be a common theme. Employers are invited to address the class, participate in panel discussions, or in some instances, a field trip to the employer's location is scheduled.

COURSE   TOPICS

Interview Types
Interviewing Strategy
Interviewing Styles
Job Campaigns
Job Market Analysis

Job Requirements
Job Satisfaction
Job Search Techniques
Job Specifications
Labor Market Conditions

Leisure Activities
Life and Work Goals
Long and Short-Range
    Goals
Minority Group Preference
Mobility

Mock Interviews
Occupational Choice
Occupational Trends
Organizational Structures
Placement Service Procedures

Positions Available
Professional Growth
Professional Schools
Psychological Tests
Salary Expectations

Salary Negotiations
Self-Assessment
Self-Inventories
Small Groups Counseling
Supply and Demand

Transition from College to
    Work
Value Systems
Videotaped Interviews
Vocational Choice Theory
Vocational Counseling

Vocational Development
Women in Careers
Work Classifications
Work Ethics

As in most college classes, students are requested to visit individually with the instructor. Many classes build these sessions into the course structure. The idea is to give students some individual personal counseling that they might be hesitant to seek in a group setting. Another effective related approach is small group sessions in which students are encouraged to discuss career-related plans with a trained moderator. Videotaping for development of job interviewing skills is a widely used technique.

Whether in large or small groups, use of audiovisual materials is highly recommended. Professionals who have used audiovisual techniques report exceedingly positive student response. Since many of the programs are given over and over by different placement staff members, the audiovisual approach reduces preparation time and provides consistency in materials presented. This includes use of transparencies, color slides, videotapes, films, film strips, cassette tapes, chart boards, etc. Information is available from CPC's publication titled *A/V Media in Career Development*.

Assignments. Most classes require some type of exercises. These projects often fall into the self-assessment, career exploration, or placement phases of the career planning process. They may involve taking a battery of vocational tests and, after consultation with a professional, incorporating the results into a written self-assessment. They may be projects designed to explore one career field in depth or to take a cursory look at several potential alternatives. For students with firm career plans, the project may involve various phases of the job search and evaluation of potential job choices.

In credit courses, where grades must be given, the projects may be graded. A few courses also provide for written examinations and objective tests based on lectures, discussions, and required reading.

Materials. Several textbooks are now available. Selection of a specific book depends upon the nature of the audience and the course content which is to be emphasized. Because of the varied nature of philosophic approaches and the necessary limited scope of any one publication, no one book is likely to satisfy all needs. Most college textbook publishers will provide course instructors examination copies to review.

Many colleges also require a career workbook for students to use in conducting course exercises and projects. Use of these depends upon the nature of the course. Occasionally, some industrial organizations distribute free workbooks which placement services distribute to students. The quality may be excellent, but it can also be quite shallow if the material is interpreted to be employer advertising. For certain programs these publications may be excellent resource materials. The workbook idea is an excellent way to get students involved in the career planning process.

Many classes also supplement the textbook and workbook with government publications such as the *Dictionary of Occupational Titles* and *Occupational Outlook Handbook for College Graduates*. These publications are designed as reference books rather than as an integrated approach to career planning, but they greatly aid in the career exploration phase of career planning.

Among the publications which are periodically distributed to placement services are the *College Placement Annual, Business World, The Graduate,* and *Placement Manual.* All provide articles and information pertinent to students graduating from college.

In many cases, the classes serve also as a springboard to the use of placement services. This group approach greatly lessens the individual counseling burden in the career planning and placement service.

Placement Seminars

Not all placement services enjoy the option of a career planning course. Staff limitations, lack of materials, no academic tie to a department, and lack of faculty support are common reasons some services have difficulty in getting formal courses started. Without some course-oriented motivation, many placement professionals find it difficult to interest students in career planning.

A well-functioning placement service is not without appeal to students. A high percentage of students require help in finding employment. Career planning concepts can and should be integrated into placement seminars. Given growing interest in using the placement service, group seminars are often the only way to economically and effectively handle the onslaught with limited staff personnel.

A number of placement services offer weekly seminars on the topical headings shown on pages 54–55. Enrollments may vary widely at first but they will grow as the program gains stature and respect. Over a period of time, programs on resume preparation, employment contacts, and interviewing techniques interest a large percentage of graduating students and some underclass people looking for help. The programs may be repeated every four or five weeks. The important point is to have a planned program on which students can rely.

In practice, placement seminars may be oriented more toward placement readiness than career planning. The objective of providing group counseling is much the same. Participants who later return for individual counseling find the sessions more productive. Group counseling, whether in career planning courses or placement seminars, is an important tool to use in the career planning and placement service.

Vocational Testing

Vocational testing is a service provided by about one-third of all career planning and placement services. Vocational testing is more common in small colleges than in larger colleges. Many large colleges have separate offices of psychological counseling or specialized testing services. In such instances the placement staff may refer students to these offices and, through cooperative arrangements, the results may be returned to the placement staff for review or analysis with students.

Vocational testing is more likely to be found in offices that deal on a regular basis with freshmen and sophomores. Vocational testing is an important tool to be used in the self-assessment and the exploration phases of career planning. It is critical that the staff administering and interpreting the results is adequately trained in this field. A later chapter deals more specifically with this service.

Career Library

Obtaining career information is a focal point in the career planning process. Although most career information may be obtained from any public or college library, seldom is there a central section of the library devoted solely to career information. Browsing through literature of various types aids in the career thought process. To facilitate this learning process many placement services purchase and maintain a central source of information related to a wide variety of career alternatives. The concept of the career library service is explained in more detail later.

The career library can be an excellent resource for individuals, but it also is an expensive and difficult service to develop and maintain. Materials rapidly become outdated or lost. The constant monitoring of the library may become too expensive and difficult for the placement service. A few offices maintain a budget for purchasing new materials, but rely on the main library to control access to them. Several bibliographies located in the placement service aid students in gaining access to the materials. Occasionally the main library will set aside some space for career information.

EMPLOYER SERVICES

An initial reaction to employer-centered services might suggest that they are not directly related to the educational mission of the college. Employer services, however, must be viewed in the broader context of a total career planning process. They are necessary in order to provide the reality testing that is an essential component of a career decision.

Employer services create the important motive that involves the employer in the total educational process. In a democratic free enterprise system, employers cannot be directed to participate in certain activities, even though the state believes that may be advantageous to society. Altruistic motives sound great in theory but in the free enterprise system they seldom work effectively in motivating any employers with the exception of a few giants who might fear government pressure.

Students need the help of employers for the purpose of both career decision making and employment upon graduation. Society is best served by cooperating with employers rather than ignoring their potential input into the educational process. Incentives generate the involvement. The incentives are the employer services offered by institutions of higher education.

Only a few of the potential employer services can be covered here. The methods and approaches being used by colleges in involving employers in the educational process vary, based upon the unique academic and placement programs of the college. The few services specified here are widely utilized but far more innovative approaches continue to be offered by colleges. Many of the more successful experimental employer services are covered in articles in the *Journal of College Placement*.

Job Listings

A central activity in every placement service is bringing job information to the attention of graduating students, alumni, and faculty. The job information may be posted on bulletin boards, sent as memos to appropriate parties, or circulated in a periodical bulletin that is widely distributed to interested parties.

Job opening information is frequently summarized from longer job descriptions and specifications sent by employers. The job opening announcement usually contains the following information:

Contact Information	Job Specifications
Employer	Job title
Address	Degree level
Telephone	Major(s)
Contact person	Experience
Source of lead	Description of duties
	Salary range
	Other factors

Employers are advised that the opening will be circulated widely within the academic community. In limited instances, employers prefer that openings not be widely advertised because they want specific referrals only. In such cases it may be appropriate not to identify the employer and to list the job as a "blind announcement," with a staff member's name given as the primary contact. The staff may inform the employer as specific qualified candidates contact the placement office.

Job Bulletins. Most offices publish a job bulletin on a regular periodical basis, usually at least once per month. Many offices, however, make the bulletin a weekly activity. The job bulletin is often sent to alumni who request or subscribe to it and is placed in a location on campus where many students, especially seniors, may pick up a copy.

Typing and editing job listings in a bulletin format is a time consuming activity and in large offices may be a full-time job for one or more of the clerical staff. Some consistent format needs to be used in order to achieve an immediately recognizable publication on campus. Logos, colored paper, good spacing and layout add to the readability and effectiveness of the publication.

Bulletin Board Notices. Bulletin board space is a precious commodity for the placement service. Material must be attractively displayed and information rotated regularly to keep students interested in reading the appropriate notices. Since space is restricted, often job information must be summarized to fit a 3 x 5 inch card which is removed every week or two. The bulletin board is more often located near the placement facilities and in a high traffic pattern. When well managed, bulletin boards with placement information are among the most widely read at the college.

Special Memos. In some cases, a job opportunity may have a very limited audience, which would tend to make the bulletin board or job bulletin approach ineffective. If an opportunity applies solely to a small academic discipline, another population group, or is for information only, a note to appropriate faculty, staff, alumni, or students may be the best method of disseminating job information. In such cases, the special attention often helps build respect for the placement service.

Whatever method is used for distributing job information, it is very important to the placement service that the information published is accurate and that credit is received for the service. Recognition usually takes care of itself. Accuracy, however, requires more follow-up. A great credibility gap may develop if some attempt is not made to remove a listing once the job has been filled. Some employers report back, but most do not. It is important to continually remind parties using the information to provide feedback. Unfortunately, feedback comes only in a small percentage of cases.

Dating each job opportunity received is the next best way of advising job candidates of the appropriateness of the job lead. Depending upon the economic climate, most jobs are filled within four to eight weeks, and applicants should be so advised.

Further Information. When candidates see jobs posted for which they feel qualified, the placement service is invariably contacted for further information. To avoid being contacted by each inquiry, most services file a copy of the original source of the job listing in a notebook or file directly accessible by job seekers. This information is most frequently filed in alphabetical order by employer name.

A log needs to be kept of all information in the files because the files must be purged on a regular basis, usually every two to four months. This may be done on a daily basis by pulling old job information when new information is filed.

Career Information. Job notices have time value but the information contained in notices may have much longer lasting value. Job notices represent one of the most realistic career information sources available and may become an integral part of career counseling sessions.

Many placement offices cross classify all job notices. One classification is by job sector: business, government, education, and other. Another classification may be by type of position: accounting, marketing, engineering, teaching, etc. Others prefer to classify by academic qualifications required, such as computer science, liberal arts, education, business, etc. The specific classification used depends upon the characteristics of the campus and type of employers who utilize the services most frequently. Job applicants and underclassmen wanting career information often spend hours reviewing these files.

Job Development

In past years, placement services waited until employers contacted them about referring qualified applicants or recruiting on campus for a specific job opening. The tables started turning in the Seventies. Placement services must now "beat the bushes" to identify employers with job opportunities whose specifications match the needs of students. This is a role that most placement officers under forty years of age never experienced before. Job development means aggressively soliciting job openings from potential employers on behalf of graduating students.

Regular systematic programs must be developed to inform the employment community of the availability of a highly trained source of potential employees. This competitive spirit is a new phenomenon and a service to students that is likely to continue to grow. Placement services can no longer passively wait for jobs to be called into the office. The available jobs will go to less qualified candidates simply because they happen to be on the employer's doorstep or because another placement director contacted the employer first.

Aggressively searching for job openings does more than re-shuffle a fixed number of openings to the more aggressive colleges. It opens up new jobs. Stories abound of employers finding or creating a job because they did not want to lose a good person. Employers also upgrade existing jobs which in the past might have gone to a high school graduate. Employers instinctively want the best, and they make necessary adjustments when they are convinced of a certain person's credentials.

Some placement directors are persuasive and have been known to influence an employer to give a young college graduate a chance. Given a chance, most graduates can produce.

Job development is here to stay for some time. There will be cyclical shifts in supply and demand. But the more successful placement staffs will not wait for good times. They will do their best to solicit job prospects at all times.

Job Referrals

Employers expect to receive two major types of assistance when they contact the college placement service: publicity on the job opening and specific names of candidates who appear to be qualified for the position. Many placement offices know every graduating student on a personal basis while others know only a few students. Much depends on the size of the graduating class and the organizational structure of the placement service.

A number of job candidates may be recommended by telephone. More frequently the placement office will send resumes of candidates to the employer if job specifications and candidates' backgrounds match. Occasionally a mention of the candidate's special characteristics in the reply letter, with enclosed resumes, is made for each candidate referred.

Employer desires vary greatly. Some prefer to see only one or two resumes with glowing recommendations for each opening. Other employers prefer resumes of many applicants which they can screen. The placement officer's approach depends upon how well the employer is known.

In large placement centers with many staff members, no one person can possibly know all candidates. A system needs to be developed whereby each opening is circulated to appropriate staff personnel for referral notes. One person is frequently designated to make the actual reply to the employer.

The importance of having the staff know every job applicant on a personal basis cannot be overstressed. Knowing who to refer greatly influences the decision of the employer to again utilize the placement service. If quality referrals are received consistently, the employer will continue to work with the college.

Resume Files

A common placement service is to offer employers open access to the resumes of job applicants. This, however, should not be done without the knowledge and consent of each registrant.

Keeping open resume files of alumni is a more difficult task. Almost all are currently employed. If their current employer discovered that they were seeking other employment, the candidate might risk being fired. As a result, few offices maintain open resume files of alumni seeking employment. Most simply request the job specifications, screen possible resumes, and send or give employers appropriate resumes. Some offices do permit employer screening but carefully pull out resumes that might cause embarrassment.

Employer Files

Graduating students and alumni look to the placement service to provide contacts to use in the career search process. Contacts serve as a primary source of development of job leads and often represent years of careful consultation with a large number of individuals who might be important in an employment search. These contacts include employers and individuals who might be instrumental in bringing together students and employers.

Contact information gives the organization name, individual name, title, address, type of positions usually offered, and other information that might be important to use in a job search campaign. Information is not limited solely to current job opening notices. Contact information comes from campus recruiting, alumni, faculty, employers, directories, employment brochures, etc.

Over the years, placement services spend many hours and hundreds of dollars developing information which students and alumni may use in making employment contacts with potential employers. Employer files are important to both the campus recruiting operation and the job development side of the operation. Employer files offer job candidates one of the best sources of leads to potential jobs and, therefore, must be up-to-date and accurate.

Employer files may be cross classified in several different orders to aid applicants in determining which contacts are most likely to be productive for their purposes. The master list is maintained in alphabetical order so that it can be updated on a regular basis. Employer files may be cross classified by geographical location, major, degree level, type of position offered, industry, or any combination of the above. Cross classifications greatly aid candidates in identifying specific contacts, and this process may turn a cold contact into a warmer job lead.

Because of the many cross classifications, numerous placement services prefer to maintain the information on computer files. Updating one master set of computer cards, tapes, or discs enables the other listings to be prepared in an updated form almost simultaneously. Employer files frequently contain several contact names for each organization, depending upon location, job title, or other designation. A properly programmed computer can provide the exact contact that a student may need. A few placement services have been fortunate enough to obtain on-line capabilities with a computer terminal, enabling students to access information directly.

The size of the employer file varies by size and reputation of the college. Perhaps more important than size and reputation is the quality of the contacts maintained in the employer file. Some placement services maintain everything while others are highly selective. The files may contain only those organizations with which the college has worked closely. Obviously, this type of contact is more meaningful to the candidates, but it often puts all the eggs in only a few baskets. The scope of the employer file is an individual college choice and is based upon circumstances unique to the institution.

The employer file is not only used by job candidates. In most facilities it serves as the main contact list which the placement service employs to generate specific job openings. The employer files become an important tool in the total employer outreach program of the placement service.

The time spent in developing and maintaining them is usually well worth the sizable investment in time and money.

Faculty-Employer Liaison

In many ways the career planning and placement service is the window to the work environment. The service is situated at a crossroads between the so-called "ivory tower" and "world of work" communities. An important service performed by the function is the bringing of the two communities together so each can see the real concerns of the other and destroy the false stereotypes surrounding each environment.

Feeding information about career possibilities to the faculty is a major responsibility. Feeding employers information about academic program changes and other facets of college life is an equally important responsibility.

One effective way to create this flow of information is to bring the parties together. This frequently is accomplished during the campus recruiting season at coffee breaks, luncheons, or evening programs. Another step is to encourage employers to invite faculty to their facilities for observation and exchange of ideas. Although less common, the placement staff may assist employers in identifying faculty who may have something to contribute on a paid consulting basis.

Bringing the parties together as frequently as possible also has some placement fallout benefits. The placement staff needs faculty support and direct assistance. Over the years many students find employment because a faculty member highly recommended a student to an employer acquaintance. The faculty-employer liaison role of placement plays a strong and important part in providing a quality service to all constituencies.

Alumni Placement

Over 85 percent of career planning and placement services offer their services to alumni in addition to current students. The range of service is frequently restricted by the geographical location of the two parties. Some offices simply cannot handle the volume of work brought on by large numbers of enrolled students, and therefore, restrict certain services, such as campus interviewing, to current students. Most placement services formally register alumni, refer resumes, send job opening information, and give career counseling as requested.

Some of the reasons why a few offices do not actively serve alumni include: resources are not available; a different approach to the job market is needed; competition with private agencies may be construed as unfair.

Alumni may be extremely valuable to the placement service, both in the short and long run. Alumni can provide jobs for current graduates and serve as important internal contacts for employment purposes. Alumni financial contributions can be a significant part of the college budget. In the case of public institutions particularly, alumni may be influential in legislative matters. A strong case can be made to encourage a placement service to offer a wide range of services to alumni, even if there is a charge for the services.

The principal services which alumni seem most interested in using are career counseling, including resume preparation, job leads, bulletins, job referrals, and for the younger alumni, campus interviewing. Opening these services to alumni undoubtedly takes a significant amount of staff time and resources away from students. In career counseling alone, most alumni need more hours of help than almost any student. Since resources are often fixed, decisions have to be made in drawing a balance between serving alumni and students. There is no simple formula or meaningful national average to determine how the resources should be optimally divided. Decisions must be made based on the unique circumstances of each college.

As times change, the need for expanded and new services for employers may change again. Although there is concern about balancing the level of service between employer and student groups, the actual implementation of this concept is straightforward. The services offered to employers invariably help students and vice versa. Because of the interrelatedness of the parties, the key word is service without regard to the constituency being served.

PART II

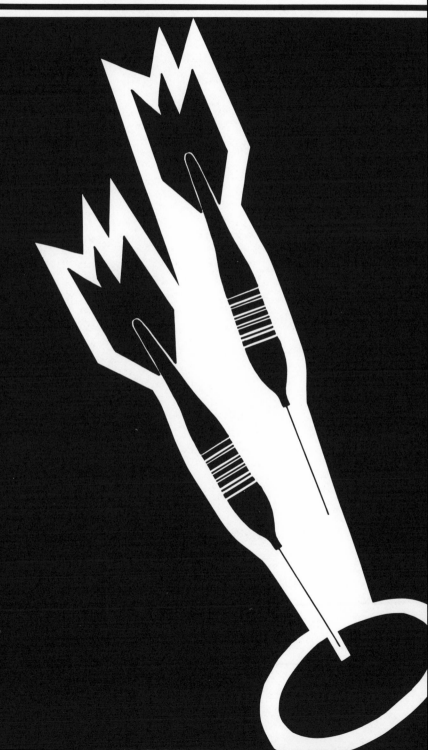

CHAPTER 4

CAREER COUNSELING

C AREER COUNSELING IS one of the most exciting and dynamic fields in higher education today. The career development needs of students are apparent and pressing. Colleges and universities nearly always include in their statement of mission the total development of the student. Institutions increasingly are realigning priorities to provide much-needed comprehensive career services. The demand for qualified counselors to participate in planning and providing for these services has never been greater.

The college environment is rich in opportunities for career planning assistance. The resources are varied and the student has maximum freedom and flexibility for the exploration required in career planning. Career counseling activities are most effective when coordinated within a campus-wide network of resources which may then be linked to the larger community. Many campus resources for career development, now latent, may be activated by a thoughtfully conceived plan executed by energetic and determined career counselors.

Career services should be comprehensive, yet not overpowering, in their presentation. The student must perceive the activities being offered as "manageable packages" which they can "buy" given the amount of time and effort they wish to spend. Career planning programs that are most effective are student centered, beginning where the student is and then moving toward an individualized goal, usually with the help of a skilled counselor. Programs are best presented in a manner in which the student may choose among many activities with some sense of coherence and in which there is a logical system of activities that have direction and purpose. Career counseling programs, which students have helped design, are particularly popular and helpful.

Career planning processes go on for millions of persons with or without the aid of career counseling assistance. Most campuses suffer from the scarcity of professional counseling assistance at a time when college-age persons are most receptive to such assistance. The career counseling enterprise today is a process-oriented educational endeavor. Career planning includes self-assessment, career exploration, and placement activities. Many campus agencies, united by the common theme of total student development, provide comprehensive services for various student needs. Ideally, since these services are coordinated and interrelated, the student activates the entire network regardless of the student service agency entered first.

The rationale for career counseling is to be found along a continuum between the poles of theory and practice. The assumptions and theories of career counseling based on the counselor's personal philosophy will determine, in large measure, the implementation of counseling skills. Observation of counseling behavior illuminates, and personal experience tends to modify, the theoretical basis of counseling. A rationale for career counseling may then be approached from two perspectives: theoretical and practical.

THEORY

Human growth is essentially positive and tends to move in developmental sequences that are increasingly enhancing and self-actualizing. This developmental movement is by no means a steady process and, in fact, may reverse itself at times and then spurt ahead at moments of crisis and decision. The nature of development is such that the individual searches for a sense of reality that will bind together the episodes of life in some meaningful way. Frequently, this search focuses on significant personal relationships and activities, including those experienced or anticipated in a work environment.

There is no single comprehensive theory capable of incorporating the observed facts of human behavior regarding career development. Empirical findings are scattered, lacking order and comprehensiveness, and are difficult to fit into a single logical framework. A variety of theories or approaches have been proposed for career counselors, based on more general theories of counseling. These include trait and factor, client-centered, psychodynamic, developmental, and behavioral approaches. The purpose here is to briefly review the major tenets of these approaches as they might influence career counseling behavior. A more detailed history and description of these approaches and theories may be found in journals and texts devoted to the systematic discussion of career development theories.

Trait and Factor Approach

The trait and factor approach is perhaps historically the earliest attempt to match individuals with specific jobs. It is based on a careful diagnosis of test profile information along with subjective items of personal history collected in an individual interview, as well as on information obtained through other sources. This represents a rational, empirical approach based on the psychology of individual differences. It is a straight-forward approach to gathering information about the individual and the pertinent occupational world and then making the most logical decisions based on these facts. In this approach, the counselor at least implicitly assists the student in determining the probabilities of success and happiness in a particular work-related decision.

Client-Centered Approach

The client-centered approach is based on self-theory and has enjoyed a long period of acceptance among counselors. This approach proposes certain necessary conditions in counseling to allow for constructive change. Two or more persons must be in psychological contact. The person being assisted is in a state of relative incongruence and is more or less vulnerable or anxious while the counselor is more congruent and integrated in the relationship. It is necessary for the counselor to experience unconditional positive regard for the student. An emphatic understanding of the student's internal frame of reference is experienced by the counselor who attempts to communicate this personal experience to the student. Communication of the counselor's understanding and regard for the student is necessary if counseling is to be effective.

The client-centered approach lends itself to the particular skills and personality of the individual counselor and it tends to maximize, at the same time, the self-directional needs of the student. The goal is to enhance the immediacy of personal experiences which facilitate a new awareness of identity and direction, allowing for more realistic and satisfying choices. In its conception, the client-centered approach places more responsibilities on the student than do any other approaches. It may be used more effectively in the stages of career counseling involving self-assessment activities and the preparation of the student for more specific training exercises.

Psychodynamic Approach

The psychodynamic approach to career counseling is based on psychoanalytic theory which gives attention to the underlying dynamic factors in the student's development. This approach allows for the significance of chronological development and the psychological factors influencing the various stages of development. Since much attention is given to the internal factors in career decision-making, the process may become fairly intensive and complex. The psychodynamic approach calls attention to the deeply personal nature of career concerns of individuals. The goal of this approach is to examine all influences affecting personality development so as to produce positive personality change and career decision. The use of these techniques may involve relatively long-term activities on the part of the counselor and student, and specific skills in analytic counseling are required.

Developmental Counseling

Developmental career counseling has gained considerable attention and popularity and represents an eclectic approach which draws heavily on self-concept theory. It begins with the student at any particular stage on the developmental continuum and then attempts to move with the student through succeeding stages of growth. Developmental career counseling proposes that, by reducing excessive anxiety, assisting the student in clarifying feelings and gaining insight, and thus helping attain some success in developing a feeling of competence in any single area of life, there will be a generalizing effect on other aspects of living, bringing about improvements in one's general adjustment. This approach rests squarely in the mainstream of developmental theory characterizing much of student personnel work today. It is compatible with the proactive thrust of most student developmental models.

Behavioral Counseling

Behavioral career counseling is one of the more recent approaches and is growing in popularity. It consists of an active and pragmatic set of techniques based on learning theory. This approach emphasizes the acquisition of decision-making skills where they have been deficient. The behavioral counselor attempts to reduce the debilitating anxiety of the student through counter-conditioning methods before attending to the skills of the decision-making process.

The goals of behavioral counseling are particularly related to the needs of each individual and, as such, are specific and observable. With specific goals established, progress through the sequential steps of the career-decision process may be determined.

The theoretical approaches briefly discussed above are only representative of the better known and established positions. Career counseling theory rests on more general theories of counseling and personality, and, like that on which it rests, will undoubtedly continue to evolve dramatically in the near future.

THEORIES OF VOCATIONAL DEVELOPMENT

Several theorists have attempted to systematize the results of their investigations into the career development process. Certain theorists have significantly influenced the direction of research and have stimulated innovative practices.

Among them are Eli Ginzberg and Associates, who reported the results of their investigations in *Occupational Choice: an Approach to a General Theory* in 1951; Donald E. Super, whose book *The Psychology of Careers* in 1957 stated his early position; and John L. Holland, who in 1966 set the stage for new empirical studies with his book *The Psychology of Vocational Choice*. The major aspects of these positions are presented as examples of the thought-guiding career development activities.

They are not meant to be exhaustive and certainly do not cover the entire range of theories.

Ginzberg's Theory

Based on developmental psychology, the Ginzberg Theory stresses the importance of the adolescent period as a time of vocational choice. Emotional factors are recognized as playing significant roles in the career development of individuals and frequently account for difficulties in career decisions. The basic theory states that vocational choice is a process, occurring over time, which moves through stages or periods of development. The process incorporates compromises between wishes and possibilities as one progresses through the sequential stages. The entire vocational choice process is essentially irreversible. The three major stages of the process are called Fantasy, Tentative, and Realistic periods.

The Fantasy period characterizes the play activity of very young children as they emulate adult models, most of whom are in working roles. The identity with significant adults through activities that fantasize "working" is rewarding in that it momentarily overcomes the limitations of size and skill and reduces the sense of frustration and inadequacy. This represents an early attempt at dealing with role stereotypes. At this stage play activities are pleasure oriented and unconcerned about reality variables that are later necessary for career decisions.

The Tentative period is divided into the stages of interest, capacity, value, and transition. These activities mark adolescent considerations of career matters. During the interest stage, there is a sorting of activities according to the degree of enjoyment related to the activity. This is naturally integrated into the capacity stage to test out how well one is able to perform the preferred activity.

A variety of role models are considered. The value stage introduces the relative importance of various occupations, not only in satisfying personal needs, but in their potential for contribution to others which may be a significant factor in the value structure of the adolescent. As the time for vocational choices with lasting ramifications draws nearer, the person becomes more aware of the time perspective involved in particular career choices which are perceived as committing one to a pattern of life-long activities.

A transition stage introduces a new awareness of the realities involved in career choice and preparation. More adult stances are taken in relation to decisions and one develops an understanding that responsibility for the consequences of decisions is very personal.

The Realistic period evolves from earlier stages and characterizes the young adult years. The tasks of this period are most often faced by the traditional college student, who is confronted with the task of establishing independent personal identity. The tasks have been divided into the stages of exploration, crystallization, and specification. The career exploration activities of the early college years typify the first stage. This is a time of narrowing fields of choice among career alternatives. It is frequently a time of high anxiety due to the press of competing developmental tasks calling for attention. It is also a time requiring accurate and adequate career information. Many students are particularly able to utilize personal and career counseling resources at this stage.

The Crystallization stage emerges somewhat out of necessity. The normal progress through the educational system has precluded certain decisions such as type of training or college, choice of major or specialized training program, etc. Development through the Crystallization stage naturally, if not easily, leads to the final stage of Specification. It is here the individual selects a more permanent career direction and accepts a specific job in the chosen field.

Throughout the entire process, it is evident that many compromises and tradeoffs from earlier positions must be made as new information is obtained. Many choice points cannot be reentered due to the limitations of time, opportunities, abilities, and other reality factors which contribute to the irreversible nature of the vocational choice process. The theory allows for persons to make career-related changes. In so doing, however, they must build on earlier decisions and developmental accomplishments.

Super's Theory

Super's Theory attempts to combine the relatively static differential psychology of occupations, the developmental psychology of careers, and the self-concept theory into a workable vocational psychology. He has stressed the importance of two major, vocationally relevant stages: exploration and establishment.

The exploratory stage includes career development activities which are defined as tentative, transitional, and involving trial with little commitment. The establishment stage continues with the substages of trial with more commitment, stabilization, and advancement. The order of these stages suggests the importance placed on the sequential and developmental nature of vocational maturity.

The tasks which need to be satisfied in this process include crystallization, specification, implementation, stabilization, consolidation, and advancement. The crystallization stage includes the increasing awareness of the need to bring ideas of vocational preference together so that they may be assessed meaningfully. What information is needed regarding the preferred occupation? How consistent is the preference in relation to interests, values, and other factors?

Specification of a vocational preference calls for more explicit educational planning and the reality testing of the plan to the point of implementation. The implementation stage includes activities preparatory to entering the preferred occupation and, in fact, gaining an entry-level position. The stabilization stage further confirms the career choice by achievement in the chosen field so as to establish credibility and with it a sense of being settled. The final stage involves consolidating one's status and advancing in the occupation.

Vocational maturity is relative to the particular age and stage of development. The adolescent considering the factors of personal interest, values, and tentative vocational preferences, while securing information about occupations, is relatively as mature as the middle-aged person advancing through a series of stable career positions. Career development is integrated with other personal growth tasks.

Although Super's Theory does not claim to be all-inclusive, it seems to provide for the interaction of many influential factors which impinge on the individual's total development. The work of Super and his colleagues suggests the possibility of self-concept studies and the theory which supports them, ultimately providing a framework from which to view, understand, and evaluate vocational approaches.

Holland's Theory

According to Holland's Theory, vocational preferences and interests are expressions of personality. The choice of an occupation expresses an individual's motivation, knowledge of a particular occupation, and personal abilities. Stereotypes are used throughout this system because people tend to agree on the meaning held by vocational stereotypes. Persons within a given vocation have developmental histories and personalities that are similar. Due to the many personal similarities among those who enter and persist in a given occupation, it follows that the characteristic patterns of communication and interaction established will form a unique work environment. To the extent the work environment and worker's personality are congruent, the prediction is for increased satisfaction, stability, and achievement in relation to the vocational choice.

The theory makes three assumptions: that people can be characterized by a particular type of personality, that environments in which people live and work resemble model environments, and that the pairing of people with environments allows for the prediction of vocational choice, stability, and achievement.

A personality type is described as a cluster of personal characteristics defining how an individual typically copes with life's tasks. For purposes of the theory, persons are categorized as being a Realistic, Intellectual, Social, Conventional, Enterprising, or Artistic type. The six types form models by which an individual's pattern of behavior may be compared for relative similarity. Although the scheme identifies the major personality type, it also allows for more complex configurations where patterns of behavior reflect similarities to different types in varying magnitudes.

There are six corresponding environments: Realistic, Intellectual, Social, Conventional, Enterprising, and Artistic. Generally, persons of the same type are found in each of the environments. The characteristics of a particular environment reflect the personal attributes of individuals in that group.

The main thrust of the theory is that persons move toward work environments that permit them to develop abilities, project personal values, and become involved in activities of interest. This movement toward a compatible work environment usually occurs over a period of time. Interactions of persons with environments belonging to the same type or model tend to promote better personal stability and satisfaction. In addition, vocational choices become more stable and vocational achievements higher.

COMBINING THEORY AND PRACTICE

The basic principles of career counseling are firmly rooted in general counseling theory and practice. When one considers persons from a holistic point of view, as with current student personnel approaches, it is frequently unnecessary to delineate between "career" and "personal" counseling. Benefits accruing from counseling endeavors in any sector of life produce gains that tend to be generalized to other areas of life functioning. Although counseling practice may be focused in a particular setting for career or personal concerns, excessive categorization may be unrealistically restrictive. The particular skills and purposes of the counseling staff and the problems presented by the students will determine programmatic emphases.

Counseling theory is important for the counselor because the student's total behavior is viewed from the particular frame of reference of theory held by the counselor. One would expect the student also to come with a theory about the problem and how it might be resolved. It is important that perceptions of the situation, as held by the student and the counselor, are as accurate as possible. Early counseling activities are aimed at clarifying these perceptions since they tend to prompt attitudes concerning the effectiveness of the career counseling relationship.

An adequate career counseling theory can serve the counselor well. It is an important part of the total rationale for counseling in that a good theory, well conceived and modified by personal experience, helps to reduce the complexities in counseling interactions to more manageable proportions and assists the counselor in dealing with an otherwise overwhelming amount of information. The present state of the art in career counseling theory suggests that theory be employed much as an untested hypothesis, a sort of conceptual model to be used as a guideline, not as a rigid discipline.

Many positions or approaches may be combined, depending on the personal preferences of the counselor, the individual's personality, and the particular needs of the student. For example, developmental and behavioral elements of theory may be combined and applied effectively. Both approaches rely on the prior establishment of good rapport and an open relationship. The developmental approach is subject oriented and aimed at understanding the particular individual while treating subjective realities with concern. Behavioral elements add to this general orientation by stressing the importance of observable realities and the need for objectivity. This application can be particularly useful in setting obtainable short-term goals in career counseling.

The general, theoretical base underlying the activities of a particular counselor tends to determine the methods and outcome criteria of counseling. Methods are determined as goals are set in any particular counseling relationship. Most practicing counselors continually interweave two or more positions with a variety of methodologies. It is helpful for the counselor to understand and to be able to employ as many approaches as situations determine. It is not necessary to choose a single position to the exclusion of all others. The development of an eclectic approach is most popular among pragmatic professional career counselors.

Career counseling theory is designed to provide a rational system for managing the events, observations, and experiences encountered in practice. A useful theory gives a handy framework in which day-to-day matters may be placed for evaluation, consistency, and utility. The usefulness of the theory is determined by how well it can generate pertinent predictions or questions concerning the events being studied. Although in an unfinished state, there is much available to the counselor from the experiences and ideas of present colleagues and from the records of predecessors. The career counselor today stands on the shoulders of giants who have labored for the development of general theories of personality and counseling as well as the formulation of theories in the area of career counseling.

The theories on which counseling activities are based frequently stem from the counselor's view of human nature, even though this may be in a continually evolving process. A quick review of one's basic position and attitude in these areas is relevant to the development of a working theory and a choice of methods in the practice of career counseling. The student's problem or behavior is viewed through the particular counselor's frame of reference, and the theoretical positions held influence counseling behavior, whether or not there is full awareness of the influence.

As the individual counselor is able to increasingly identify the basic assumptions supporting practice and then examine actual counseling activities in the light of that information, it is possible and desirable to move about on the continuum between theory and practice. Theory and practice may interact in this fashion and provide a very useful and constructive criticism for each other and for the benefit of career counseling. Practice checks and verifies theory, and theory checks and judges practice. With a carefully examined theoretical stance, the counselor better knows what is going on and why.

The blending of the theoretical and practical provides the base for important "in house" research which allows for the checking of counseling outcomes and the reasonable modification of programs. Good theory encourages practical research and allows for data-oriented practice. The career counselor need not be a "thinker in the clouds," but should be able to make reasoned decisions among alternatives for counseling practice.

Career Counseling Defined

The approaches and methods of counseling vary with the needs of the particular student. An eclectic approach is perhaps most useful in that it allows the counselor maximum flexibility to use more direct, rational techniques or more reflective and analytical approaches, depending upon the nature of the problem and the student's particular stage in the counseling process. Career counseling is essentially an educational and developmental process which is strongly dedicated to student self-realization and self-direction. It is aimed at developing insight and understanding of self as necessary to more effective functioning.

Counseling is an art. It is learned by doing. Much as theory and practice go hand and hand, a study of counseling principles must be accomplished by counseling practice in order for the counselor to become an effective helper. Career counseling is a helping process which has as its objective the mobilization of sufficient student resources to attain the counseling goal. It aims to help the student make satisfying choices and utilize the self-fulfilling aspects of personality. There are certain basic skills needed by the counselor if the counseling relationship is to enable the student to achieve a clearer perception of the problem and a deeper understanding of self, so that the individual can arrive at more effective and satisfying personal behaviors and career plans.

Career counseling as proposed here is probably best described as developmental in that it follows sequential stages or skill levels achieved by the counselor and reflected in the developmental growth of the student. To the extent that each stage or level is completed or worked through satisfactorily, the succeeding stage has a higher probability of success.

Overview of Counselor Skills

There are certain counselor skills that are widely accepted as necessary in facilitating student growth. A brief overview of counseling skills is presented here. A more detailed discussion will follow. Included is the pre-counseling skill of attending to the person who comes for assistance. This calls for giving one's self to the other as entirely as possible without physiological or psychological interferences. It also expresses one's ability and desire to work with the other person.

The next necessary skill is the ability to respond to the student in ways that permit the exploration of problem areas more clearly and in more depth than was possible outside the counseling relationship. Responding in these terms requires genuineness and warmth which convey respect for the student as a person.

There are no particular conditions which the student must meet in order to be accepted in counseling. The counselor attempts to meet the student at any particular point of need. Although this may not be possible in an absolute sense, it should be effective to the degree that a tone or attitude is set for the relationship permitting the establishment of rapport. The student experiences a special condition of trust and confidence which promotes the sense of personal value and significance in the relationship. The immediate goal for the student is to explore the various individual experiences with career planning or personal matters that are related to the problem under consideration.

Another important skill for counseling is that of empathy and effective communication of understanding to the student. This skill is built on a variety of counselor behaviors, including self-disclosure and immediacy or dealing with the "here and now." In self-disclosure, the counselor's own experience is shared when appropriate and when it assists the student's grasp of personal experience. Confrontation also helps the student see the distortions and conflicts in thinking and feeling. The goal for the student at this stage is to appreciate new dimensions of behavior and pattern of response, and to emerge with new alternatives for action, to see more clearly what can be done about the problematic in life.

Counselor skills involving spontaneous and open collaboration with the student in the development of action programs constitute the final necessary step in career counseling. As the student attempts to make career decisions or implement a plan of action, there may be need for the continuing encouragement and support of the counselor or the career-oriented group.

The student's goal in this stage is to assume the risks of trying new behaviors, to begin acting. As the student begins the action program the counselor may assist in a variety of training experiences. The career counselor may provide training and assistance in acquiring career information through a variety of approaches outlined elsewhere in this book. The counselor may also assist in the development of skills required in job-search campaigns. These include certain communication skills, letter writing, preparation of resumes, and the development of a natural interview style.

This model for career counseling is developmental in that the goals of the student are successive ones, each building on the last, until the task to be accomplished is clear and there are sufficient skills to begin with reasonable self-assurance. These goals are attained within the context of a supportive, well conceived career planning operation where a variety of career services are available, not the least of which would be effective, highly skilled career counseling.

Summary

Career counseling, based on any one or a combination of approaches, is a special condition of interpersonal relationship whose purpose is to assist students in their search for self-realization and self-direction in matters of career planning. Such counseling is aimed at developing student insight and understanding as necessary to behavior change or reaching realistic decisions. Change in behavior, including decision-making behavior, is a function of learning, and in many respects, the counseling interaction is a special kind of learning situation. In most cases the student is capable of modifying behavior as new possibilities of response and alternatives of action are learned.

Career counselors most often deal with persons in the normal range of human development. Counseling activities are thought of essentially as a preventive, not a remedial process. Therefore, more attention is given to developmental concerns than to rehabilitative functions. Career counseling is dedicated to the concept of self-realization, new learning, and a willingness to accommodate methods to the needs of the student in all counseling interactions.

BASIC SKILLS

Career counseling is an activity one learns by doing. Counselors may have adequate academic grounding through courses and graduate programs in psychology, counseling, and other fields related to the helping process, but they still may feel inadequate in practice. The skills required in career counseling are basic human relations skills. The skills one needs for effective communication and involvement with other people in any setting are extended in special ways to provide for career counseling.

Most of these skills are well known and for many the assimilation of these skills in their practice has been a thing of long standing. The purpose here is simply to review these basic skills and to be reminded that they are transferable to many situations. The skills of good human relations are applied in special ways to the career counseling relationship to effect positive outcomes in terms of student goals.

As outlined and briefly discussed earlier, these skills are integrated, systematic, and developmental in that succeeding activities in the counseling relationship build on them. For example, it would be premature to leap immediately into an action program without adequately exploring the problem, understanding resources, and examining the variety of alternatives for action.

Just as in good human relations, effective career counseling demands much of us. It assumes that the counselor is relatively "together," at least for the time committed to career counseling. The quality of the counseling relationship will depend in large measure on the condition and characteristics of the person of the counselor.

The basic raw material necessary to the counseling relationship is one's own personality in all its uniqueness and resourcefulness. So even though theories and approaches are discussed as though they were clear-cut and easily replicated, in fact each counselor devises an approach based on one's individual personality, the particular student, and the resources available. Nevertheless, with all the idiosyncratic approaches, it is possible to delineate basic skills which appear to be common to most career counseling situations.

The Individual Interview

The individual interview is perhaps the most basic element in all career counseling programs. All of the basic skills of the counselor come together and are put to the test. It is the point at which the most specific attention is directed toward the individual student. Along with small group counseling, the individual interview places a great demand on the counselor for the competent use of acquired skills. Individual career counseling calls for facilities which allow for private interaction with the student and allows for follow-up sessions to maintain the benefits of counseling over a period of time.

Although individual counseling is expensive in terms of staff time, it is essential in certain cases where the student does not have the initial resourcefulness or assertiveness to make gains in a group situation. Furthermore, it is possible that certain individual concerns are not appropriate for short-term group interactions. When individual counseling is performed, process notes should be kept by the counselor to allow for more accurate recall prior to succeeding interview sessions. An interest and concern for the person is conveyed when the counselor is able to begin where the student is without loss of time and energy on the part of both participants.

When information given in an individual counseling interview may be helpful to other advisors or helpers, permission must be secured from the student to share or release information to them. Usually, if the student understands that the sharing of information with other persons involved in career planning activities would be helpful, there is no problem. In cases where information is to be released to others, the explicit content of such communication should be discussed with the student before it is released.

Attending Skills

Helping another person in an interpersonal relationship demands a genuine sense of presence. Attending fully to another person demands much energy and is not a common experience in everyday life. In ordinary human relations one often feels that another has not listened or has not been fully aware of what was being said. The counselor is committed to providing a very special kind of attentiveness. It is similar to that found in friendship, but differs in at least one important respect. Whereas in friendship there is a mutuality, a give and take, an ebb and flow of ideas and feelings, in counseling the immediate needs of the counselor are recognized by the counselor but are withheld for the most part to allow focus and continued concentration on that which is problematic in the life of the student. This attention is so unusual that it tends to prompt the exploration of problems on the part of the student and facilitates the establishment of trust in the counseling relationship.

Attending involves certain physical behaviors by the counselor. It is assumed that basic physical needs have been taken care of and that the student is reasonably comfortable in the physical setting. The counselor must provide an appropriate meeting place so the relationship will be free from unnecessary interruptions and distractions.

The position and posture of the counselor convey a readiness to respond to the student's needs. Posture tends to reflect attitudes and feelings within. The counselor may feel better toward the student as the physical distance is reduced by coming out from behind a desk and arranging chairs for proximity. Interest in the student's presence and in what the student brings to the counseling relationship is expressed, in part, by the relaxed but alert posture of the counselor.

Attending psychologically is the next step after caring for the physical situation. In psychological attending, one is communicating undivided attention to the student. One of the best ways to convey this attention is by maintaining good eye contact. As the counselor is aware of using visual contact, the student is encouraged to do the same. Each is able to check out the cues given by the other so that all expressions are better understood or are readily clarified as the counseling process moves on.

The counselor communicates much to the student by the expressions projected by skillful attending. When intently involved with the student's concerns, while maintaining a relaxed stance, the counselor communicates the desire to be with the student. This is much more facilitating than the nervous fidgeting which conveys a desire not to be present.

In attending to another person it is essential to be aware of one's own behavior, to "tune in" to feelings and needs and to see that these are satisfied or managed prior to the counseling contact. The counselor must be relatively comfortable with intrapersonal matters to provide high level attending behavior.

The development of good attending skills is a vehicle for conveying respect to the student. Being able to face the person, maintaining eye contact, listening without distraction or interruption, and conveying an intent involvement with the student all play a key role in facilitating productive counseling interactions. Most people are sensitive to inattention and tend to be turned away by others who are preoccupied or obviously not attending to their concerns. On the other hand, high level attending skills provide powerful rewards for continuing in counseling and persisting in the work at hand.

Thoughtful reflection on physical and psychological behavior in interview situations may be instructive. Many counselors find it helpful in professional workshop settings to check out their counseling behaviors through critiques from colleagues and by videotaping counseling sessions. Career counseling effectiveness is developed and improved as counseling behaviors are regularly examined.

There are no rigid formulas for attending, for each counselor must adopt a unique style. In any case, attending is demanding work. Helping people in career counseling is not simply a relaxed informal procedure. The counselor's attending behaviors are crucial to the early establishment of rapport. The effective counselor is aware of the influence of body language in counseling and the maintaining of psychological attentiveness.

Listening Skills

Listening is the activity going on while attending to the other person. We "listen" not only to verbal messages but to nonverbal behavior as well. The high level counselor will be alert to a variety of nonverbal behaviors such as body movements, facial expressions, tone of voice, the pace of the verbal expression, emphasis, and many others. The counselor responds to the student's total behavior, not merely to the words or content being presented but also to the manner and feeling which is present in the process. Listening to the person with this involvement allows for the reflection of content and feeling at levels which facilitate the exploration of ideas and experiences relating to the problematic in the person's life.

Listening to material as it is being presented requires active listening on the part of the counselor. It also means the counselor must withhold critical judgment, learning to pause and to wait for a response. The ability to refrain from rushing in with an immediate response and to remain relaxed while waiting conveys a concern and thoughtfulness on the part of the counselor for the work the student is doing. The effective counselor is fully present and open to the student. Establishment of trust is enhanced and the base is laid for further work in career counseling.

Responding Skills

Counselor response skills set the stage for more complete exploration by the student of material relevant to the career counseling process. The counselor's skills of responding facilitate the communication of empathy, respect, and genuineness. Empathy involves the counselor's ability to see the world somewhat through the eyes of the other person and to get a feeling for what the world is like from the perspective of that individual. This understanding is communicated sufficiently to allow the student to know that the counselor understands the personal experiences and the feelings accompanying these experiences.

The ability of the counselor to be empathic has a positive effect on the student and encourages continued self-exploration. Empathy and genuineness promote a sense of trust and assure the student that the counselor is present even at levels beyond verbal expressions. This does not mean that to be empathic one should attempt to interpret hidden meanings in the student's words or behavior. Rather, the counselor should simply communicate the understanding of what is being expressed. It is quite appropriate for the counselor to ask the student if this understanding is accurate. There is no place for pretense in the counseling relationship, pretending to understand when one does not. It is much better to ask the student to go over that material again for the counselor's benefit. This may express care for the material being presented and respect for the person.

Developing the skill of empathy enables the counselor to get beneath the immediate or superficial understanding of the content or experience of the student and reflect some of the connections in what seem to be fragmented ideas and other expressions. By employing high-level empathy, the student is enabled to see response alternatives and to experience new dimensions of the particular situation.

Confronting Skills

Following closely, and perhaps intertwined with the activities of self-exploration, come those of self-understanding. Understanding is necessary in the consideration of alternatives for action. The skills that enable the counselor to assist the student in achieving this goal include confronting, immediacy, some self-disclosure, and the continued use of empathy.

After rapport has been established, one of the counselor's most potent skills in assisting the student to new levels of understanding is the activity of confrontation. It is here that the counselor, by the techniques of questioning and restatement, assists the student in examining some of the distortions or inconsistencies that have emerged in the immediate counseling situation. It is a time when the counselor may ask the student to elaborate on a theme or pattern of behavior that seems to have self-defeating elements about it or is an evasion of some issue which tends to block the forward movement of the student.

Confrontation must be closely coupled with accurate empathy, so that one is not leading the student in directions selected by the counselor or following so far behind to suggest the counselor is not keeping up in the process. When all the previous skills have been operative and are still functionally available at this stage in the counseling process, confrontation and understanding go hand in hand. Some of the most significant gains for the student are possible at this stage in the career counseling process.

The additional skill of immediacy can be very helpful. This is a way of testing the counseling relationship at any point along the way. It amounts to calling attention to the "here and now" of the relationship, looking at the qualities and dimensions of the immediate interaction. In this way, the counseling relationship provides a laboratory experience in which one significant interpersonal relationship of the student may be examined with very minimal threat and certainly without consequences of action. Immediacy allows the counselor to check the student about feelings in the interaction or about the material being presented at the moment. It also enables one to deal with issues as they arise, such as trust, resistance, difficulty in expression, and so on.

Revealing one's own experience in the counseling context should be done with great reserve, but on occasion the process may be advanced if relevant experience of the counselor is disclosed at a time and place in the relationship that is not threatening to the student. This communicates the counselor's willingness to give of self to assist the student. The counselor should be cautioned, however, to keep such self-disclosure at a minimum and to avoid the danger of lengthy discussions concerning personal experiences.

Constructive Action

The goal of career counseling is to enable the student to launch an action program based on new behaviors which carry the potential of more productive and enjoyable life experiences. In terms of career counseling, this may mean the development of a strategy that leads the student to success in a first-job placement or in developing a methodology for career planning that goes on serving needs beyond the immediate concern. To the extent that the counseling activities through the preceding skill levels have been successful, the student is prepared to enter or to continue problem-solving behaviors with specific goals in mind.

In review, career counseling has assisted the student in identifying and clarifying the problem and exploring alternatives and dimensions. With this exploration comes deeper self-understanding, a greater trust in one's own resourcefulness, and a greater sense of self-assurance. Based on these new plateaus of understanding, the student is now able to establish personal priorities for action grounded on that which is most important to the individual.

The established priorities and the help of the counselor permit specific goals to be named. These goals are clarified in the counseling relationship as being realistic and obtainable. The student is then assisted in reviewing the various resources available to achieve these goals. As the action program proceeds, it may be desirable to recycle selected counseling process elements to mobilize certain personal resources or to deal with incidental problems. The student is encouraged to use the resources of the total community in the attainment of set goals.

After the assessment of various resources, the student, with the help of the counselor, selects the most effective means available to attain the goal. These avenues of action should be in keeping with what is important to the student in terms of personal values and should be action goals assessed as reasonably attainable. It is the counselor's responsibility to assist in confronting and challenging unattainable goals in the context of the counseling relationship, as well as the exploration of personal resources.

At this stage in the decision-making process, it is helpful to establish very specific outcome goals so that the action program can be evaluated. Frequently in the beginning it is helpful to have short range and specific goals that are very attainable so that the continual support and encouragement offered by a counseling relationship allows the student to develop the increasing confidence necessary to take on higher risk goal problems. As goal attainment is realized, the self-image of the student is enhanced and additional personal resources tend to be released and become available for use.

The developmental model provides for goal attainment based on prior achievement. In this way, the system of reinforcements encourages continued individual growth along lines established by the student, not imposed by advisors, counselors, or outside agents. These experiences of the student in counseling through exploration, understanding, and then acting on best alternatives, provide training in a methodology of decision-making and behavioral change which is essentially educational in nature and goes far beyond the attainment of an immediate goal.

It is important to note that in career counseling the counselor does not jump prematurely to action programs on the one hand or never get to them on the other. This should be preceded by an adequate amount of prior insight and development of student resourcefulness. Action programs follow very naturally, and grow out of the student's own frame of reference and system of values. This allows for the fullest expression of individuality, and conveys, even in the final stages of an action program, respect for the student.

The comprehensiveness of career counseling is one of its

most exciting aspects. Not only does the counselor work with the student through the early stages of frustration, conflict, and pressures and the surrounding confusion, but the counselor also accompanies the student through exploration and the attainment of a solid base of understanding where the individual reaches a plateau from which to operate in a more realistic fashion.

In career counseling, the helper is able to share in the action plan and to assist the student in shaping behavior in ways that are more personally rewarding and vocationally satisfying. Effective career counseling assists the student in attaining the goal selected or changing the behavior that has been self-defeating for new behavioral responses that are self-enhancing and lead to a happier and more productive life.

Confidentiality

Career counseling is to be marked by confidentiality. Confidence is earned in the counseling process and cannot be assumed to be granted by virtue of title or the simple declaration of confidentiality. Only as the counselor's respect for the student is sensed is it possible to assume that the productions, thoughts, and feelings of the relationship are also respected and will be treated with the same measure of trust as experience suggests. The sense of confidentiality is necessary for the student to feel safe in the relationship.

The counseling process is a private process, whether with an individual or in a group context. It is a process marked by a code of behavior for all participants. It is essentially the counselor's responsibility to see that the code of ethics of good counseling practice is followed. The counseling relationship should not be interrupted by other matters extraneous to the concerns of the student. The burden of maintaining confidence and privacy is on the shoulders of the counselor.

Counseling Limits

A subtle but very important aspect of any counseling relationship involves limits. Counseling implies the willingness of the counselor to accommodate the student in relation to time, place, and pattern for the counseling relationship. In effect, the counselor is committed to a rather specific amount of time for the relationship and attempts to maintain an appropriate psychological climate in order to be helpful. The career counseling relationship is a special helping situation where the counselor suspends attention to personal needs and attends as wholly as possible to the needs and concerns of the student.

An essential safeguard to both student and counselor is maintenance of limits on time committed to the counseling activities. When counseling is an active process all persons involved are expending much energy and usually sense they have been working. This sort of relationship differs from the usual mutuality of friendship where there is more give and take and limits of time are less crucial. In its total setting, counseling is thought of as a learning experience, and the matter of dealing with limits is a very important one for reality testing and student learning.

Awareness of Cultural Diversity

Career counseling should be provided all students, including those from special populations with diverse cultural backgrounds, as well as students who do not fit a traditional pattern in terms of age, socio-economic status, or other stereotypic variables. As higher education becomes more accessible, it is important that career counselors be prepared to relate to the particular needs of subgroups within the student population. The basic theory, approaches, and skills used in career counseling are appropriate for all special groups.

All persons who seek the assistance of career counselors have common characteristics. In other respects, however, every individual is quite unique. When there are pronounced cultural differences, counselors need to exercise special attentiveness and preparation to be effective. Special subgroups within the general population of the United States include, among others, blacks, American-Indians, Mexican-Americans, and women. Each group has certain special features deserving of consideration in counseling approaches.

In counseling black students, counselors should be aware of the considerable body of literature that has been produced in recent decades and that contributes to our understanding of the black student. For many, counseling assistance has been less than fully available because of a lack of understanding of black cultural values and the unexamined biases and attitudes of those involved in the educational process. The sensitive counselor must be aware of the biases that may exist in both parties where interracial relationships are involved. These may be very subtle in nature, particularly resistant to conscious awareness, and difficult to manage.

It is important to remember that, in counseling relationships, the student by definition is placed in a rather vulnerable position during the exploration of strengths, weaknesses, and other personal characteristics. The career counselor must be particularly attentive, understanding, and sensitive to the dynamics of the student counselee. For many students in this special group, the encouragement and support of a mature and effective counselor can be a rewarding experience.

American Indians bring a special cultural background to counseling relationships. Knowledge of Indian culture and language is most helpful for counselors assisting Indian students. The student's responses to the counselor may be atypical due to cultural patterning which would lead the counselor to certain expectancies which may not be present in other special subgroups. The basic skills of counseling, particularly those of empathy, are called for in these cases. Effectiveness will be enhanced by attempting to see the world through the eyes of the student client so that counselor responses are more appropriate and directed to the perceived need of the student.

Counseling Mexican-Americans calls for specific information concerning their cultural background. Career counselors in the American Southwest are more involved with these special populations and recognize the importance of understanding their language and the continuing effects of their cultural heritage. To work effectively as a career counselor with Spanish-speaking Americans, the counselor must be able to focus on the points of conflict between the typical American cultural issues and those of the student client.

Assisting special groups within the student population calls for resourcefulness. A mark of the professional career counselor is willingness to face personal limitations in counseling and a readiness to refer clients to other qualified persons within the career resources network. Wherever sizable special populations of students exist, it is most desirable to employ competent career counselors who share that cultural background. Where this is impossible, special sensitivity on the part of the culturally different counselor is required.

Women have been engaged in a long and difficult struggle to gain equal rights, particularly in the career area. One role of career counselors is to assist female students as they cope with choices concerning life and career planning. Decisions concerning marriage, a career, or a career in some combination with marriage are frequently difficult. It is vital that the career counselor respond to female students as individuals rather than with stereotypical and biased responses based on previous or distorted perceptions. Counselors must be aware of their attitudes about women and the role of women in contemporary society. The counselor's unexamined biases can be particularly troublesome and hazardous in the career assistance of female students.

The career planning and placement office should provide assistance for students coming from culturally different backgrounds and for non-traditional students who are entering or reentering the higher education system in mid-life. In these cases, the basic approach and skills of the counselor are the same. The presenting problems and perceived needs may be different when compared to traditional students. The career counselor must be sensitive and respond appropriately.

If special subgroups of students appear challenging, the appropriate response of career counselors should be to expand knowledge and increase effectiveness. Career counseling may be an area where these special persons receive individual attention not provided elsewhere in the system.

Summary

The assimilation of the skills of attending, listening, responding, confronting, and empathy into the unique personality of the counselor provides for high-level assistance in career counseling. One of the goals of this activity is increased self-confidence and self-direction in the student. Positive outcomes are to be expected. The professional career counselor will certainly be prepared by academic background along guidelines established by the profession. The skills of career counseling, however, grow out of a willingness to learn and an openness of personality that enable the counselor to employ a variety of techniques and develop the wide repertory of skills necessary for effective counseling.

As the career counselor prepares for more professional and effective counseling activities, it is important to reemphasize the person of the counselor. In fact, attending to the counselor's own needs in the area of career development and other personal matters may be most significant. It seems that, to the extent the problematic areas of the counselor's life remain unresolved, there is risk of these areas interfering with open counseling activity.

Most counselor training programs allow for the didactic counseling of the counselor-in-training. This activity is highly recommended to achieve in the counselor the sensitivity and the experiential knowledge so vital to effective functioning as a counselor. No amount of reading or other intellectual pursuit totally divorced from the experiential will allow for the development of the practicing counselor.

To the degree that the counselors own career is not secure or the counselor feels insecure, there is risk of interference in helping other people resolve career problems. Training programs for career counselors should give much attention to the selectivity of counselors based on their openness and relative good health.

Professional associations providing workshops, inservice training programs, and other graduate programs with experiential components are fully recommended. Frequently, in career planning and placement operations where staff members are few in number, it is desirable to arrange for inter-institutional association to provide the stimulus and opportunity for the career counselor to continue growing in personal and professional stature.

GROUP COUNSELING

Group counseling is becoming very popular in career planning and counseling offices due to the large number of students who desire the service of these offices and because there are certain advantages of group counseling that are not available in individual sessions. Group counseling is emerging as one of the most significant means by which career counseling personnel are able to achieve their program goals.

The variety of objectives which may be met by group means is extensive. Many career planning and placement offices are using group approaches to provide instruction in the methods of career development through formal courses and a variety of special purpose groups. Career counseling groups are based on the same assumptions and principles as other forms of career counseling.

Group techniques have been employed over the years with varying degrees of success, from large assemblies called to disseminate information concerning placement and career planning operations, to college-wide career days, to departmental meetings with selected alumni, to more specific group programs within the career planning office. The career counselor may choose among a variety of techniques for larger group meetings, including the forum, panel, symposium, or any combination that may fit the specific occasion where large groups are involved.

The focus here, however, is more on the use of small groups in career counseling. The collective experience of a number of career counseling operations is utilized to provide information and guidance. Particular attention is given to the process and content of small groups employed to achieve career planning goals.

Description

Group counseling in nearly all settings is a dynamic interpersonal process by which individuals interact with a peer group, usually with the assistance of a professionally trained counselor. Most often group participants are involved with exploring problems and feelings with a view toward modifying attitudes and developing programs of action that allow them to better deal with developmental problems.

The dynamic interpersonal process emphasizes that each individual is an integral part of the group, and the group becomes more effective as each individual feels an increasing involvement. Participation must be active. However, each individual is not expected to be anxiously waiting a chance to talk, as even the nonverbal participant is reacting emotionally to the various forms of interaction going on within the group.

In order to provide for this process, a relatively open and permissive atmosphere is established and maintained, primarily through the facilitation of the group leader. In this climate, the individual members sense enough security to explore themselves and to interact and thus receive feedback from other members of the group to acquire a high level of accurate self-knowledge which assists them with developmental tasks. The open atmosphere typically leads to high levels of group acceptance and consequent encouragement of the freedom of expression and self-evaluation.

Group techniques which facilitate the group process provide dimensions of emotional support not present in the individual interview. In effect, the group setting is a laboratory for the testing of personal and social realities. The particular feedback and reinforcements applied by peers within the group provide for strong motivation in the continuing exploration and discovery that self-assessment activities require.

The group increasingly becomes its own counselor as it is being assisted by the skilled career counselor. In fact, the trained counselor becomes a sort of participant-coach in the team activities represented by the group. The entire group acts to reflect feelings, to clarify problems, and to allow the individual to find a solution. The process is not that of a counselor counseling an individual within a group setting. Rather, by means of the group structure, various individuals counsel each other by sharing feelings, ventilating problem areas, supplying support, and the various other activities that go on with the group interaction. Group members identify with each other as well as with the counselor.

The group size has been a matter of discussion among counselors for a long time, but in general, the group must be small enough to permit each participant the opportunity to contribute to the group process and yet have time between contributions so that the pressure is not too intense for everyone to be involved at high levels. If the group is very small, persons may feel too much is expected. On the other hand, when the group is large, it is possible for individuals to hide from the interaction. Counseling groups that are based on the small group experience ideally range in size from eight to twelve members.

Group Counseling Skills

The demands placed upon the group counselor are heavy. The person must be skilled in both group dynamics and counseling. All the various counselor skills outlined earlier involving general counseling come into play in this setting. In addition, facilitation skills in group dynamics are required.

In providing for a group, it is essential that the career counselor create a nonjudgmental atmosphere and work to achieve the ideal of shared leadership within the group. The counselor will perhaps summarize discussion of the group, highlight significant trends, or work to maintain the group's focus. The counselor will also attend to the group process to insure a positive and forward moving direction. The group facilitator permits as much freedom within the group process as is possible, depending upon stated goals of the group.

The counselor is able to facilitate the process by using skills similar to those used in other forms of counseling. High-level attending is particularly important. It is also rather demanding for the counselor to attend to six or eight persons in a group. The counselor must be very active in picking up eye contact of all members of the group, not in a mechanical fashion, but in an easy, relaxed yet intent manner. It is essential to continually read the cues for communication, most of which are nonverbal, since if six or eight members are present in a group only one may be speaking at a time. The nonverbal cues become extremely important in facilitating the process—such as body posture, facial expressions, and physical position in the group, including relative proximity to particular individuals. The counselor becomes aware of these cues and attempts to attend to the pressing issues of the moment which may go beyond the content of the exercise itself. In all of this, the counselor becomes very active, although not necessarily in leading the verbal productions of the group. Group members may be quite active in assisting each other in discussion and clarification of attitudes and in the exploration of problem areas and what is important to them in their career planning, while the counselor is, in a sense, on the sidelines facilitating the interaction.

GROUP OBJECTIVES

Career counseling centers may offer a wide range of group activities with stated objectives. A group may meet to explore information available in a given area and discuss procedures for securing additional and particular occupational information. In this approach, attention may be given to open and free discussion related to the selected topic. The leader then becomes a resource person, interjecting methods and resources not supplied by other members of the group.

As one moves along the continuum from more structured to less structured groups, an intermediate group may meet to clarify work values or explore decision-making methods and processes. In these cases, the process of the group interaction becomes as important as the content. The participants learn from shared experiences and behaviors within the group in the "here and now" as well as from the outside content which may be introduced.

The positive reinforcement available through the social interaction is frequently a necessary ingredient to encourage some participants to continue in what can be a difficult, although exciting, exploration of their own attitudes toward work, self, and other significant persons. In groups such as this, a variety of approaches have been tried in recent years, and materials have been published by career counselors to assist in group exercises to clarify values, evaluate personal abilities, and arrive at a better understanding of the meaning of personal experiences and what effect these may have in future planning.

Career counselors are encouraged to devise their own exercises to facilitate the exploration of characteristics important for the student in the assessment of personal liabilities and assets for realistic career planning. In providing such workshop group approaches, the career counselor must be aware of the different levels of participation. Although content and structure may be provided by an exercise introduced to the group, the skill of the counselor is required to attend to the process elements of the group interaction. The group may become bogged down by an overly talkative, quiet, or hostile member unless the counselor's knowledge of personal and group dynamics is adequate and available. The members will expect leadership from the counselor, even though they may not know what leadership is needed.

Unstructured Groups

Relatively unstructured groups may also be planned. These are frequently helpful for students who are indecisive about career goals or other personal situations. The career counselor may assist by providing an unstructured group designed to run for a specified number of sessions for the purpose of personal growth and self-exploration but with no specific career planning goals established at the outset. The group may agree to establish goals or it may decide to leave the work of the group open-ended. The exploration, development of communication skills, and examination of typical behaviors as exhibited in the group setting afford the participant the opportunity for experiential learning through the group process.

An unstructured group may be facilitated by certain exercises that are designed for further acquaintance and communication but are non-specific in terms of goal outcome. Simulation problems permit a small group to explore typical problem-solving behavior. The leader or members of the group will present a problem that the group might address. A specific time might be set for the group to interact while the counselor and perhaps other observers are named to note the interaction of participants in the role-play simulation.

Following a brief interaction of this sort, the role-play participants receive the benefit of the observations of counselor and

observers, providing a "mirror" for the reflection of typical behavior patterns. Videotaping of these exercises may also be
helpful, not only for group review but for individuals to see and
hear their participation in certain group situations.

Beyond any specific exercise or simulation, the skillful career
counselor allows the group to explore the problems and feelings of participants. The emphasis should be on gaining a
deeper understanding of the self, not simply solving the problem. In most instances, it would be premature for the group to
solve the problem area immediately. As attitudes are modified
and new information is acquired, the student becomes better
able to solve problems in various areas of life, including those
of career planning.

Laboratory Learning

The small group becomes a powerful laboratory learning opportunity and is therefore a form of experience-based education
in which the group members learn primarily through the activity of the group and in the practice of communication skills,
rather than from lectures or books. The students who take part
in small face-to-face groups interact with and receive feedback
from each other in ways that assist in the development of
human relations skills. Through the group experience, the participant has the opportunity to experiment with and get a feeling for one's own style of personal interaction.

The group counseling situation is a laboratory in that the
participants are able to examine or research their own behavior
and experiment with new and more satisfying kinds of behavior
facilitating growth. Through insight provided by the group experience, individuals are able to launch their own personal action programs. Follow-up with individual counseling by the
professional counselor may be highly desirable after group experience or concurrent with it.

Most often the experience of the unstructured group is a
new kind of learning for most students. Theory about human

behavior is being translated into practice. The acquired human relations skills that each participant possesses at the time are being put into action with a view toward the development of new skills. In order to enhance this exploration, the group leader should be careful not to impose an authority of "right and wrong" behaviors. By being alert to the particular interactions of the moment, the leader should be able to clarify and reflect on behavior that may be blocking the group and interfering with the open expression of feelings or concerns of a particular member.

Through these processes, the career counseling group is able to provide a culture of its own where it is permissible for members to contact each other directly and provide feedback on the effect one member has on another. When these interactions are allowed in a climate of constructive and cooperative work as initially established by the skilled leader, there need be little fear that the group will become too threatening or harmful to members as they disclose themselves, express their feelings, or react to the behavior of others more directly. There is, of course, need for vigilance by the trained counselor to monitor and prevent potentially harmful or destructive interactions. These are relatively infrequent and, in most cases, the group takes care of itself and will maintain a level that that facilitates growth for the participants.

The trained counselor is prepared to accept any initial hostilities and anxieties that characterize most any group in its beginning interaction stages. The anxiety experienced by the participants and felt by the group leader is an important motivating force to assist the group in its forward movement. The experience of anxiety may become a matter for open and free discussion, with a view toward discovering what is stressful within the group and thus is producing the anxiety.

As these process elements are dealt with in the relatively unstructured group experience, the participant learns to more fully utilize personal resources in a variety of problem-solving situations, both within and outside the group. The exhilarating feeling typically experienced by members in well-planned, low-structured groups assists them in beginning other self-development programs or becoming more fully functional in the academic, personal, and career planning areas of life.

Summary

The career counselor providing leadership for the small group is offering a powerful and important vehicle in the accomplishment of career counseling goals. As the student becomes more self-knowledgeable and able to initiate methods of inquiry into occupational information and experiences, that person also becomes more adept at making reality-based decisions about career direction and satisfying lifestyle.

The range of group activities moves from a fairly highly structured, goal-announced group, to the moderately structured group that allows participants flexibility in proceeding with patterned exercises, to the relatively unstructured group where more emphasis is placed on the personal dynamics, communication, and human relations skills and their development. All forms of group counseling require the skilled counselor to facilitate the group in a manner that will encourage the positive growth and forward movement of each group member.

It is imperative that career counselors have experiential knowledge of group process as well as of individual counseling. Most counselor training programs incorporate the experiential as an integral component in counselor preparation. A minimum level of skill in this area seems essential for career counseling to meet the requirements of today's students.

PEER COUNSELORS

Peer counselors are being employed with increasing frequency for a variety of counseling outreach programs. Student counselors can effectively extend the arm of career counseling programs if certain conditions are met. It is essential that student counselors be selected carefully, receive adequate training and supervision, and that the paraprofessional program be effectively evaluated for modification and continuation.

Although student counselors have been employed by many campus services such as student housing, admissions, orientation, and ushering at campus events, the use of student counselors in the counseling and career planning offices is relatively new.

There are a number of advantages for employing students in career counseling services. The professional counseling staff has the advantage of regular student perceptions and suggestions in the formulation and implementation of programs. Another advantage is the personal growth and development of human relations skills this opportunity affords the student counselor. It also provides work experience which allows for the exploration of particular vocational goals much as an internship program in any field would provide. Most importantly, peer counselors provide much needed direct service.

Role of the Student Counselor

Peer counselors may provide service to a variety of student groups with particular developmental goals. In serving individuals the paraprofessional may be involved with intake interviewing and be the first staff person to greet the student coming to the Career Services Center. This activity could produce preliminary information regarding the student's concern and offer referral to the appropriate campus resource.

The peer counselor may also be trained to offer specific assistance to small groups of individuals. Direct service of this nature may be related to a residence hall unit, a particular class of students, or a group of advisees working in coordination with a faculty advisor. Co-leadership with other professionals in campus situations provides an opportunity for the peer counselor to offer counseling assistance while adding to the credibility of student advising programs. Co-leadership also fosters mutual support among counseling and advising personnel.

Peer counselors may become adept at assisting career groups in certain exercises and paper and pencil tests that lead to the exploration of values, interests, and other topical areas found in career exploration situations. The alert career counselor will discover many areas of valuable service for the paraprofessional in the career planning and placement office.

Certain levels of personal counseling and the use of career information should be reserved for the professional counselor. Dealing with the limits of the student counselor's competence is essential for the protection of the student counselor as well as the one who comes for assistance. The credibility of the career service is judged by the professional management of the paraprofessional program much as it is by the relevance and outcome of other program efforts. Usually, very positive results are reported where well trained and supervised student counselors are employed.

Recruiting Student Counselors

Selection of the student counselor is approached by clearly defining the position being offered. The duties and responsibilities of the position need to be specified, along with the particular competencies required prior to selection or the skills that need to be acquired during training. The professional career counselor involved in selection and training of student assistants must identify the functions that are to be performed and indicate how these are clearly related to professional goals and not simply support or clerical services.

To use student-to-student counseling, the student counselors need to feel centrally involved in the essential mission of the service and that they are performing a truly paraprofessional role based on the particular skills they have acquired.

Recruiting of student counselors may be approached in several ways, but in every case a base for reward needs to be established. Rewards may be financial, academic credit for training and service combined or, at the very least, adequate recognition for services. The form of reward may be related to the extent of service provided and the necessary time demand on the paraprofessional.

Generally it is unwise to depend upon volunteer student service for peer counseling. The role, to be truly helpful, will be a demanding one and the student should not be asked to serve without adequate reward. Experience suggests that the overall time demands on students are so great that even the most well intentioned volunteer will have difficulty keeping commitments during the press of other duties in the academic year. Therefore, a solid financial or other basis needs to be arranged before announcing the position.

Recruiting may be done by a general announcement on campus of the position openings. Faculty or other campus groups may be asked to suggest names of persons who may be interested and qualified for such positions. These persons may then be contacted more directly, indicating they have been nominated by a faculty member or other person as one who might be interested in this position. This particular process tends to be a strong encouragement to persons who might otherwise be hesitant in stepping forward to apply for such a position.

The application process and further information should be readily available. On some campuses this might best be implemented by having a general meeting of all interested applicants. The career counselor should outline the program and the use of student counselors, including the kinds of time and other commitments in a very direct way so that the potential student counselor understands clearly the expectations of the role. Application forms can be made available at this time for those who remain interested.

This information period is also a good time to clarify the qualifications for the position. These may include certain background experiences if required, the acquisition of particular skills, or the willingness to function in certain areas, such as conducting small group meetings or working individually with peers. The professional counselor may find it helpful to state the general philosophy and approach of the career counseling service so that students may determine if their approach is compatible.

The final selection of applicants to train for the position should be announced promptly with tactful notification of those not selected, expressing appreciation and the possibility of future participation in the program.

Training the Paraprofessional

The professional career counselor who plans to initiate a peer counseling program must be genuinely interested in and open to working with students as paraprofessionals. The most important key to success is the open, mutual relationship that exists between the supervisor and the peer counselor. The success of the program will partially depend upon the counselor supervisor being able to organize the work of the paraprofessionals and provide a structure for their training and service. Supervision must be an ongoing process since the paraprofessional will need continuing corrective and supportive interaction with the supervisor. The program of training and supervision should be well thought through, planned, and prepared even before the selection of candidates for peer counseling.

The training and supervision will call on the best teaching skills of the counselor. The training program normally includes a general orientation to the skills necessary for the peer counselor in a variety of helping relationships. Basic policies of the career service and specific ethical issues, such as confidentiality in contacts and records, are explained. The aim is to develop a sense of staff cooperation for mutual referral and assistance.

The initial training dealing with specific task-oriented skills should be specific to the particular work assignment. In a peer counseling outreach program, basic interviewing skills are of first importance. A carefully selected manual to help with the rationale of the approach can then be integrated with experiential elements. In the case of peer counselor training, the experiential is the most important element. It is essential that carefully defined skills, such as the use of restatement in elementary interviewing, be practiced.

Simulation exercises that are devised by the career counselor may be most effective. The behavior or skill to be acquired is first demonstrated by the professional counselor. This modeling behavior sets the stage for the role play between peer counselors in experiencing the specific skill to be acquired. Based on the professional counselor's own experience, selected elements are chosen for the initial training of the peer counselor.

The effect of simulated exercises and role playing is to improve not only the skills of effective communication but to enhance the self-confidence and the feeling within peer counselors that they truly can be effective in their role. The availability of videotaping may assist in the modeling of specific skills, such as the effect of nonverbal cues and posture in the interview situation. This is effective also in recording role playing situations for better feedback to the participants.

Supervision of Peer Counselors

The particular tasks to be accomplished by the peer counselors need adequate structuring. As the work is spread over a period of time, regular workshops or group meetings should be scheduled as an ongoing training function. Because in-service training occurs along with service on the job, the main purpose is to update and increase specific skills of the participants. Through group and workshop experiences, common problems may be shared and dealt with in ways which provide a vehicle for the trainer to facilitate the acquisition of new skills or attitudes.

The qualities required for the supervisor of the peer counselor are essentially the qualities for the professional counselor, with particular emphasis upon the role of the educator or trainer of the paraprofessional. The career counselor should attempt to train the paraprofessional only in areas where there is a high degree of competence and where there is first-hand knowledge of the position and functions necessary for the peer counselor to perform the job. The keys to a successful peer counseling program are the structuring of appropriate functions for the peer counselor and quality of supervisors.

PART III

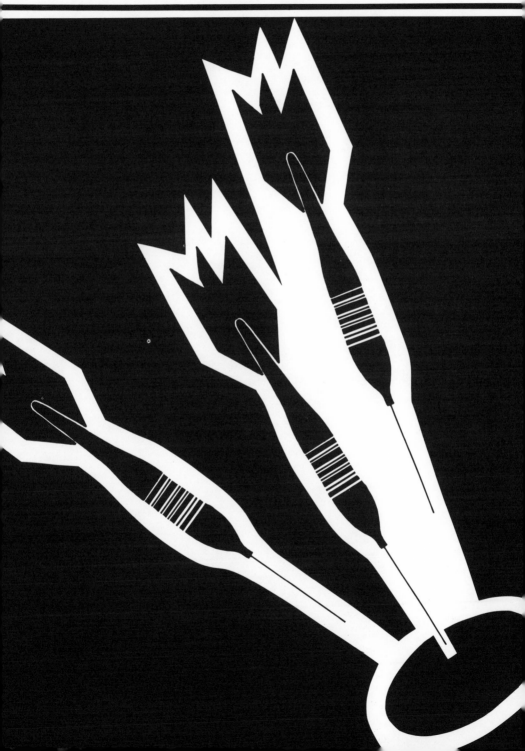

CHAPTER 5

CAREER PLANNING RESOURCES

THE SELF-ASSESSMENT AND career exploration phases of career planning are greatly enhanced by the availability of adequate and pertinent resources. Psychological tests provided by trained counselors and up-to-date information regarding careers are essential aids for students involved in career planning.

Vocational assessment, frequently in the form of standardized psychological tests, assists the student in gathering information about self prior to further career development activities. Tests, inventories, and exercises relevant to vocational choices not only provide an economical means of self-knowledge but also may increase motivation for further assessment or exploration. Test results supply specific information structured in ways which help organize the information gained.

Career planning tasks are encouraged when the process seems organized and directional, with one activity logically leading to the next. The skillful use of self-assessment instruments within the context of career counseling is a valuable service offered by the career specialist.

Career information is a necessary resource for persons making vocational choices. The adequacy and accuracy of career information influence the quality of career decisions and, therefore, the personal satisfactions derived from vocational choices. Career information resources deserve the continuing attention of the professional career service staff. A good information system, including personal contacts and publications, comes into being after careful planning, adequate funding, and persistent effort. The importance of the service is evident based on students' needs in the area of career exploration. The task is to present timely information in a format that is acceptable and readily used by students.

PSYCHOLOGICAL TESTS

The use of psychological tests as effective tools in career counseling depends upon the background and training of the career counselor and the counselor's attitude toward the use of measurement devices in the counseling process. Tests are useful to the extent the counselor knows the scope and limits of the tests available. When tests are to be used it is essential that the student have a role in selecting the test or inventory and understand the purpose of the particular instrument. This will assist the counseling process and help avoid unrealistic expectations from test results.

The counselor should be able to explain what tests are available to assess different areas of personal functioning. There are hundreds of standardized tests for psychological assessment. For career counseling purposes, tests may be grouped according to the functions they perform, including the measurement of achievement, aptitude, interest, intelligence, and personality.

Achievement Tests

These are perhaps most familiar to students since they are typically used in academic settings to test one's mastery of a subject and in many cases are standardized, such as the College Entrance Examination Board's Achievement Tests in the areas of English, mathematics, chemistry, and many other subjects. The achievement test is not designed primarily for prediction, but is intended to measure the individual's actual learning in specific subject matters after a period of instruction.

Achievement tests provide objective measures of progress and, as such, have been valuable in determining individual difficulties in learning, in the discovery of strong scholastic interests, and in assessing special abilities or disabilities. They also permit intergroup comparisons which may be helpful in educational career planning. Examples of standardized achievement tests include, in addition to the College Entrance Examination Board tests, the Stanford Test of Academic Skills and the Wide Range Achievement Test.

Aptitude Tests

Certain personal characteristics are measured to indicate an individual's capacity to acquire some specific knowledge or skill, such as the ability to perform as a musician, do mechanical work, or speak a language. These tests measure the capacity to acquire certain skills or proficiencies, based on innate ability and past experiences.

Examples of aptitude tests include the Seashore Measures of Musical Talent, the Bennett Mechanical Comprehension Test, and the Modern Language Aptitude Test. The Scholastic Aptitude Tests or the American College Tests are perhaps most familiar to college-bound students as these represent a standardized national testing program for scholastic aptitude. They are administered to groups and have time limitations.

An example of an untimed power test of scholastic aptitude

is the Ohio State Psychological Test. The Employee Aptitude Survey Test Series measures perceptual ability for persons such as drafting personnel, engineers, electronic technicians, and individuals whose work requires the use of complex schematic diagrams. Tests in this series are used extensively in personnel selection. Aptitude tests cover a wide range of abilities related to most areas of the world of work.

Vocational Interest Inventories

These are perhaps most popular among career counselors since they have specific content relevant to the career-related questions of students. Inventories of vocational interests are not tests of aptitude. They indicate only the extent of similarity between interests and preferences expressed by the student and those of persons successfully employed in the specified occupational areas.

The principle underlying interest measurement is that, to the extent an individual has a pattern of interests similar to a particular professional or occupational group, the chances of work satisfaction are greater as the person enters an area related to these interests. The prospects of succeeding in the chosen area of work are also enhanced, providing the person has the necessary aptitude to perform the given tasks.

Inventories frequently used in career counseling of college students include the Kuder Occupational Interest Survey and the Strong-Campbell Interest Inventory. Machine-scored and interpretive reports now facilitate the feedback of results to students and require little time of the counselor except for the integration of test results into the counseling process. As in all situations of test interpretation, students must be cautioned about the limitations of the measures being presented.

The Self Directed Search is another interest related career counseling tool based on Holland's theory of personality types and environment models. The person involved in taking the Self Directed Search is able to see what is being assessed and to participate in the scoring and interpretation of the instrument. It has the further advantage of providing immediate results in the self-assessment exercise.

The Self Directed Search may be employed in small group or individual counseling situations. Two booklets are used to assist the person in evaluating interests, activities, competencies, and self-estimates. The results are integrated into a three-letter code, permitting a search of the classifications for a wide range of occupations. This instrument may provide a valuable adjunct to individual career counseling activities or serve as an independent learning experience for students needing no further assistance.

Interest inventories may naturally lead to the exploration of career-related information. Materials suggested by the inventories used most frequently may be acquired for the career information library. This exemplifies for the student how various career planning activities and resources are integrated into the total plan for the individual.

Intelligence Tests

The measurement and analysis of individual differences in intelligence marked the beginning of psychological testing. Several group and individually administered tests of mental ability have been developed. The most widely used test is the Wechsler Adult Intelligence Scale, which is individually administered and yields several sub-test scores as well as a general measure of intellectual functioning. Additional information regarding personality characteristics are also gained by use of individual tests. Tests of general intelligence, whether individual or group form, are primarily concerned with the complexity, level of difficulty, quality, and rate of mental activity.

Personality Testing

Within the context of career counseling, personality testing most often takes the form of a paper and pencil test, such as the California Psychological Inventory, the Edward's Personal Preference Schedule, or the Career Maturity Inventory. Less frequently, projective methods are employed, such as the Rorschach or Thematic Apperception Tests. Projective methods are sometimes helpful in eliciting feelings, values, and motives.

The California Psychological Inventory may be particularly helpful in providing descriptive information concerning personality characteristics relevant to the self-assessment activities of career planning. The scales of the inventory produce measures of social poise, intrapersonal characteristics, achievement and interest modes. Personality tests are to be used in the context of counseling where results may be fully understood and assimilated.

The counselor using personality measures must be fully prepared by training and experience to competently administer the tests selected. To the extent the counselor is comfortable with the use of particular tests and the student has participated in their selection, the informational gain from the activity can greatly assist the career counseling enterprise.

Evaluation of Tests

A number of criticisms have been leveled at the use of tests:

1. Tests as evaluation tools disturb the counseling relationship and interfere with the release of growth forces in the student.
2. Tests tend to cast the counselor in the role of an authority and promote student dependence on the counselor and the counselor's tests for answers and information.
3. Existing tests lack precision and tend to measure insignificant factors.

Many of these objections may not be so much directed toward the tests as to their use.

In career counseling, information is not so important, per se, as is the student's perception of it. Test information is primarily for the use of the student and meant to promote independence and self-understanding. Just as the counselor needs to accept the presenting problems or concerns, so must the feelings and attitudes of the student toward test information be accepted. This emphasizes the importance of using tests only in the context of counseling relationships. With all of the difficulty tests impose, to reject their use is to reject a useful tool for student growth.

Norms. A test is essentially a standardized set of measurements of a person's responses to a group of tasks from which more general inferences can be drawn. In order to facilitate interpretation, good psychological tests will provide tables of norms, or percentile ranks, or standard scores, depending upon the purpose of the test.

A norm is the average or typical score (mean or median) on a particular test obtained for a specified population: for example, the average score on a mechanical comprehension test for a group of applicants for process training jobs in an oil refinery; the mean score on a diagnostic reading test for a group of college freshmen. The test manual and other literature supporting most well-established tests used in career counseling provide normative data which are frequently derived from college-age populations.

Other normative measures include the percentile rank and the standard score. A person's percentile rank on a test indicates the percentage of scores in the total distribution which appear below it. Therefore, an individual having a percentile rank of 30 is positioned above 30 percent of the total group. In other words, thirty percent of the group fall below this individual's rank. The percentile rank makes it possible to determine at which one-hundreth part of the distribution of scores any one individual is to be found. This technique of reporting also permits scores on two or more tests which are presented in different units of measurement to be transformed into values that are comparable.

The standard score measures, in terms of standard deviation, how far a particular score is removed from the mean of the distribution. The average is taken as the zero point and the standard scores are given a plus or minus designation. Assuming a normal distribution of scores on two or more tests, the standard scores may be compared.

A widely used variation of the standard score is the T-score. This method sets the mean at 50 instead of the standard score value of zero. The T-score is derived by multiplying the standard score by 10 and adding or subtracting it from the mean T-score of 50. Since practically all standard scores are within five standard deviations of the mean and each divided into ten units, the T-score is based on a scale of 100 units and, therefore, usually avoids negative scores.

Test-users will most always want to have the percentile equivalent of any scores given to facilitate interpretation. Meaningful comparisons are more easily made between scores on different tests for an individual when the percentile rank is used.

Reliability and Validity. All testing involves errors of measurement, and the counselor must be sensitive to the reliability and validity characteristics of the test selected. Most test constructors go to some length in reporting the studies of reliability and validity completed on the particular test being presented. These results are usually found in the test manual along with reports of other research involving the usefulness of the test in specific situations.

Reliability is concerned with how consistently the particular testing instrument measures the same event or characteristic in successive measurements. However, knowing that a test is reliable is not enough to enable one to assess its value as a measuring instrument. It may be highly reliable and still a very poor instrument because it lacks validity.

Validity determines the extent to which the test measures what one thinks or says it measures; that is, how closely the results of the test correlate with the given criterion. For example, scholastic aptitude test scores should correlate highly with actual academic achievement, and vocational interest inventory scores should correlate highly with actual occupational interests of the student.

Career counselors using tests should know certain essential facts about the instrument. Much of the information is found in the manual for the particular test. Counselors must know the purpose of the test and the groups for whom it is intended. They must attend to the reliability and validity measures, paying particular attention to the kinds of external validating criteria, such as instructor's grades, supervisor's ratings, or other standardized tests.

The population sample on which the test has been standardized should be examined for appropriateness of age range, socioeconomic distribution, educational level, or other types of limiting and biasing factors. The best source of evaluative information on practically all tests in print is *The Mental Measurements Yearbook* by Buros. This reference book can be found in most college libraries.

Test Selection

The test selection process takes place in the context of counseling and takes into account the individuality of the counselor and the personal preferences for the use of certain instruments. The selection process also acknowledges the particular needs of the student. The tests chosen should serve these needs. The following steps are recommended in the test selection process:

1. Provide sufficient interviewing time to explore the needs and determine the kind of information desired.
2. Use pertinent information readily available.
3. Explain the functions of available tests to the student.

4. Relate information needs to the counseling tests available.
5. Suggest specific tests.
6. Provide for the administration of the tests selected.

The use of tests in career counseling may be accomplished by establishing a close working relationship with other counseling and testing agencies on campus. This arrangement is helpful when the career services staff is limited in number or by training and is unable to provide testing services. In interagency cooperative arrangements, it is essential that the career counselor insures continuity of services from the student's viewpoint. This may be accomplished by maintaining close working arrangements with other counseling personnel to whom the student is referred, so that the student is directed back to the referral source for the integration of all career planning activities. Referral services must not detract from the systematic program offered students through the career services office.

Test Administration

Career counselors who provide testing services for students are responsible for maintaining an adequate library of testing materials. *The Mental Measurements Yearbook* can be used to review and select a reasonably wide range of instruments upon which students and counselors may draw to meet particular information needs.

As each counselor develops skills and builds experience, certain tests become more valuable in the career counseling process, much as any tool increases in utility with continued practice. Most often people who administer tests find it best over time to select or recommend a few tests from the total array to construct a useful small battery for the individual student while still maintaining necessary flexibility to meet particular needs.

It is, of course, important to be aware of the ethical and legal ramifications of test administration. The proper use of all test scores is the responsibility of the counselor administering the test. The scores should be treated as the property of the person taking the test. That person should have control over the disposition of test results. The form and manner in which scores are reported to the student, however, is left to the judgment of the counselor.

All matters pertaining to handling of test results should be discussed with the student before administering the test. The counselor may be guided in matters of ethical and legal concerns by the American Psychological Association's statement on "Ethical Standards of Psychologists" published in the current *Biographical Directory* of the Association.

Attention must be given to the conditions under which tests are administered. The physical environment should be pleasant and free from distracting noises or other interruptions. The counselor should promote strong motivation for completing the test by such means as arranging interpretive sessions promptly or incorporating test information into counseling sessions in a timely manner. The administration of tests should be timed to be as meaningful as possible for the student by fitting them into the framework of the individual's total career planning program.

Psychological testing is relatively expensive in terms of staff time. It is expedient, therefore, to look for economies in test administration, scoring, managing results, etc. Increasing precision in test offerings should be developed so that time and energies are not wasted on providing extra tests which serve little purpose in career planning.

Use of Test Information

A test score is a symbol used to quantify a person's behavior in relation to others. The counselor must understand both the tests chosen and the behavior being measured. The testing instrument is only a tool to help provide information related to the behavior, attitude, or some other characteristic being measured. The particular usefulness of a test will depend upon the ability of the counselor to interpret the results. The counselor's familiarity with the test and its usage over time increases its value for the counselor and the student. The theoretical position of the career counselor will determine how often and which tests are used. The counselor should feel comfortable using any technique or test selected.

Tests have a number of counseling functions, including the provision of information to assist the counselor in surveying and evaluating behavior so as to make decisions regarding referral and predicting behavior. Test information may also aid in the development of realistic expectations about the student and help the student develop and clarify self-concepts. Although knowledge is not synonymous with understanding, it is essential for understanding. Tests also help the student identify and clarify alternative courses of action, expose gaps in knowledge, or reduce gaps in expectancies.

An example of a popular and helpful psychological profile of interests in common use today is the revised *Strong-Campbell Interest Inventory*. Male and female forms of an earlier version are now combined into a single inventory. This inventory integrates the theoretical framework of Holland's studies. Scales measuring the six model personality types and work environments proposed by Holland are provided in the augmented interpretive report. Holland's theory offers a structure around which the scores are clustered.

Some of the advantages in using the computer-printed, multi-paged, report are: since results are written in narrative format, they may be released to students; page references for the *Dictionary of Occupational Titles* and the *Occupational Outlook Handbook* are presented for the individuals' high and low scores; the interpretive report provides a basic explanation of results which frees some routine interpretation time for the assimilation of results and other counseling functions. Even with such elaborate reporting formats as provided by the computer, the role of the counselor in explaining any unique pattern of scores and offering comprehensive interpretations remains absolutely vital.

Extending the example of test usage one step further, many counselors are able to combine other personality measures, such as the *California Psychological Inventory,* with interest inventory results. The personality inventory suggested here will generate scores describing personality characteristics important for social interaction. These characteristics, considered in relation to one's hierarchy of vocational interests, may be stimulating and instructive for the career planning student. The charts on pages 134 and 135 display the names of the basic scales for the two inventories.

The content of an interpretive counseling session may deal with comparisons of results in a direct or indirect manner, depending on the nature of the counseling relationship. A possible outcome of such interactions would be to increase the free association from the limited information presented. This often leads to new perceptions of personality and the consideration of alternative occupations. Hopefully, the student is also encouraged and directed toward other sources of needed information.

Summary

There are certain guidelines for the use of tests in career counseling:

1. The counselor must have an adequate understanding of the behavior being measured and thus be able to provide the student with the best available tools to assist in the development of self-understanding.
2. The student should understand the purpose of all tests used during the counseling process, and the limitations of test results should be made known.
3. Tests should be used only for the counseling of students.

Scales of the California Psychological Inventory

Measures of Poise, Ascendancy, Self-Assurance, and Interpersonal Adequacy

> Dominance
> Capacity for Status
> Sociability
> Social Presence
> Self-Acceptance
> Sense of Well-Being

Measures of Socialization, Responsibility, Intrapersonal Values, and Character

> Responsibility
> Socialization
> Self-Control
> Tolerance
> Good Impression
> Communality

Measures of Achievement Potential and Intellectual Efficiency

> Achievement via Conformance
> Achievement via Independence
> Intellectual Efficiency

Measures of Intellectual and Interest Modes

> Psychological-Mindedness
> Flexibility
> Femininity

Basic Interest Scales of the Strong-Campbell Interest Inventory

Arranged According to General Theme

REALISTIC
Agriculture
Nature
Adventure
Military Activities
Mechanical Activities

INVESTIGATIVE
Science
Mathematics
Medical Science
Medical Service

ARTISTIC
Music/Dramatics
Art
Writing

SOCIAL
Teaching
Social Service
Athletics
Domestic Arts
Religious Activities

ENTERPRISING
Public Speaking
Law/Politics
Merchandising
Sales
Business Management

CONVENTIONAL
Office Practices

4. The counselor should not use tests beyond professional capabilities to administer and interpret.
5. Tests should not be used for purposes other than those for which they were developed.
6. Test information is the property of the student and is to be used as that person wishes within the counseling process.

CAREER INFORMATION

Information resources for career counseling are essential for adequate career planning. Resources must be carefully developed and maintained. All counseling personnel should be well informed concerning the sources of information available and their general content. Career information centers serve best when information is collected to meet the specific needs of students in the local institution. Collections of information should have immediate relevance to the academic programs offered.

Material collected should be based on the frequency of demand by students using the career information center. Career information, as career counseling, needs to be student-centered, beginning where students have questions and moving with them in the exploration of alternatives. The selection of materials also should reflect the areas of employment most often entered by alumni as well as emerging and developing career areas which students may consider.

Personal Contacts

Career information is obtained primarily through personal contacts, a variety of publications, and technical media. The most basic source of career information is the person who holds the job, who has first-hand acquaintance with the activities of that work environment. Personal contacts are time-consuming but very valuable sources of career information.

Contacts can be arranged with alumni or other campus and community resource persons. This first-hand information has a number of advantages not available in publications. The student has the opportunity to evaluate the work setting as well as attitudes and feelings of the job-holder toward the work performed. Frequently, these unspoken communications reveal important factors about lifestyle and work satisfaction which assist in determining suitability of that function and setting in one's own career plan.

An interview arranged with a worker in a particular occupational field by the student provides important benefits. First, the information obtained is current and, by the nature of the questions asked, may be tailored to meet the student's informational needs. As mentioned earlier, the interview also provides the student with a view of the lifestyle of the worker as well as the job environment, enabling the student to sense dimensions of the total work situation not available in other forms of information.

Second, the informational interview provides experience in the interview process and at the same time develops career contacts with persons in fields of interest to that student. Although the informational interview is not designed to seek employment, it does provide information about possible future openings in a particular organization and gives the student increasing numbers of contacts. Career information obtained through the interview process can be particularly valuable if questions to be asked and areas of inquiry are identified before the interview takes place.

Students can become proficient in interviewing for career information, especially with the guidance of a career counselor to assist in clarifying objectives and preparing an appropriate approach. Some colleges provide directories of alumni who have agreed to meet with students to discuss career options in their field of endeavor.

Personal contacts, although expensive in time and energy, can be arranged by students to take place during school vacation periods in their hometown area or in a selected geographical target area where several persons in their career field are located. The career information center can provide lists of persons who have indicated willingness to discuss career matters with students. This becomes a ready resource for counselors and is particularly helpful when students also need opportunities to develop assertiveness in initiating contacts to help themselves in this career planning activity.

Publications

Publications provide the foundation for career information used in counseling. Materials include directories, books, periodicals, brochures, research monographs, and employer's literature. Increasingly important are the specialized local publications produced by departments within the institution. These often give recent historic data concerning alumni and point out the occupational areas frequently entered by graduates of the department. Publications provide the most convenient collection of information by allowing a student to consider a variety of materials with the least expenditure of time and energy.

Directories

Directories are helpful in locating organizations and persons in a specific geographical area or organizations offering a particular product or service. Directories become outdated quickly so the listings and directories which are published annually must be ordered regularly. Many local Chambers of Commerce issue directories of area businesses and industries which offer detailed product and service information for a specific municipality or region. Telephone books also serve as directories of employers. Yellow Page listings, organized by categories of service, may suggest areas of employment possibilities. Current telephone books are likely to be more up-to-date than published directories in providing current addresses.

Examples of directories found in career information centers are listed below. This represents only a small sample and is intended to suggest the kinds of materials available. As with all career information materials, local institutional needs must determine specific titles acquired.

Standard & Poor's Register of Corporations, Directors and Executives. Standard & Poor's Corporation. Annual. About 37,000 corporations are included. Lists officers and directors, and gives annual sales, number of employees, and products. For several years this directory has included not only U.S. and Canadian corporations but also major international corporations. The index volume lists companies according to classification of product or business.

College Placement Annual. College Placement Council, Inc. Directory of more than 1,200 corporate and governmental employers who normally recruit college graduates with or without experience. Name and address of employer, recruitment representative, nature of business, number of employees, summer and foreign employment if offered, and openings for which the organization will recruit. Indexes: occupational, geographical, type and level of degree.

Federal Career Directory: A Guide for College Students. Supt. of Documents, U.S. GPO, Washington, DC 20402. 142pp. Presents a review of job opportunities as they relate to college majors. Offers a cross-reference by government agencies.

Guide to American Directories. Klein, Bernard (Editor), Ninth Edition, Klein Publications, New York. Provides complete information on directories published in the U.S. categorized under industrial, mercantile, and professional headings. Includes the cost of each directory.

Encyclopedia of Associations. Volume I: National Organizations of the U.S., Detroit: Gale Research Company. Comprehensive list of all types of national associations arranged by broad classification and with an alphabetical and key-word index. Gives names of chief officers, brief statements of activities, number of members, names of publications.

National Directory of Private Social Agencies. Helga B. Croner, Social Services Publications, Division of Croner Publications, Inc. Monthly supplements. Queens Village, N.Y. Lists over 14,000 agencies in U.S. by field of service and geographical location. Provides full address and service descriptions for such areas as family and child welfare, vocational services for disabled, sheltered workshops, naturalization and legal matters, homemaker and professional groups, and rehabilitation.

Directory of American Firms Operating in Foreign Countries. Angel, Juvenal (Editor), 8th Edition, Volume 2 of four volumes entitled *American Encyclopedia of International Information,* Simon and Schuster, Inc., New York.

>   Part I—Alphabetical Index of American Corporations. Lists company name and address, key executives, products and/or services, and foreign locations.

>   Part II—International Geographical Distribution. Companies listed by country.

>   Part III—Index according to products or services, from abrasives to wood products.

Directory of Career Planning and Placement Offices. College Placement Council, Inc. 238pp. Annually. Listings of approximately 1,800 two- and four-year colleges and universities with career planning and placement programs. Includes college names and addresses, CPC and regional memberships, names of placement personnel, telephone numbers, on-campus interview dates, etc.

Directory of College Recruiting Personnel. College Placement Council, Inc. 207pp. Annually. Listings of approximately 1,400 employers. Includes the name of the organization, its address, whether it is a subsidiary of a parent company, nature of business, number of employees, whether it recruits nationally or regionally and, if regionally, in what areas. Also includes names and titles of key college relations and recruiting personnel, their addresses if different from the headquarters address, telephone numbers, and CPC and regional placement association memberships.

Handbook for Recruiting at Minority Colleges. College Placement Services, Inc. 1978–79. 108pp. Biennially. A 108-page profile of 92 four-year colleges and universities with predominant enrollments of minority students. Contains data on enrollments, degrees awarded, special programs, names of key officials, recruiting activity, employment of graduates.

Special Reports

In addition to directories and periodicals, valuable information for counselors in their work with students can be found in special reports and monographs. The findings of special studies, such as those by the CPC Foundation, contain concrete data that support assumptions, dispel myths, and introduce new ideas that can be incorporated into career counseling.

Planning and Implementing the Careers Conference. College Placement Services, Inc. 1975. A 33-page booklet that describes the policy considerations, planning process, and operation of various types of career orientation conferences. Includes planning outline, budget guides, sample letters, forms, and publicity materials.

Women: Marriage, Career, and Job Satisfaction. CPC Foundation. 1978. Special analyses provide information on job satisfaction of married women compared with single women, characteristics associated with combining marriage and career, backgrounds and special plans of those who work.

Low Income Students in College and Careers. CPC Foundation. 1978. Discusses how low income populations fare in college and whether class differences persist in the careers of people with equal education.

Who Will Succeed? College Graduates as Business Executives. CPC Foundation. 1978. Reports the characteristics that differentiate those who will achieve high salaried positions as business executives from those who will not. Among factors studied are family background, scholastic achievement, college selectivity, and life goals.

Job Satisfaction After College—The Graduate's Viewpoint. CPC Foundation. 1977. Reviews levels of satisfaction college graduates experience in their careers. Topics covered include relationship of college majors to jobs, dissatisfaction with nonprofessional jobs, importance of choosing a career early, sex stereotyping of occupations.

College Education on the Job—The Graduate's Viewpoint. CPC Foundation. 1976. College graduates tell how useful their education has been for their careers and what recommendations they would make to help future generations prepare for employment.

Careers in the Private Sector—A National Study of College Graduates in Business and Industry. CPC Foundation. 1976. Reports the career patterns of men and women in private companies compared with those of men and women who chose other employment settings.

The Hard-to-Place Majority—A National Study of the Career Outcomes of Liberal Arts Graduates. CPC Foundation. 1975. Provides comparison between the employment status of liberal arts graduates and graduates in other fields.

College Graduates and Their Employers—A National Study of Career Plans and Their Outcomes. CPC Foundation. 1975. Gives comparison between career plans students expressed while in college with actual occupations entered.

Books

There are several books on the general subject of career planning for the library collection. These are frequently characterized by practical, step-by-step instructions for the evaluation of skills, values, experiences, needs, and other personal attributes. Advice for successful job-hunting is offered by some publications which review job-acquisition skills such as letters of application, preparation of a resume, and the development of interviewing technique. A few provide information about employment in a particular field. Some are more for the professional career counselor. A sample listing is provided below.

Occupational Outlook Handbook. U.S. Department of Labor, Bureau of Labor Statistics. 1978–79. A major source of vocational information for hundreds of occupations, this book describes what workers in various occupations do, training and education needed, availability of jobs in each field in the years ahead, possibilities for advancement, probable earnings, and suggestions for finding further information.

Dictionary of Occupational Titles. U.S. Department of Labor, U.S. Employment Service. 4th Edition. 1977. Focuses on occupational classifications and definitions. Includes standardized and comprehensive descriptions of job duties, related information for 20,000 occupations. Covers nearly all jobs in U.S. economy. Groups occupations into systematic occupational classification structure based on interrelationships of job tasks and requirements. Designed as job placement tool to facilitate matching job requirements and worker skills.

Career Planning and Placement Today. C. Randall Powell. Kendall-Hunt Publishing Co. 144pp. 1978. Designed to provide college students information regarding the career/educational decision-making process; entry-level careers in business; organizing a job campaign; developing an interview strategy; and graduate study alternatives.

What Color is Your Parachute? A Practical Manual for Job Hunters and Career Changers. Revised edition. Richard N. Bolles, Ten Speed Press, Box 4310, Berkeley, CA 94704. 1975. Written for adults on how to choose and find the kind of work they want in the place they want to find it. Urges concentrated approach on one employer rather than simultaneous approaches to many.

PATH: A Career Workbook for Liberal Arts. Howard E. Figler. The Carroll Press, 43 Squantum St., Cranston, RI 02920. 160pp. 1975. Designed as a career exploration workbook for college students. Through a self-evaluation and career exploration model, college students are provided a means to discover their own work values and abilities.

Graduate Programs and Admissions Manual 1977–79. Educational Testing Service, The Graduate Record Examination Board, Princeton, NJ 08540. 4 volumes.
Vol. A—*Biological Sciences, Health Sciences, and Related Fields.*
Vol. B—*Arts and Humanities.*
Vol. C—*Physical Sciences, Mathematics and Engineering.*
Vol. D—*Social Sciences and Education.*
These manuals provide concise, up-to-date information on programs and degree offerings in graduate schools. Departmental and entrance requirements, and financial aid information are provided for each institution.

How to Get the Job That's Right for You. Ben Greco, Dow Jones-Irwin, Inc., 1975. Manual outlining the processes of career selection, development, and management for the white-collar worker. Lists factors and indicators to use in evaluating a career position.

Occupational Information. Robert Hoppock. McGraw-Hill, Inc. 4th Edition. 1976. A basic text exploring the rationale for the development of occupational information systems and surveying the range of practical applications.

Theories of Career Development. (Second Edition) Samuel H. Osipow. Prentice-Hall, Inc., 1973. A review and synthesis of the major theories of career development. This text defines the basic thesis of each theory, discusses results of relevant research, considers the implications for counseling, and evaluates prospects for future development.

The Managers: Career Alternatives for the College Educated. College Placement Council. 128pp. 1978. Describes many entry-level jobs in the business world and typical career progressions. Includes interviews with recent graduates in these positions.

A Model Career Counseling and Placement Program. College Placement Services, Inc. 340pp. 1978. A guide for two-year and four-year colleges that want to establish, improve, or evaluate career counseling and placement programs. Appendix contains examples of documents and forms, bibliography for a career library, sample group career counseling programs, syllabi for career planning courses.

Periodicals

Trade or professional journals frequently describe job openings and provide information concerning activities of organizations and associations. Newspapers and magazines are also sources of career information. Although a few selected periodicals may be acquired for the career information center, students will also benefit from searching the larger holdings in the main library on campus. References such as the *Business Periodicals Index* and the *Wall Street Journal Index* will assist in finding specific information of interest.

In addition to the typical periodicals listed here, the career librarian should also provide for current graduate school announcements and catalogs pertinent to the student population being served.

Occupational Outlook Quarterly. U.S. Department of Labor, Bureau of Labor Statistics. Articles relating to job outlook on national level. Many items pertinent to college level students. Provides updating of some areas in the *Occupational Outlook Handbook.*

The Graduate: A Handbook for Leaving School. Approach 13-30 Corp., 1005 Maryville Pike, SW, Knoxville, TN 37920. Annually. This guide in magazine format is designed for the near graduate and describes many aspects of the post-college world.

Business World. University Communications, Inc., 37 W. Cherry St., Rahway, NJ. Quarterly. Timely articles concerning career options in a variety of business fields.

Counselor's Information Service. B'nai B'rith Career & Counseling Services, 1640 Rhode Island Ave., NW, Washington, DC 20036. 1975. Quarterly. A quarterly annotated bibliography of current literature on educational and vocational guidance.

Catalyst Publications. Catalyst, 6 E. 82nd St., New York, NY 10028. 1972–75. Series of 40 educational and career opportunities booklets. Primary focus is on women returning to work, but also useful for all college women.

Journal of College Placement. College Placement Council, Inc. Four issues/year. Professional magazine of placement-recruitment featuring articles of interest to field.

Salary Survey. College Placement Council, Inc. Three reports/year, plus summer supplement. Reporting service on beginning salary offers to college graduates. Covered are 24 curricula, 23 functional positions, and 18 types of employers at the bachelor's level; 16 master's programs; and 8 doctoral programs.

Recruiting Activity Survey. College Placement Council, Inc. Two reports/year. Reporting service on plans of employers to hire college graduates in current year.

Brochures and Employer Literature

The largest single category of material for the career information library is usually employer literature. These brochures and pamphlets are produced by employing organizations to describe products and services and give specific job information. Students are expected to be familiar with a particular company's literature before taking interviews. Much of this material is attractive and informative, although in too many cases it is biased as a promotional item.

Most national or regional headquarters for trade and professional associations offer free brochures and other literature relating to careers in that field on request. The *Occupational*

Outlook Handbook provides sources of information, including addresses, for most occupational areas. There are several other services offering assistance in finding sources of information, such as the *Counselor's Information Service.*

A brochure and pamphlet collection must be purged on a regular basis as outdated material is misleading and harmful. Since many do not show date of publication, brochures should be marked when received to facilitate identification of obsolete material.

Graduate school and test information is appropriately made available in the career information center. Aptitude test registration forms and information for persons making application to professional schools of law, medicine, management, other graduate programs, or government employment are usually in demand.

The publications described in the preceding pages are just a few of those which should be considered by the career services center. They are presented to give an indication of the types of material found in career information libraries. A more comprehensive list is available in two widely used, annotated bibliographies published by the College Placement Council: *What Shall I Order for Our Career Planning and Placement Library?* and *Career Information for College Graduates.*

Regularly checking the Career Media section of the *Journal of College Placement* is an excellent means of keeping up to date on the publications most appropriate for career library consideration.

Audiovisual Media

Occupational information is presented in a variety of media and formats. The College Placement Council's publication *A/V Media in Career Development* is a valuable review of the programs now available and being used by many career planning offices. Emphasis is placed on the production of local audiovisual programs. It has been demonstrated that career information programs can be developed within the limits of even moderate budgets by using campus media resources.

Locally produced materials have much in their favor when they have been thoughtfully planned and prepared with a specific audience in mind. The credibility of locally produced material is usually high as the student is better able to identify with persons and examples used in the presentation. The producer has a serious responsibility, however, to be certain that the information presented is pertinent and accurate. Career counselors should consult with the professionals in their learning resources or media center for advice in choosing equipment and in producing audiovisual and other technical media for use in career counseling.

Several technologies have converged in providing guidance materials in the past few years. A special computer card with a microfilm insert allows for the production of decks of occupational information cards which are easily sorted into interest areas. Students can view the microfilm copy of the information on a reader-printer which has the capability of producing a printed copy of the material. The computer card microfilm system offers easy flexibility and updating with minimum expense. Although entire decks of view-cards such as these are commercially produced, the college career counselor must take care in reviewing such material since much of it is developed and marketed for secondary school populations.

Computer Systems

Computer applications involving interaction with the computer and the student have made their appearance and have been used in some counseling and career information centers. The technology is fascinating and has generated considerable interest as a novel approach for acquiring information. Reports indicate mixed success in the long run due to wide differences in motivation for using such equipment. The National Vocational Guidance Association has evaluated the computer's involvement in career guidance in a monograph, *Computer Assisted Guidance Systems,* which also suggests guidelines for their use.

A typical computer-based system attempts to assist students with career decision-making by providing a cathode-ray-tube terminal through which the individual student may interact with the computer. The computer storage contains data which allows the student to examine values and tentative plans by retrieving information about chosen occupations along with predictive data. The goal is to teach decision-making strategies as well as provide vocationally relevant information.

These systems are relatively expensive to date, given the volume of student usage reported. Undoubtedly more effective and lower cost systems will be forthcoming. The potential of computer applications has not yet been realized. It is possible in the future that the entire range of career and occupational information will be available through a computerized access system.

Library Arrangements

The arrangement and management of library materials and facilities can offer an inviting resource which students will use with profit. If poorly arranged and unattended, the library could be a detriment to career planning goals. The maintenance of a library that is pleasantly appointed and easy to use is not so much dependent on a large budget as on innovative ideas for presenting career information materials.

Such career information can be made available at satellite locations in residence halls, student centers, etc., as well as in the career planning center. This is in keeping with the proactive stance of career development programs.

Filing. Career information materials are to be arranged and made available by any system that is as logical and simple as possible. The *Dictionary of Occupational Titles* provides a classification scheme which is adaptable for the career planning library. By organizing materials along these guidelines, kindred occupations are clustered together, permitting a student to view associated occupational activities. Any classification system should be fitted to serve the needs of users of the local library. Easy access to materials and a clear presentation of their scope encourages the consideration of alternatives related to an identified area of interest.

The *Dictionary of Occupational Titles* arranges titles and definitions by occupational groups using a numerical system that lends itself to computer applications. The system, using a series of digits, may be as simple or complex as the library collection requires. This approach is quite flexible, allowing for easy expansion of sections where more material is needed. A sample of the classification scheme is given below.

The filing arrangements for career libraries will be as unique from campus to campus as the career service itself. Although there may be room for wide diversity, consideration should be given the compatibility of the chosen system with other university resources. Is it possible to easily cross-index library holdings among other campus agencies and departments? A simple alphabetical filing system may be sufficient.

Professional, Technical, and Managerial Occupations

00/01	Occupations in architecture, engineering, and surveying
001	Architectural occupations
002	Aeronautical engineering occupations
003	Electrical/electronics engineering occupations
005	Civil engineering occupations
006	Ceramic engineering occupations
007	Mechanical engineering occupations
008	Chemical engineering occupations
010	Mining and petroleum engineering occupations

A library may be arranged by categories corresponding to the stages of the career planning process: self-assessment, career exploration, placement. There is no one recommended system in common use today. Most systems incorporate the organization provided by the *Dictionary of Occupational Titles* simply to avoid "reinventing the wheel." Any arrangement that keeps the needs of the information seeker in mind has a high probability of success.

Posters and handouts in the library area may facilitate use of the collection by simply explaining the organization of the materials. Information sources in the collection that are not visible, such as slides, audio-cassettes, pamphlet files, and other items, should be announced by poster or handout. New acquisitions can best be announced in a periodic newsletter to student groups and faculty advisors. Copies should be posted on prominent bulletin boards. Career counselors may wish to consult *Guidelines for the Preparation and Evaluation of Career Information Media* published by the National Vocational Guidance Association. The publication deals with printed material, films and filmstrips.

Management. The physical setting for the collection of materials should be an appropriately furnished area with chairs and tables and one that is well lighted, inviting the casual examination of items germane to the career planning process. It is important to have a person stationed in the information center to assist in finding relevant material and to make referrals to career counselors when additional assistance is required.

The secretary or librarian serving this function can conduct some of the research of new publications to bring them to the attention of the counseling staff, order new materials as they are selected, and arrange for the purging of obsolete materials. The maintenance and operation of a career information center is an ongoing, year-round process, although seasonal activities such as updating files and reordering items may occur at specified times. Attention to the usefulness of materials, as determined by student activity and requests, will highlight deficiencies which may be remedied by ordering the material requested or referring students to a source outside the center where the information may be obtained.

Summary

Serving the career information needs of students is a proactive service. The information specialist assesses the need for information by asking students directly and by checking with academic departments or key faculty members to determine kinds of information needed to supplement other campus holdings. The career information specialist may need to coordinate the various campus collections of the main library and academic departments to facilitate the interchange and cross-indexing of information.

Students should have available a single, coordinated network of information resources, both in collections of library materials and contact persons. It is important for the career information specialist to make the collection of materials known to the college community and to indicate how it can be used in conjunction with a variety of counseling and advising activities going on throughout the campus.

Some career planning offices have tried novel approaches for the dissemination of information and the announcement of services by taking mobile units around campus or stationing displays in residence units. Any approach for announcing services and the availability of information that is appropriate and tasteful should be considered. In announcing services, adequate planning is necessary to insure that the quality of the presentation adequately reflects the quality of the service being offered.

RECOMMENDED READINGS

BEAUMONT, A., A. COOPER, AND R. STOCKARD: *A Model Career Counseling and Placement Program,* College Placement Services, 1978.

BORDIN, E.S.: *Psychological Counseling*, Second Edition, Appleton-Century-Crofts, 1968.

BROWN, W.F.: *Student-to-Student Counseling*, University of Texas Press, 1972.

CARKHUFF, R.R.: *The Art of Helping*, Human Resource Development Press, 1973.

CRITES, J.O.: "Career Counseling: A Review of Major Approaches," *The Counseling Psychologist* Vol. IV, Number 3, 1974.

DELWORTH, U., G. SHERWOOD, AND N. CASABURRI: *Student Paraprofessionals: A Working Model for Higher Education*, American Personnel and Guidance Association, 1974.

EGAN, G.: *The Skilled Helper*, Brooks/Cole Publishing Company, 1975.

FIGLER, H.E.: *A Career Workbook for Liberal Arts Students*, The Carroll Press, 1975.

GAZDA, G.M.: *Group Counseling—A Developmental Approach*, Allyn and Bacon, 1971.

HOPPOCK, R.: *Occupational Information*, Fourth Edition, McGraw-Hill Book Company, 1976.

KEMP, C.G.: *Perspectives on the Group Process*, Second Edition, Houghton Mifflin Company, 1970.

OSPOW, S.H.: *Theories of Career Development*, Second Edition, Prentice-Hall, 1973.

POWELL, C.R.: *Career Planning and Placement Today*, Second Edition, Kendall-Hunt Publishing Co., 1978.

ROGERS, C.R.: *Client-centered Therapy*, Houghton-Mifflin Company, 1951.

SIMPSON, L.A.: *A/V Media In Career Development*, The College Placement Council, 1975.

TYLER, L.: *The Work of the Counselor*, Third Edition, Appleton-Century-Crofts, 1969.

WHITELEY, J.M., AND A. RESNIKOFF (eds.): *Perspectives on Vocational Development*, American Personnel and Guidance Association, 1972.

PART IV

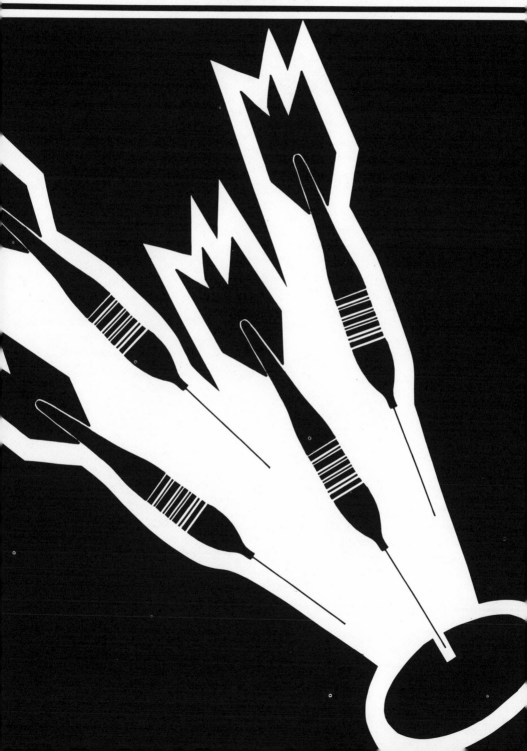

CHAPTER 6

THE JOB SEARCH PROCESS

FOR SOME YEARS the major service in many college placement offices consisted of teaching students and alumni how to get a job. Placement offices assumed that the students who came for advice already had established career goals and knew the initial type of position being sought.

Teaching students and alumni methods of organizing effective career searches remains a major and important role of every career planning and placement service. Many students have little knowledge about job campaigns and, therefore, look to the placement service to give the needed guidance. The placement service that fails to address this critical need is not meeting its responsibility for offering students a complete line of placement-related services.

Shifting Emphasis

In recent years, a few career planning and placement offices leaned toward concentrating career counseling on life and career goals. Occasionally, the important function of the career search was overlooked. The assumption was that students who can analyze self, explore the world of work, and integrate the two surely can, on their own, learn the mechanics of job seeking.

On the other hand, even though the need to provide new types of services to students emerged as a result of the changing economic and social environment, a few placement offices resisted change and failed to recognize the need for career counseling. These operations held to the concept that campus recruiting was the key activity, and the only career counseling students received came as a byproduct.

A balance needs to be restored in many offices between career counseling and career placement. One role of higher education is to provide instruction for students in areas where knowledge is lacking. The subjects taught range from physical education to nuclear theory, and one subject area that has a defined body of knowledge based on theory and supported by principles and practices is career planning. The placement function is an integral part of the career planning process.

Need for a Career Approach

A public demand for this knowledge is evident. Unfortunately, the field experienced its share of shysters, hucksters, and false prophets over the years, and this has tainted the image to a slight degree. Hundreds of poorly written books blanket the market. The advice is seldom written by individuals who are closest to the field. In many cases, the author's claim to knowledge is based solely on a few personal attempts at job hunting. Only a few have been on the daily firing line where their profession demands staying tuned to concepts and techniques.

The career planning and placement professional is closer to the actual job search process than nearly all of the authors of job hunting books. The professional possesses expertise and experience, and has access to feedback that is immediate and constant.

To teach the career search, every professional has the responsibility to study, experiment, and research a variety of approaches. Only the most effective approaches, supported by concrete evidence, should be taught to students and alumni. This is not to suggest that gimmicks, neat-sounding ideas, and unique approaches should not be utilized. Experiments with new ideas create new knowledge and approaches, but only a few of the ideas ultimately pass the reality test. Clientele being used in such experiments need to know that they are part of an experiment and should not be led to believe that the new approach has been tested in the marketplace.

Improving the System

Unlike many countries, the United States has a fairly well defined approach to seeking career-related employment in a managerial, technical, or professional capacity. Few countries have the elaborate system of personnel offices in private and public organizations, corporate college relations officers, and career planning and placement functions in colleges and universities. Functions taken for granted in America are being exported to many other countries of the world.

Because the employment system does not always work smoothly for every applicant, cries for change in job-hunting strategies abound. Problems exist in any system, and the rule of career specialists is to help make the approach work better. Rather than destroy the present system and build a new design, a more rational reaction would be to improve the current approach if possible.

One should also recognize that the design of the employment system may not be the problem. Most problems could be resolved by a more abundant supply of job openings. Increasing the number of jobs for college graduates may be a long-term role that should be addressed jointly by employer and college professionals. In the short term, the supply and demand balance is one of several constraints under which everyone must operate.

Defining the Search Process

The purpose of this chapter is to offer one approach to the career search process. The suggested approach is the widest accepted view, but many variations and differing emphases on techniques often improve this basic approach.

Recommendation of this approach, including its variations, assumes that employers and colleges desire to work within the present employment system. The recommendation assumes that employers wish to continue in an employment relationship with colleges and that colleges also wish to maintain the status quo, with improvements incorporated as appropriate. The recommendation is based on the belief that it is not in the best interests of either party to recommend approaches that bypass the other.

Career planning and job search is a step-by-step procedure followed by nearly all job seekers. The career planning steps include: (1) assessing self, (2) exploring career options, (3) establishing career objectives, and (4) specifying an appropriate position to seek. The mechanical steps in the job search include: (1) resume preparation, (2) cover letter preparation, (3) contact development, (4) employment service use, (5) interview preparation, (6) interviewing, (7) job selection, and (8) evaluation.

Nearly every career planning and placement professional is familiar with each step in the process of organizing a job campaign. Most counselors teach the approach on a regular basis in career planning classes, placement seminars, and individual counseling sessions. Ironically, until now, none of the professional publications laid out a definitive statement of the process. With minor modifications, almost everyone follows the same approach. Instruction of new personnel is given by word of mouth and recommendation of books to read.

This chapter is an attempt to develop a basic foundation which may be used by experienced and new professionals. The approach presents a skeleton upon which new techniques and modifications can be applied.

THE CAREER PLANNING PHASE

Starting a job campaign assumes that career goals have already been well defined. All too often, many individuals who wish to improve their lot in life fail to set some initial guidelines. Everyone operates in a constraint-filled environment. Without some goals based on a realistic plan, even individuals with the best intentions simply stroll through a sundry of jobs wondering why they do not get ahead. A better job is always desirable and lets one feel that there is upward movement. There are direct and indirect routes to get from point A to point Z. Staggering off track results when there is no realistic plan.

A successful job campaign begins with the development of a career plan that starts with direction and builds-in appropriate monitors to indicate deviations. Career planning is the key.

Career Planning Defined

Conceptually, career planning is a continuous decision-making process that feeds upon an ever-increasing awareness of self, with continuous inputs from the world of work. From a practical standpoint, individuals continually think about what they want to do and how they might improve themselves.

Career planning involves three activities for every individual: (1) discover what they want out of their working life, (2) explore what is available in the work environment, and (3) organize a plan of action that integrates needs and occupations.

The element that brings the self-analysis and work analysis together is a decision-making framework. Decision-making involves five basic steps: (1) define the problem, (2) develop the alternatives, (3) evaluate the alternatives, (4) make the decision, and (5) evaluate the decision as new information becomes available.

Certain events in life trigger the career planning process. A student graduates from high school, trade school, college or a professional program. A person is unhappy in his or her current job. A person gets fired or laid off. An individual senses a need to advance. Upward mobility is a cornerstone of the American way of life. The continuous desire to upgrade or improve one's standing in society sparks career planning.

Objectives

The primary goal of career planning is to provide a simple framework that may be used to appraise career potential, explore various alternatives, and implement a plan to achieve the career goals. Although the focus is often on the third phase of career planning, implementing a career search process, the initial two phases are no less important.

The specific approaches recommended here relate most closely to managerial, technical, or professional occupations for which training or experience beyond high school is desirable or required. The general approach used in organizing a job campaign is common to many occupations. Career planning is a natural human process, and career planning concepts impact upon all occupationally trained individuals, regardless of their career interest.

The ideas pertain equally well to persons contemplating careers in business, education, government, or non-profit organizations. Career planning pulls dangling career fibers together in a meaningful manner.

Self-Assessment

The overall goal in career decision making is to obtain a career position consistent with academic training, past work and

life experiences, personality, abilities, aptitudes, values, interests, etc. These background characteristics are not always easy
to identify or evaluate.

Career planning merges information about self with information about careers. Logic demands that sound decisions on career and life planning can only be possible if facts about the
two parts are available.

The process of developing information about self is called
self-assessment. Putting it all together is a personal project.
Laying out the framework and the approach may require
the help of others. Some of the methods used in self-assessment include developing a chronological autobiography, preparing a topical autobiography, completing a personal inventory, and taking psychological tests. All of these methods
attempt to classify strengths and weaknesses, assets and liabilities, attitudes, aptitudes, personality, etc.

Individuals are far more likely to be able to integrate their
backgrounds with career characteristics if a sound understanding of self is available. Self is one half of the career decision equation.

Career Exploration

Career exploration is the process of developing information
about career alternatives. For every occupation there is a
wealth of information about factors that may influence success
in the field. Unfortunately, no single source could ever cover
information for all occupations. Career exploration involves
digging into a mass of information in order to cull out the most
pertinent facts that might influence a person's decision.

One of the questions most frequently asked of career counselors is, "What job possibilities are available for someone with
my background?" Questions often asked by an employer are,
"For what position are you applying?" and "What qualifies
you?"

Job candidates who ask interviewers what jobs are available

usually terminate employment consideration because there is no mutual starting point. The career objective must be set before the interview.

Career exploration analyzes information about the world of work. The process may be an in-depth analysis of a given career option or a cursory view of occupations clustered in a broad career field. The problem is to display the information in a logical format that is useful for decision making.

Sources of Career Information

The type of career information needed includes job titles, job descriptions, duties, responsibilities, qualifications required and desired, current market outlook, training provided, and advancement possibilities.

People and publications, including a variety of media, are the two sources of career information. Information from people comes from general observation (role models), informational interviews, cooperative education, internship, part-time, summer, or other temporary work arrangements. Helpful publications include books, association pamphlets, government publications, and employer brochures.

The *Dictionary of Occupational Titles* and *Occupational Outlook Handbook* are key resource documents but must be supplemented with other sources. *Career Planning and Placement Today* is an excellent resource for understanding the world of work and selected occupations. The *College Placement Annual* provides a realistic view of what employers seek. Numerous books in libraries go into significant depth on various career fields, occupations, and specific job assignments.

Frustrations begin as individuals try to match self-knowledge with career information because rarely do the pieces fit neatly together. Integration involves compromise in a decision process. The decision becomes the career objective statement on a resume and further specification produces a few job titles consistent with long-term aspirations.

Placement Process

The word "placement" is a misnomer but it adequately translates into the process of organizing a job campaign. Placement is an integral part of the career planning process because it continues to add new, real-world information into the self-assessment and career information components of the career planning equation.

A common occurrence is a change in career specification (usually not in direction) once the placement phase is in operation.

Placement provides the road map. It serves as a feedback loop that reinforces or alters the career goals established earlier. Placement represents a testing of earlier decisions through a real-world exposure.

The placement or job campaign includes resume preparation, cover letter design, contact development, interviewing, and evaluating actual job offers.

Organizing a job campaign must be viewed in the total framework of the career planning process. A runaway placement strategy connotes getting a job (not starting a career) at any cost and taking whatever is available. A sound approach to career planning pays off in future job satisfaction, higher earnings, and a happy life.

The placement process is time and decision oriented. Success depends upon matching career goals with job requirements and forecasting a realistic career path. Without compromise, the match rarely occurs. Time pressures force career choice.

For individuals unsure of their career goals, a return to the self-assessment and exploration phases of career planning is in order. Since career planning is not always a do-it-yourself project, career counselors and other professionals offer individuals assistance in integrating self with occupations. Many workbooks and psychological tests greatly assist in the process of arriving at a specific career goal.

Summary

Career planning is a continuous process that feeds upon sound approaches in three basic phases: (1) self-assessment, (2) career exploration, and (3) job placement. Career planning occurs in an integrative, decision-making framework based on constraints which force compromises.

The job search process assumes that definitive occupational choices have already been made. Moderate changes in career thrust may be made, but if major decisions are altered radically, important contacts and other employment resources may no longer be useful. Going back to the well repeatedly for job-related assistance rapidly depletes the supply of help from important contacts.

The topics covered in the search process include: (1) designing the job resume, (2) creating the letter of application, (3) developing contacts and strategies, (4) using professional employment assistance, (5) preparing for job interviews, (6) conducting the job interview, and (7) follow-up. The conclusion of a successful job campaign means obtaining one or more offers of employment in a capacity consistent with career goals. This is not the end, however. The career planning process continues throughout life.

DESIGNING THE RESUME

One of the most essential components in anyone's job campaign is a resume, the basic communication tool of an effective job campaign. A resume is a carefully designed and typewritten summary of a person's background characteristics that appear to be most relevant to the type of position being sought.

This digest of qualifications is written in a style and format that quickly focuses attention on the key elements that qualify an individual for a specific job interest. Although there is no one universally accepted format, general guidelines do exist.

Most resumes adopt a free form, yet a highly structured approach designed to highlight assets while minimizing liabilities.

Purpose

No one is hired solely on the basis of a resume. Personal interviews, tests, transcripts, references, etc. go into the hiring decision, but the resume is the key to opening the door. Its purpose is to whet an employer's appetite to the extent of wanting to provide a job interview.

The resume is occasionally used as an interview instrument where an employer's application has not been completed prior to the interview. Resumes rarely exceed two pages in length except for very high-level management positions, and most often are limited to one page. They are never rambling discourses about one's life history. The purpose is to obtain—not substitute for—an interview. An employer must readily see that credentials match job requirements.

Style

Graphically, the resume should be easy to follow. Sentences may be incomplete. Brief, concise, short, to the point are words to keep in mind as one writes a resume. Eye appeal should be emphasized. The reader quickly searches for key points, so the resume needs to be uncluttered, neatly blocked, and logically organized.

All unnecessary words should be eliminated including the use of "I" and "my." This can be done by starting sentences with a verb. Some words, particularly action-oriented activities, hold a more positive connotation than passive verbs or forms of "to be."

Action-oriented, self-descriptive words help the resume

come to life. Some of the key action words include active, direct, expedite, plan, organize, solve, supervise. Key descriptors include aggressive, ambitious, creative, enthusiastic, logical, reliable, tactful, etc.

Resumes should be reproduced by photo copying or offset printing on the highest quality of copy affordable. Carbons and special paper copies that fade or smudge easily should be avoided.

It is not necessary or expected to send an originally typed copy each time. There can be absolutely no spelling, typing, or grammatical errors as these always reflect negatively on even the best qualified applicants.

Some experts recommend a passportsize, but higher quality, photograph for the top of the resume. The purpose for this is to assist the employer in recalling candidates after interviewing many applicants for hours. Remembering from a photograph is much easier than recalling from notes or resumes.

Pictures also present problems as they serve in identifying race and sex. Therefore, employers are forbidden by law to request pictures, although there are no laws against the voluntary inclusion of a photograph on a resume. Some employers might have to cut it off, however, before placing it in their files. The decision to use a photograph is a personal judgment. The resume format recommended by several regional associations does not include a photograph.

Most resumes are printed on 8½ x 11" paper and reproduced on white, light gray, or beige paper of 20–50 pound weight. Odd size resumes and ornate designs rarely please discriminating employers. The most effective resumes do not state salary requirements, past salary history, reasons for changing jobs, and geographical limitations. The resume must place emphasis on the positive aspects of one's background. Other details come to the forefront at the time of the interview.

A resume is a sales device and justifiably takes time to prepare. The best resumes are written by the individuals themselves although advice from others and various publications is helpful. The resume must present a positive image!

Resume Elements

Every resume contains several major elements, each of which must contribute to the process of getting the interview. Every word is important. Each component must highlight the most positive assets which relay a message that the individual is well qualified for the job in question. Each element is briefly described below.

Identification. Contains contact information such as name, home address, telephone number, business address and telephone (if pertinent), and occasionally a permanent address of parents or relatives.

Many employers and agencies retain resumes for years, and a call in the future is not impossible. This is the reason for using the permanent address for people who tend to be highly transient, such as students.

Personal Data. Includes marriage status, birth date, condition of health, physical limitations, photograph, family background, and other related information. The decision to include these items is entirely optional. Many experts recommend that they not be included. In fact, it is illegal for employers to request this type of personal information. However, since the resume is a personal document and an individual's right of free speech is protected by the U.S. Constitution, it is not illegal for an individual to volunteer the information.

If the candidate feels that these items might have a positive impact on the employment decision, including them on the resume could be useful. For example, a family background in a given profession (such as a doctor) could positively influence an employer (such as a pharmaceutical firm) to interview applicants since they are applying for a career in a field in which they have lived. Because employment preference is sometimes given to minorities, women, and handicapped people, some individuals prefer to take advantage of that fact by indicating it on the resume.

Career Objective. Tells the employer the specific position being sought as well as longer-term aspirations. This is one of the most important parts of the resume because it is the first thing used by the employer in matching job interests with current job requisitions.

If there is no match, the rest of the resume may not be read. Without a clearly defined career statement, the resume simply says, "Here are my credentials, so what do you have for me?" Few individuals will accept just any job, and few employers will read any further.

The career objective, particularly the specific job desired, must be narrow enough to match a specific job opening and broad enough to show sound career direction. The tight rope is critical!

The remaining parts of the resume must continually reinforce and support the career objective. Where there are multiple career goals, it is wiser to prepare a separate resume for each interest. Care must be taken to insure that any one employer sees the most appropriate resume.

The career statements should reference several of the typical job titles used in the specific area of interest. It is helpful in the career statement to include some of the common buzz words found in the occupation. The final sentence of the career statement often relates to longer-term goals. Several sample statements may be found in *Career Planning and Placement Today*.

Education. Lists the complete educational history, with the most recent and highest level listed first. This section should list all colleges or trade schools, major subjects, degree(s) earned, graduation dates, dates attended, and grades.

In a section under the listing, it is common to include honors, scholarships, specific courses and grades relevant to the career objective, and comments about grade trends or performance if they are positive. Professional licenses, exams, certifications, and publications should all be acknowledged.

Activities. Describes civic or college extracurricular activities. Activities reveal certain values, concerns, leadership, teamwork, respect, and commitment that go beyond the scope of college or everyday routines.

These activities may include sports, fraternal organizations, associations, clubs, politics, service organizations, etc. It is especially important for college students to show such activities because of the lack of significant work experience.

Experience. Gives the name, job title, and description of all previous employment. The most recent work experience should be listed first. Included should be the organization's name, address, position title, brief description of duties and responsibilities, hours worked (full or part-time, summers), and the dates.

For students, it is not necessary to list every single little job or to go into any detail, but it is necessary to present a representative sampling. Even if the jobs seem menial and not job related, they often signify a commitment to a goal, desire to work, and other important work-related values.

References. Lists individuals who are willing to offer a positive statement about abilities and attitudes. Many resume experts recommend stating "references furnished on request," but good references are not to be minimized. For students with few work references, they can mean success or failure.

If references are listed, they should include the name, title (if applicable), current employer, address, and telephone number. References should always be advised that their names are being used. References should be familiar with academic and work capabilities. Especially effective are people with high social and professional standing—professors, teachers, counselors, bankers, lawyers, business executives, managers, etc.

Summary

A high percentage of hires are introduced via the resume. Care in writing and construction is essential. The resume must be a credit to the individual and designed to sell potential to an employer. The potential to handle a given assignment is based on a subjective feel by the employer, based on an assessment of career interests, education, activities, work experience, and references.

CREATING THE LETTER OF APPLICATION

The cover letter, sometimes called a letter of application, is a one-page letter with a business format designed to introduce a job applicant to a potential employer. A resume always accompanies a cover letter.

The purpose of a cover letter is to obtain a job interview, not to obtain the job offer. A large number of other factors, including the resume and interview, go into the final selection decision by an employer, but the cover letter is often an important consideration.

A good letter encourages the employer to read the resume and gives the employer a brief opportunity to appraise writing abilities. Personnel officers often receive many similar inquiries each day so they use the time available to quickly scan for details that roughly match specifications of current job openings.

Given this brief screening process, only a very carefully worded, highly organized, to-the-point letter stands a chance of surviving the initial screen.

Use of Letters

A high percentage of hires, especially at the entry level after college, result from mailing cover letters and resumes. Success depends on a quality letter and resume, coupled with a well-planned approach in deciding which employers to contact.

A cover letter should not reiterate everything in the resume. The letter must complement and expand on the resume and finally support why the employer should consider the applicant for employment.

Cover letters are usually sent as a result of a recommendation by a third party (professors, teachers, friends, agencies), a follow-up to an employment advertisement, or maybe a simple unsolicited inquiry. Letters are part of an overall job search strategy that includes several other methods of making contact with potential employers.

Approach

A direct mail, letter-writing job campaign can take two forms: a rifle or shotgun approach. In the rifle approach, a list of selected employers who normally offer employment in the designated field of interest is used to initiate contact. This special list may come from a college placement office, want-ads, teachers, friends, etc. The focus is on employers where a known opening exists or where there is a high probability of an opening. The list of contacts is not always extensive in numbers. Rather it is highly selective.

In the shotgun approach, inquiries are mailed to hundreds of potential employers in hopes of finding a job match or stumbling on more solid leads. Contacts come from annuals, directories, and professional occupational rosters. With today's mailing rates, this is an expensive approach, but it may be the only recourse for people in narrow job markets. The typical response rate in the shotgun approach to a 100-letter mailing is less than four or five replies. Most of the positive replies simply indicate that the employer will be happy to interview the candidate whenever the individual is in the area.

Because of the expense of replying to hundreds of inquiries, many firms do not send negative replies. If no reply comes in two or three weeks, it can be assumed that the employer does not have any appropriate job openings.

Cover letters must be personalized and individually typed to be effective. A reproduced form letter should never be sent. Whenever possible, the letter should be addressed to a specific person. Only as a final resort should functional titles, such as personnel director, president, sales manager, etc., be used. Specific names are available from college placement offices, teachers, and friends. Most large libraries frequently carry directories that provide specific contacts.

Content

The cover letter should not exceed one page. Key facts and brevity are watchwords. In the applicant's own words, the letter should say, "I am interested in you. Here is why you might be interested in me. May I have an interview appointment?" Each cover letter contains an introduction, body, and close.

Introduction. The first paragraph must attract attention. The reason for writing is the first thing the employer needs to know. The applicant should name the specific position being sought. Failure to commit to a specific job is a prime reason used by employers in rejecting applicants.

The employer is interested in knowing which job openings available best meet the candidate's background. Rarely will an employer take the time to review an applicant's entire background, mentally scan through all of the current job requisitions, and then come to a decision. The luxury of such time is not available.

The first paragraph should also state the source of information about the specific job (newspaper, agency, directory, etc.). If the contact is being initiated through the recommendation of a specific person likely to be known by the employer, that person's name should be mentioned.

Body. The body should never be more than three, possibly four, short paragraphs in length. Concrete reasons should be expressed for wanting to work for the employer. Specific interests and career goals need to be quickly stated to build a foundation of briefly stated educational and work background.

As in resume preparation, certain key words may be used to spark the imagination of the employer. Successful candidates use self-descriptive words and phrases that create an image of an aggressive, hard working, self-starting individual.

The resume data should not be repeated any more than is absolutely necessary. Only a few seconds are available to capture the employer's interests, so wasted words must be avoided. In one of the paragraphs of the body, the employer should be referred to the resume for details.

Desire, interest, and ability must come through loud and clear. The message to relay is that the requirements for the job being sought match the applicant's credentials. Only if the match is clear will the employer feel that a personal meeting is worthwhile for both parties. A logical, rational case for consideration must be made in the body.

Close. The purpose of the closing paragraph is to request an appointment. The last paragraph must force the reader to act by contacting the applicant immediately by letter or telephone. It is not easy to make a person want to do something in a letter. Because of that, phrases like "if you have any interest, please write" seldom generate a response.

Follow-up

In most cases, the next course of action is still up to the applicant. Tell the employer that you will call soon. Tell the employer you will be in the area on a specific date. Ask the employer to give you a specific name to contact in your area. Ask the employer to return a postcard questionnaire. In other words, make the next step easy for the employer. Suggest an appropriate follow-up. One technique is to end the letter with a question.

Few employers encourage applicants if there is only a marginal chance for employment. Sometimes, however, marginal chances pay off. If an interview involves travel of 50 to 1,000 miles, most employers figure the applicant does not want to gamble. Employers need to be told when and where candidates are available for an appointment. Incidentally, the travel expense for the first appointment is always the responsibility of the applicant.

Summary

The effective cover letter always keeps the reader in mind. The letter focuses on a specific position and is directed to the person most likely to be responsible for filling the position or doing the initial screening. The letter must give enough information to entice the employer to read the more complete resume. The letter must request a specific response.

Cover letters are an effective way to make contact with employers, but it is expensive, time consuming, hard work, and often discouraging. Cover letters do work and those who get discouraged, quit, or seek gimmicks probably will not be given consideration. A direct mail campaign is only one of several different approaches to initiate contact with employers, but it is one of the most widely used.

DEVELOPING CONTACTS AND STRATEGIES

The best resume and cover letter are effective only if they reach the proper person. Identifying potential employers to contact is one of the most critical areas because development of the sources of jobs creates the target group. Approaches directed to a carefully designed population of potential employers have a much higher probability of success. The time and money spent in the job campaign are reduced significantly.

Job leads come from direct contacts with employers and contacts with third parties who know potential employers. Everyone has a network of people who can be called on for assistance in the job search. The first task is to develop the network of contacts that may prove helpful.

Most job seekers do not have direct personal linkages with employers for whom they wish to work. If they did, they would no longer be job seekers but employees. Of course, direct contact can and should be initiated with potential employers, but frequently an emissary or go between is helpful. The direct mail and walk-in methods are two direct approaches to organizing a job campaign, but they are difficult for the job hunter.

The Contact's Roles

Contacts often serve in a brokerage capacity and play a simple but important role in the employment process. They are not god-like figures directing a group of players. They only act, react, advise, and recommend. Contacts are influential, but contacts do not get anyone a job. Only the solitary job candidate can accomplish that task.

Contacts can see that resumes get read. Credibility with potential employers normally is high because of past excellent working relationships. The result is that the contact's advice is taken seriously by employers.

Use of an influential contact can insure that the potential employer will read the resume. In many instances, contacts make appropriate introductions and/or arrange specific interviews. This intermediary is extremely useful in bringing the two parties together. The role of the intermediary can often be the commonality that starts the first interview flowing well. It breaks down the cold barrier occasionally found when two strangers get together to see if there is a mutual interest. Wherever possible, a job seeker should make use of all potential contacts who are in the position of playing an intermediary role.

Another important role that contacts can play is in giving positive recommendations to an employer about a prospective candidate. The contact has to be certain of the recommendation because one poor recommendation may destroy a long-term relationship with an employer. Consequently, it is in the best interest of contacts and employers to maintain an honest, truthful, and open channel of communication.

Personal Contacts

Who are contacts? Contacts are people who know people. Most job matches come from someone who knows someone important, putting two parties in touch because there appear to be mutual goals that can be satisfied. Every person has a wide array of contacts. Some are in the official business of being a contact while others are simply ordinary people whose daily life places them in touch with large numbers of other people.

The most important sources of contacts are friends, families of friends, teachers and professors, counselors, fellow workers, politicians, professional associations, and service organizations. For college graduates, the best sources are faculty, counselors, friends, and family.

Every acquaintance may become part of a network of contacts that can be expanded many fold simply by exploring with each acquaintance individuals they know who may be of assistance in a job search. A very high percentage of job placements come from such contacts every year. There are other sources of contacts, but these are some of the most effective since the referrals are on a more personal basis.

Approaching Contacts

The job seeker should approach each contact on a personal basis, asking for advice on how to approach the job market. As in resume preparation, a firm goal should be established because this will greatly facilitate the communication process and get right down to the issue of whom to contact.

Each contact needs to be provided with a letter (before or after the discussion) explaining the position being sought, soliciting ideas, and appreciation for help given. Attached to this letter should be about five resumes with the request that they be shared with anyone deemed appropriate.

A typical job campaign often takes about three months. During this time each contact should be advised by letter or phone of the current job status. Contacts will not follow through until convinced that the search is serious.

An important technique in using contacts is to keep soliciting advice. People enjoy helping others. It is not uncommon for a job seeker to be eventually hired by the person approached for advice. The request for advice is actually a subterfuge for requesting employment.

Strategy

The most successful job campaign begins with a timetable. The initial career planning process of self-assessment and career exploration generally takes a long time. During the planning process the individual goes through a lot of give and take before coming up with a specific career goal. The career planning process is important because over a period of time it builds the motivation and desire to make the actual search and the placement component function properly. It builds commitment! Without this commitment the job campaign loses credibility with contacts. Most job seekers cannot afford to waste contacts.

Once the commitment to change jobs or find professional employment after college is made, a strategy needs to be outlined. Strategies require targets—targets in a time frame as well as targets for creating the contact network.

Timing the Strategy

Once the career planning process is completed to the point that definite career objectives have been set and specific job titles consistent with the individual's background have been identified, the actual placement or job campaign step may take from thirty to ninety days. For the graduating college student the process should begin during the first term of the final year because the employer's lead time is much longer.

Resume preparation takes one to three weeks from conception to reproduction of final copies. Because cover letters must be individually typed, the preparation of a complete set of letters may take from one to four weeks, depending on the number to be typed. Personal contacts who assist in developing employment leads must also receive personally typed inquiries and thank you letters.

Developing the contact network may be the most time-consuming process of all. The contact network serves as the mailing list for dissemination of cover letters and resumes. This mailing list must contain columns to record dates sent, dates replies received, and types of response. Creation of a contact network rarely takes less than two weeks and often requires six weeks.

Obviously, there is some overlap in timing, for several activities can proceed simultaneously. Even the casual observer can see that a well-planned and orchestrated job campaign takes considerable time and effort. The thirty-to-ninety-day time frame is not unrealistic.

The time frame is more complicated when job searchers must conduct the campaign on a part-time basis because school work or a full-time job occupies the majority of their time. Most spare time is spent on the job campaign and rarely does the less-than-serious candidate succeed.

Summary

Fortunately, some of the work can be short-circuited by relying on professional assistance and publications. The wheel does not have to be invented each time. In addition, people who have been through the process once usually build upon earlier learning and find new shortcuts. No matter who the person is and how much other people can be relied upon to help, the process takes time and energy.

The development of a list of personal contacts and a strategy for using that list is an integral part of the search process. Even for individuals planning to rely strongly on referrals from faculty, friends, and others, the network of contacts needs to be prepared.

USING PROFESSIONAL EMPLOYMENT ASSISTANCE

The most astute job hunter soon learns that doing all of the work on a job campaign alone takes more time than available. Turning toward professional sources of employment assistance is a natural course. The assistance boils down to using the library for helpful publications which give advice and individuals whose daily activity centers on helping people make contact with potential employers.

As with personal contacts, none of these sources get anyone a job. Only a dedicated individual with a sound approach can be successful. Intermediaries only serve in a capacity of advice giving and brokering between employers and job candidates.

Publications share information that others have found useful and provide potential names and addresses of potential employers. Personal contacts share information gained from others that proved successful and make arrangements for interviews. Beyond that scope, the job search is a solitary experience.

Publications

Generating a comprehensive yet potentially effective contact list requires more than talking to people. A wealth of information, although not as personal, has been printed which will help generate specific names. The three major sources of specific job leads are newspapers (Sunday editions), trade journals, and professional publications. Each runs classified advertisements.

For the cold contacts, but hot from the standpoint of being a potential employer, most libraries contain many different types of directories. There are even directories of directories! Although these directories are not employment related, they do give names, titles, and addresses needed in the direct mail job campaign. Two directories often overlooked which may be somewhat more personal are directories of employers published by college placement offices and directories of members of professional associations.

Although cold contacts are not as effective as referrals from within the personal network for many types of jobs, they can serve as primary job leads. If cold contacts are selected with a particular career focus in mind, the returns can be greatly improved.

Libraries located in public buildings, colleges, or college placement offices open up resources that most individuals do not know exist. Directories vary from *Who's Who* to association membership lists. There are directories on foundations, hospitals, associations, educational institutions, public agencies, corporations. The people listed in the directories often have some relation to the occupational field of interest to the job seeker.

Libraries contain books on the job hunting process which may give a different approach than that suggested in this book. Differing viewpoints permit the individual to adopt the approach best suited to solve that person's specific employment objectives. There are thousands of books on various career fields which may be more germane to the early career planning process but which also offer excellent suggestions on how to break into the occupation.

Different occupations occasionally offer a unique method of entry into the profession. For example, entrance into the legal and teaching professions requires an initial certification which, if not obtained, bars employment regardless of the best laid job campaign strategy.

Reading moves the job seeker one more step into organizing a successful job campaign. Of course, reading must end and actions begin for success to be realized. Reading represents a learning process which can only enhance the chances of conducting a successful approach.

Employment services offer the same type of advice found in libraries. Employment professionals gain their knowledge from a combination of books and experience. While publications provide names of contacts, intermediaries often go a step beyond and arrange for the parties to get together for an interview.

Placement Office Services

For college students, and often alumni, the college placement office is the one best source for obtaining employment assistance. Services provided and the policies governing who is eligible vary widely but most placement offices offer to arrange appointments with employers visiting campus. Graduation from college is one of the very few times in life where the employers initiate contact with job candidates.

Most placement offices assist students in a wide range of career planning. Most provide current job listings, descriptions of hundreds of careers, directories of contacts, annual reports, and employment brochures from many employers. Except for credential reproduction, seldom is there any cost for the services. There are three key areas where they are most effective.

On-campus Interviews. For graduating students, campus interviewing is the most convenient, least expensive, most effective means of obtaining the first job after college. It is a once-in-a-lifetime opportunity.

Unfortunately, less than half of college students get their first job this way because they either fail to take advantage of the service early or there are not enough employers visiting campus to hire everyone. Of those who actively utilize the service, a very high percentage obtain employment and all learn more about the pressures of an employment search than possible in any other way.

Referrals. Most placement officers maintain close contact with alumni and local and national employers, and cultivate close working relationships with a host of potential employment contacts. Referrals to employers are made on a personal basis, so this process can be even more effective than campus interviewing.

Services. The services of a college placement office are much broader than either of the above. Their key thrust is to teach people how to help themselves. Career planning goes far beyond the job hunting process and the concepts taught in career planning build the foundation upon which a successful search is built. Most services teach these concepts and techniques.

Two books serve as key references. The *College Placement Annual* contains the current names and addresses of over 1,200 employers of college graduates. Included is a listing of the job openings normally available, along with the degree level and major required. The *Annual* is cross classified by geographical location and by major field of study.

The other major reference book is the *Occupational Outlook Handbook for College Graduates*, which contains titles and job descriptions for all occupations normally requiring a college degree. The *Handbook* describes the work duties, the places of employment, qualifications required, employment outlook, and sources of additional information.

Employment Services

A job campaign must utilize all avenues of potential career search assistance. Each method may translate into success, and no one approach is ideal for everyone. An individual should do as much spade work as possible, but there is no reason for the person not to approach and use employment services. Three of the most frequently used sources are discussed below.

Public Employment Service. Government-operated employment services suffer from the stigma of being unemployment offices useful primarily for "blue collar" workers. The facts no longer justify the allegation. Employers with government contracts must list professional openings with the services. The services are free to both candidate and employer.

The quality of the service varies by office. Their basic role is to advise job seekers of potential openings and refer the candidate's paperwork to employers. Employers follow up by contacting and interviewing candidates.

Private Employment Agencies. Agencies maintain two files: one of job applicants and one of job specifications. Ideally, as a match occurs, candidates are contacted by the agency which sets up an interview with the employer. The agency's basic service to an employer is its ability to screen out unqualified candidates, which frees the time of the employer.

In an imperfect world, seldom are matches perfect. The agency, therefore, plays the role of a middle-person adviser who prepares candidates and talks employers into modifying specifications slightly. Such a role may be extremely helpful to candidates.

The service is paid for by one party or the other. The fee is at least 10–15 percent of the annual salary and is due within three months after employment. Some agencies also charge applicants for counseling and other services. If the job market is very tight for a given career field, the employer pays, but otherwise the applicant usually pays. Applicants should be cautioned that employment agency contracts are binding.

An applicant should contact several agencies but work regularly with one that seems most helpful. If referrals fail to come, change agencies. Since persistence pays off, contact should be maintained on a weekly basis. Most professional and managerial placements are in the $10,000 to $25,000 range.

Search Firms. Search firms do not contract with individuals, although many individuals like to send resumes to search firms to get into their file. Search firms work on a contractual agreement with employers to find a special person for a given job assignment. Most search firms have exclusive rights and get paid by the employer whether or not the person is found. Jobs are always over $25,000 and require extensive experience.

The search firm's responsibility is to the employer. Candidates are aggressively interviewed and screened and often candidates seeking an employment change are contacted. Obviously, search firms are useful only to a very small percentage of the population.

Summary

The ways to locate and contact potential employers are many, and each approach has certain advantages. Each job hunter should utilize every approach that closely matches the individual's career interests. The whole concept of employment searches and job campaigns rests upon the use of a network of contacts, college placement offices, and employment agencies. Developing the network of contacts is one of the most essential parts of the employment process.

PREPARING FOR JOB INTERVIEWS

The best prepared resume and cover letter only serve to open the door to a job interview. Even the most influential benefactors or contacts rarely impose their will on a friend who has a job opening available. Obtaining the right job requires a highly successful personal interview. The job interview is becoming more and more the most important selection factor in the employer's decision to hire.

Evaluation

An interviewer is interested in what makes applicants think, react, and behave, particularly as these points impact the work setting. The interview brings out the subjective factors in contrast to the objective factors listed on the resume and application.

Many employers elect to interview only those candidates whose resumes indicate that they have all of the abilities needed to handle the job. The interviewer assumes that the applicant "can do" the job and must determine if the applicant is "willing to do" the job. Evaluating interest, attitudes, personality, aspirations, and motivating factors is a key factor in the selection process.

The importance of the job interview cannot be overstressed, and yet many applicants take it as a casual affair requiring little or no advance planning. The most successful interviews are planned ahead of time.

The resume summarizes the essential background facts. Good interviewers probe in depth some of the points listed on the resume in order to appraise a wide range of qualities. The questions relate to motivation, personality, values, attitude, speaking ability, leadership, and ambitions. The object is to assess the applicant's willingness to handle assignments.

Presentation

The secret to successful interviewing is a sound presentation supported by facts and examples. Good presentations require advance preparation. Employers tend to remember reasons why *not* to hire while the applicant must continue to reinforce reasons why *to* hire. At the conclusion of the interview, the interviewer must be able to list several points that show why the applicant should be hired. A strong, long lasting, verbal presentation is possible only with advance preparation.

Preparation takes homework about one's self and about the employer. An honest, sincere story comes after the self-assessment that was discussed in the first part of this series. Without a self-evaluation, complete with strengths and shortcomings, taking a job interview is like selling a product about which nothing is known. Discussing a life history that can show how the points relate to a job is impossible without some pre-conceived plan. Without it, all an employer gets is a stumbling, rambling dissertation, and that does not turn into a job.

Preparation

If one knows the employer well and what is being sought, organizing a presentation that draws upon positive job-related traits and omits negative traits becomes an easier task. Essential items that should be known about the employer include the position available, the job description which gives duties and requirements, training program if any, and basic facts about the firm.

Basic facts about an employer include some financial data like sales volume, net assets, and profit levels. An applicant needs to know the various locations, products made and distributed, competition, industry position, past and potential growth in sales and profits, etc.

Adequate preparation for a series of interviews may take five or six hours of concentrated thought and writing. Each interview requires about one hour of advance preparation and a 15–30 minute review just prior to the interview. Essential preparation means knowing what information to give about self, presenting a clear statement of career goals and immediate job interest, and knowing facts about the employer.

Sources

Sources of information include annual reports, investment advisory publications in the public library, teachers, friends, employment advertisements, and present employees. Applicants having information in advance can more readily interweave background characteristics and interests with what the employer needs.

Factors Being Evaluated

To obtain a managerial, technical, or professional job, many applicants go through a series of interviews. The initial interview is with a person, often in personnel, who conducts a preliminary screen and refers qualified candidates to operating personnel in the department with an opening. After a series of interviews with several people in the unit, a committee or consensus decision is made.

The most important factor being appraised is technical competence which relates to education, grades, test scores, and experience. Other predictors of success include an evaluation of motivation, ambition, intelligence, teamwork abilities, initiative, adaptability, habits, leadership potential, and ability to communicate.

Strategy

Interviewing success requires a plan of attack. This strategy anticipates the likely circumstances that may occur and maps an approach for dealing with each expected event. Every possible question relating to an applicant's background or job requirements can be anticipated with forethought.

The strategy includes making a list of every likely question and preparing in advance a reply that is truthful, organized and yet best represents what the employer wants to hear.

Most interviewers ask open-ended questions, that is, the questions are topic oriented. The topics likely to be important to a given position rarely change from interview to interview. A brief presentation should be prepared around each of the topical headings. When a specific question is asked, however it is phrased, the gist usually centers on one of the topics. With a short preface, the presentation about the topic can be inserted as a reply to a given question.

The most frequently recurring topics are listed below:

Career objective	Education
Initial assignment	Experience
Employer knowledge	Geographical flexibility
Personal qualifications	Past achievements
Career choice rationale	Social/civic activities

Personal Appearance

Proper personal appearance is not a minor part of interview preparation. Appearance is the easiest problem to solve, but many applicants get hung up on this issue. Appearance is the strongest nonverbal cue in an interview that an employer can evaluate. Appearances relay messages which the employer must consciously or unconsciously process, depending upon a preconceived point of view.

The best guideline for appearance (dress, grooming, manners, etc.) is: Present yourself in a manner that is consistent with how most employees currently on the job present themselves.

Confidence

Job candidates must first convince themselves that they are right for the job and prospective employer before there is a chance of convincing the employer of the ideal fit. All job applicants are nervous and employers overlook initial flutterings. The only way to minimize nervousness is to eliminate the uncertainty that creates it. Uncertainty disappears as the interview follows a pre-planned pattern.

The pre-planned pattern comes from a sound, well-conceived, and carefully designed presentation. No one would face an audience of friends or peers without a speech outline and without rehearsing the presentation. An interview often has a longer lasting effect on a person's life than a speech. Interviewing demands no less advance preparation!

Summary

Getting ready for an interview is a large part of the preparation. Knowing what to expect and how to react to it is another important part. Successful interviewing is really a psychological state of mind. The level of success is somewhat dependent upon the level of control exercised by the applicant. As control dissipates, confidence diminishes, and nervous rambles replace a planned approach. Success seldom follows. Control involves knowing what is going to happen and how to influence the situation.

CONDUCTING THE JOB INTERVIEW

A job interview is nothing more than an exchange of information between two people with specific goals that is designed to explore whether there are mutual areas of interest. An interview is not a battle of wits between two fighters, but a friendly communication effort by two individuals trying to match human qualities with job characteristics.

The thirty-minute interview often has a major impact upon both parties so the decisions to be made must be decided with as much information available as possible.

Career success may depend upon the results. Each party must understand the goals of the other. Many employers spend hours training interviewers. Effective techniques of interviewing for the applicant seldom get taught but are equally as important to both parties. An interviewer much prefers talking to prepared applicants. The difficult selection task becomes easier and the applicant finds success more often.

The advance preparation lays important groundwork for conducting the interview. A strong preparatory strategy increases the confidence level of the applicant and permits control to be exercised by both parties, creating the desired two-way channel of communication.

Interview Stages

The typical interview has four recognizable stages. The introduction is designed to establish rapport and smooth nerves. It usually consists of small talk related to the weather, sports, common identities, etc. The background stage moves the interview into a mutual exchange of information about the candidate's background, with the employer giving some information about the organization.

In the evaluative stage, each party attempts to match job requirements with human talents, hoping to satisfy each other's needs. The closing stage leaves room for final questions and covers anticipated follow-up procedures. Although each interview has unique variations, the pattern is usually consistent.

Employer Questions

The mid-section of an interview contains numerous probing questions by the interviewer that can be recognized by why, where, when, and how types of leads. The questions may not all be job related because the goal is often to evaluate self-confidence, ability to communicate, and adaptability to a new situation.

In a factual, sincere, and candid manner, the answers to probing questions should be pre-planned and designed to reveal high levels of motivation, job-related abilities, strong interests in the job, appropriate career potentials in the career path, and values common to society-defined maturity standards.

Saying things that reveal qualities often sought by employers sounds boastful but that is the essence of job interviews. Job interviews sell the abilities of applicants to employers and vice versa. Bluffing through an interview and still showing the above talents is not possible. It takes a planned approach to communicate talents in these areas to an interviewer.

Interviewers watch for special skills that may not be needed in the initial job but which may be required in subsequent promotions. The most common skills sought in people being promoted are responsibility, supervisory talent, ability to work with and through others, communication (speaking and writing), perseverance, and dependability. Candidates who talk about these skills seldom succeed. Candidates who discuss each of these talents in an example-oriented presentation often find understanding employers.

An excellent technique is to prepare multi-page written responses to questions that touch on areas such as background, career goals, education (course, grades, trends), work experience (full or part-time, summer) and college activities. Rehearse a presentation as one would a speech until it falls in a two- to three-minute time frame. Try it on a friend or with a tape recorder. Evaluate it and then use a modified version or outline in an interview.

Asking Questions

Asking questions is not any less important than answering questions because the evaluative process continues. The information to be gained by each question should be important enough and needed for decision-making purposes to justify its use in a time-critical activity. If a question appears insignificant or the information could have been obtained in the normal interview preparation process, the interviewer gets the impression that the candidate lacks true interest.

Appropriately phrased questions frequently tell the employer something about the pre-planning that came before the interview and thus show real interest. For example, a training program question might be prefaced with statements that show extensive knowledge about the program but which indicate that additional information is needed. Such questions show the interviewer that advance homework was done and that a high interest is present.

Most appropriate questions focus on the initial assignment, the advancement potential, and further information about the employer. Most experts recommend that questions about salary and fringe benefits should be avoided in the initial thirty-minute interview. These questions are value laden and relay messages that are more important for follow-up interviews with operating managers.

Nonverbal Cues

Interview evaluation is not conducted solely on what is said. Two people can communicate without talking. Nonverbal communications include gestures, facial expressions, posture, perspiration, eye contact, and mannerisms. Dress and grooming send signals to the employer. Most nonverbal cues can be planned in advance from a concept perspective just as verbal communication can. Above all, one should recognize the items that send messages and exercise some control over them.

Knockout Factors

The reasons why candidates receive turndowns provide a helpful feedback loop. Fifteen common factors consistently emerge. A candidate may be lacking in one of these basic areas: goal definition, technical knowledge, expression, achievement, preparation, interest in employer, location, personality, aggressiveness, money, questions, realism, evasiveness, maturity, or appearance. Frequently, there is evidence of an overriding "halo effect" where one negative transmits negative feelings to other factors which might be really one of the strengths of the interviewee.

Individuals also are turned down through no fault of their own. An employer may find a slightly stronger candidate or simply select someone in a toss-up.

Employers rarely tell applicants why they were not accepted. That is unfortunate because often the feedback could be of major help in solving a problem. Employers are not professional counselors, however, and when forced into that role, the applicant often becomes defensive. The best sources of honest appraisal are the college placement offices, teachers, employment agencies, search firms, friends, and relatives. Employers will occasionally give a trusted third party valid information.

After the Interview

The initial interview is usually only the first hurdle as several subsequent interviews often follow. The interviewee must recognize that the end is not present and must make plans for the future.

Every interview, whether initial or secondary, should be followed by a note-taking process. The name of the interviewer and others met at that time must be written down or business cards requested. An evaluation needs to be written that covers all major points discussed, an opinion of the strengths and weaknesses, and the expected follow-up procedure. If one is taking several interviews, as is usually the case, remembrances get hazy after the first couple and ideas discussed run together.

An accurate recall is likely to be necessary if further interviews or a job offer result, and few people enjoy being embarrassed later.

Thank-you letters after an interview are not necessary, but for special circumstances a follow-up thank you is a polite gesture. The letter can include information that was overlooked in the interview. A thank-you letter can also include new information that may have developed since the interview.

Summary

The job interview plays the most central role in the entire job search process. The resume, cover letter, and contacts open doors. The job interviews serve as a major selection tool in the decision. Attention to the job interview phase is essential. Advance preparation, developing a presentation, planning anticipated question responses, and outlining strategies and techniques in advance, all must be present in successful interviewing.

EVALUATION

The job search process does not end with the interview. Successful completion of the initial interview brings more interviews and, as these become more successful, other factors enter into the search process. Consideration must then be given to a chain of written communications, ethics, factors to consider in selecting employment, further education, and the return to the career planning cycle.

Communications

Passing the initial interview completes a major hurdle in the job campaign. A series of further interviews follows but the preparation and techniques in conducting these vary little from the initial interview. One thing that some individuals fail to recognize is the need for follow-up communication.

Some of the correspondence after the interview includes arrangements for secondary interviews, follow-up letters with expense statements and appropriate thank-you notes, acknowledging offers, and accepting or declining offers. Many placement offices maintain files of such sample letters to expedite the process. Sound business communications play an important role in deciding who obtains an offer.

Decision Factors

Making the employment decision is often the most difficult decision ever faced in a person's life. Some of the factors most often used in the evaluation include advancement potential, responsibility, training, type of work, autonomy, salary, colleagues, security, benefits, working conditions, etc. The relative ranking of such factors is an individual responsibility which is complicated by the fact that few of these factors can be objectively evaluated.

Before making the final selection one should return and discuss the circumstances with the individuals who were most helpful in the job campaign. Insights often are offered by others that assist in the decision-making process. For college graduates respected faculty and placement office staff provide an excellent sounding board.

Whatever the ultimate decision, the career planning process does not end. Career planning is a cyclical event that continues to recur as an individual gains a more defined opinion of personal goals and processes this opinion with new career information. The cycle frequently includes organizing a new job campaign which may lead to another job change or a decision to maintain the status quo. The career planning concepts of self-assessment, career exploration, and placement provide principles around which a plan of action can be drawn.

Summary

This chapter on the job search process attempted to lay a foundation around which the total career planning process can revolve. Improvement, additions, deletions, and alterations can easily be made to the approaches discussed, but the basic concept of a process based upon accepted principles and current practices remains somewhat stable.

Although this chapter was undoubtedly much too basic for the experienced professional, its usefulness lies more in the development of a common body of knowledge acceptable to a high percentage of the profession. To those entering the profession, the approach may sound familiar, but the organization and structure put the various elements together in a manner readily teachable to others. Although the information is not new, it has served many years as the backbone of many career planning and placement services.

CHAPTER 7

CAMPUS INTERVIEWING SERVICE

D URING THE FIFTIES and Sixties, campus interview visits by employers consumed a high percentage of placement staff time on hundreds of college campuses. Even during recessionary years, the trek to campus by employers each term hardly slowed from a well-worn path. The system thrived largely because the supply of college-trained talent never kept pace with increasing demands for college graduates. Many placement services were born during these times, and the small but growing staffs found it hard to manage the hectic activity.

Only a few colleges spent much time with career counseling. Students knew they had a choice of several job possibilities, so few really took the time to undertake serious planning as we know it today. The motivation to conduct career planning was not always present. Times changed, however, as a balance in supply and demand developed, starting in the Seventies. Many of the hours spent in managing a large campus interview program were diverted to development of programs more geared to student needs than to employer needs.

The shift came gradually and, indeed, on many campuses it still is in process. Employers began the shift by dropping smaller, less-productive colleges from recruiting schedules. The recession in the early Seventies speeded up what might otherwise have occurred on a slower basis over time. Some employers halted all college visits and others drastically cut back their programs to only a few limited colleges. As employment needs returned to more reasonable levels, employers exercised great caution in rebuilding recruiting itineraries.

Employers soon discovered that their needs could be met by fewer campus visits because of a greatly increased supply of graduates at many schools. The recession also brought graduates to the employer's door instead of vice versa. Employers cut recruiting to a minimum to reduce costs per hire, which meant that only the most productive colleges remained on itineraries.

Many employers confused college recruiting with college relations in the early stages of the shift in the supply and demand balance. A few recruited on campus when no openings existed or were anticipated. In many instances, resentment built up against employers following this strategy of keeping the company name visible on campus. A more prudent course might have been to pursue college relations through a non-recruiting avenue.

College recruiting is far from dead, however. On some campuses in the late Seventies, recruiting thrived like never before, even exceeding, in some cases, the level of activity in the Sixties.

The scope of campus interviewing is influenced by economic factors, the academic mix of the graduating students, and the size of the college. These are factors which a placement service is powerless to change. But the scope of recruiting activity is also influenced by factors which are within the control of the placement service. Employers return to campuses that have been highly productive in terms of both quality and quantity of students recruited. In short, employers visit campuses where there is a quality level of service.

A service reputation is earned. Reputations change. Recruiting itineraries experience a high state of flux. Room for addition or deletion of a given college always exists, and employers continually evaluate current positions.

College recruiting is a proven method of finding quality personnel. Employers cannot abandon the concept. Properly developed, college recruiting is the most economical method an employer can use to meet the needs of a professional, technical, or managerial nature. Advertising, employment agencies, walk-ins, and referrals cost more on a per hire basis because of the larger number of applicants that must be seen to hire one highly qualified person. A number of reasons make campus recruiting the most effective source of personnel.

Quality Level. The key differentials are quality level and organized structure. Quality personnel do not just walk into a personnel office or contact employment agencies. Aggressive recruiters on campus skim off the top candidates before they ever think of leaving campus. Employers who think that they are seeing top-quality graduates by waiting for them to contact the organization have their heads in the sand. Laggards may be satisfied with the level of quality walking in off the street, but that is far from being the best quality available. Competition for quality graduates is always keen, even in extremely soft job markets!

Productivity. The cost of college recruiting is low compared to other sources of employment because of the highly structured nature of the activity. Seeing a schedule of quality personnel every half-hour throughout the day is more productive than an off-and-on stream of applicants, some of whom get five-minute interviews by preliminary screeners and others who waste hours of executive time.

Reliable Supply. Another important plus factor of college recruiting is the reliability of the supply source. As a rule, wide gyrations in supply on a given campus rarely occur. A consistent number of potentially qualified applicants graduate each year.

Preselection. Colleges have a reputation to maintain. The reputation is based upon the standards set by the faculty. Although higher percentages of high school students are entering college, not all of them graduate. Quality institutions cannot afford to rubber stamp diplomas and turn out graduates like an assembly line. Standards vary from institution to institution. In general, only the best qualified make the entire road to graduation. To be sure, a few who are not well qualified survive, but the standards at most quality institutions are such that students who earn the degree are truly a preselected group of individuals.

This is not to say that levels of quality among graduates from any one institution do not vary. By definition, some people must graduate in each quartile regardless of the yardstick. The graduate from the institution at which the employer elects to recruit is already among a highly selected group of individuals. By and large, the lesser quality candidates have been screened out of consideration by the faculty.

Cost. Campus recruiting services are free to both students and employers. Of course, there are indirect costs, but these expenses are generally far less than those found in any other method of employment search or method of recruitment. With public and private colleges sharing the costs of personnel, resources, and facilities, it is highly doubtful, given the high level of service offered by college placement offices, that any other recruiting source could compete on a cost basis.

Service. Most U.S. colleges are committed to the encouragement and fostering of close alliance between higher education and external constituencies. Cooperation is a two-way street. One of the commitments on the college side is to serve employers by assisting them in finding qualified employees. That commitment falls on the career planning and placement service at most institutions of higher education.

Placement services should be staffed to handle this responsibility, and they should make a point to accommodate employer needs and desires whenever possible. Naturally, there are financial and facility limitations and other constraints, but rarely do these obstacles impede effective operations. The degree of service varies to a small degree among colleges but, through the professional associations, responsible guides have been established that offer some consistencies from campus to campus.

College Recruiting Programs

Traditionally, the college recruiting program tends to follow a pattern of serving the large national employer who seeks college graduates in academic fields that are technical or vocationally oriented. The service is open to smaller, local employers, but the larger, national employers hit the campuses first with the strongest recruiting efforts. A major challenge facing placement services is to involve more employers in the process that many larger employers have carved out as a private domain.

The logical case for campus recruiting previously discussed clearly applies to all employers regardless of size. The placement service must tell a positive story to a new audience. Although the job listing and referral service has better aided smaller employers than campus recruiting, the future may find new adaptations of campus recruiting directed to assist specific employer clients. For example, a variation of campus interviewing might be to invite all local employers to participate in a two-day employment conference on campus with student participation. The last part of the conference might consist of specific interview schedules.

For students, campus interviewing is the most convenient, most efficient, and least expensive method of making contact with potential employers, especially for students at colleges located in non-metropolitan areas. At no other point in life is the opportunity likely to repeat itself. Later career decisions are made on a job-by-job basis, not after a collection of several opportunities which can be objectively evaluated. A strong campus interviewing program for students who have established initial career goals is the greatest service which a college can provide graduating students.

Campus interviewing is one of the most educational experiences available to college graduates. The reality sensing and appraisal that occur during this phase of career planning frequently follow students throughout life. Even for graduates who do not find their initial job after college through the campus interview process, the experience of having learned about life and careers cannot be duplicated in many other types of settings. It truly offers a unique learning opportunity.

From an academic as well as service perspective, it behooves every college to invest in this educational experience. The program is more difficult to develop on campuses where the academic programs are not vocationally oriented, but the effort to achieve a viable campus interviewing program is well worth the cost. Fair numbers of predominately liberal arts institutions have strong campus recruiting programs, which illustrates that the path is open to all types of institutions. In other cases, a modified recruiting program, such as a one- or two-week conference or consortium arrangement with other institutions, may be an excellent approach for smaller non-vocationally oriented colleges.

Recruiting Activities

The underlying concept behind campus interviewing is educational and service oriented. The actual implementation of a program is clearly management oriented. Professional management skills and organizational abilities wax in importance over teaching and counseling skills. Management is the key behind successfully run campus interviewing programs. Important interfaces develop between career planning and interviewing, but the counseling aspects can be developed as a spinoff and feeder into the interview process.

One point of view suggests that colleges should hire a professional manager to run the office operations of the campus recruiting program and a professional educator and counselor to run the career planning program. Putting the two programs together in a team approach might then provide optimal results for employers, students, and other constituencies.

Obviously very few career planning and placement services can afford the net addition of new staff to manage on-campus interviewing programs. The professional counseling and placement staff must be trained in the principles of managing an interview program. The major advantage of this approach is the ability that many professional staffs have in integrating counseling and placement. A new population of students often is reached because many who might not come in for counseling will come in for placement assistance. Interweaving the two programs often provides the impetus students need and, properly developed, adds a new dimension to the total program.

Because of the management nature of campus interviewing, the system is procedure oriented. A highly organized structure permits the maximum number of people to use the service with a minimum of staff time. The less time that professional staff devotes to system management, the more time available for use of other professional talents.

The major parties involved in this process are students and employers. In many ways, the central role of the placement service is to bring the parties together in a brokerage role. To aid in establishing appropriate guidelines and procedures, the text first covers the employer's mechanical process and then turns attention to the student practices.

Recruiting Dates

The first step in the recruiting system begins with the employer establishing a specific date to visit campus. Interviewing space is limited. Employers who consistently recruit on campuses regularly establish recruiting dates 12 to 18 months prior to the actual visits. Establishing dates far in advance almost assures a spot on the school's calendar and permits employers to build a recruiting itinerary that is travel, time, and cost conscious. Employers who wait until the last six months to establish dates frequently must accept only those few open spaces in the school's calendar, and these times may not coincide with other schools in the same general vicinity.

Prime recruiting dates at colleges with extensive recruiting schedules fill rapidly. Nearly all colleges operate on a first-come scheduling arrangement, but there are some minor variations. Some colleges give preference to employers who have been consistent supporters of the school for many years. Some colleges also like to group major industries, such as public accounting, retailing, banking, etc., and rotate the employers' recruiting dates within a given time frame. Perhaps the most common practice is for colleges to ask employers who visit campus if they would like to maintain equivalent recruiting dates for the following school year. The majority say "yes," which explains why dates are set 12 to 18 months in advance.

Employer Literature

Most colleges request employers to send employment literature about two months prior to the campus visit. Students are encouraged to read the materials before signing an employer's interview schedule. This self-selection process by students reduces the shopping around and the number of unqualified candidates on recruiting schedules. Informed job candidates make the interview much more productive for both parties.

The two most common materials sent by employers are annual reports and employment brochures which describe available openings in some depth. Occasionally employers send product information and more detailed job descriptions. As a rule of thumb, employers should send a supply equal to one and one-half times the number of students expected to sign up.

This allows one copy for each interviewer plus copies for students who reviewed the material but decided not to sign up. If schedules exceed the expected number of interviewees, additional copies should be forwarded as soon as the decision to send additional recruiters is made.

Employment information is extremely valuable to students. Storage space is always a problem at colleges, but every effort should be made to accept and distribute all information received from employers. The cost for one copy of each annual report or employment brochure is far greater than most people think. Wasting this valuable source of career information would be disgraceful. If a college cannot disseminate the materials, the employer should be so advised.

Many colleges maintain one copy of all material sent by employers in a permanent file with limited access to students. Even if the employer's last brochure copy is labeled "Do not Remove," it frequently disappears. The permanent reserve file allows students a library checkout type of privilege and keeps information available.

A few placement offices prepare a large, three-ring notebook which is placed in the career library. These binders contain the latest annual report, employment brochures on various career fields, employer personnel policy handbooks, internal publications, product information, recent news articles, etc. A major problem is keeping them up to date. The most common practice in updating is for the employer's recruiters to fill in the new material each time a visit to campus is made. Because of space limitations and in order to achieve consistency, a few placement offices provide a notebook or file box for each organization with which they work.

Maintenance of employment literature requires significant space and staff time, but the activity is highly important to the recruiting program. The commitment in terms of resources is one of the many items that must go into the planning of budgets and staff if a first-class program is to be offered to students and employers.

Campus Recruiting Information Forms

The campus recruiting information form (CRIF) is the basis upon which an employer's campus visit is publicized and schedule organized. Although the name of the form varies from college to college, the purpose is the same. The campus recruiting information form (CRIF) is the most important document that an employer sends to a college.

The Appendix includes some sample forms. Some follow a questionnaire format. Others are checklist oriented. A few are designed for computer input. Some are free-form versions. Most placement offices do not retype the form.

The CRIF is widely circulated throughout the campus to faculty and students and is the basis upon which campus publicity is built. Ironically, many employers spend thousands of dollars on brochures and advertising to college students, but only minutes on the document that is most likely to influence the greatest number of students to sign on an interview schedule.

The CRIF gives students the information about various positions available and the related job specifications. This form is used by students in deciding whether or not to interview the organization. It is used by the staff in signing and screening students on or off appropriate schedules.

Employers may limit the number of signups by the specifications placed on the CRIF. Students self-select themselves on and off schedules by estimating the probability of their receiving a job offer. Narrow job specifications in terms of major, degree level, grades, etc. may be so limiting that very few candidates sign up. If specifications are extremely broad, many more students than physically possible to interview may want to be on the schedule. Employers need to determine the optimal match on a campus-by-campus approach. On many campuses, the recruiting information form is the tool to use to monitor schedule signups.

School Information

Most placement services send employers information about the college's academic and recruiting programs on a regular basis. Employers need and want this information if they expect to be effective recruiters. Sometimes the information is sent to the employer's college recruiting headquarters and may not reach the person doing the actual recruiting on campus. In such instances, it is the employer's responsibility to inform recruiting personnel of unique circumstances.

Many colleges prepare a "Recruiting Packet" which is mailed to each recruiter prior to the campus visit. This packet may include recruiting instructions, maps, lodging information, parking permits, recruiting handbook, school bulletins, potential faculty contacts, luncheon plans, etc. Advance information aids in effectively utilizing the placement services.

Interview Schedules

Most colleges have interview schedules prepared at least one day prior to the visit so that the number of signups can be checked and any necessary final arrangements can be made. Most offices type the final schedule the day before the employer's visit, although a few have stopped typing them because of campus cost-cutting programs. Upon arrival on campus the sequence of events is similar to the activities stated here.

Registration. The recruiter is requested to complete a sign-in card which is used to advise job candidates and faculty of the recruiter's name, title, and address. The day's plan is usually discussed at this point. Many placement offices make arrangements for lunch with faculty and placement staff at this time. Interviewing schedules normally start between 8:30 and 9:00 a.m., with morning and afternoon coffee breaks. Usually there is a one-hour lunch break. Interviews are regularly scheduled on a thirty-minute basis unless other arrangements are discussed in advance.

Recruiting Schedules. Besides the interview schedule, the recruiting packet contains a resume or college interview form for each applicant. Although the practice is rapidly declining due to the Family Educational Rights and Privacy Act of 1974, a few colleges provide faculty recommendations for each student. Several schools request employers to complete an evaluation of each candidate which is returned to the placement staff for use in career counseling individuals. To encourage honest and candid evaluations, the employer is not identified in the feedback counseling sessions.

Transcripts. The procedure to obtain transcripts varies on each campus and is discussed with recruiters at the time of the campus visit. Many colleges provide transcript release forms which students may sign as requested by employers. At other schools, students must request to have transcripts sent to employers. There is usually a charge to students or employers for the reproduction of transcripts.

Faculty Contacts. The placement service can be instrumental in assisting employers with making appropriate faculty contacts. Where the employer already knows faculty, it is wise to call or write individual faculty prior to the campus visit and make appropriate arrangements directly. Where contacts are not known, many placement services will suggest appropriate faculty for employers to contact in advance or make the contact themselves. About the only free time available during the day is the lunch hour or the brief coffee breaks. As a result, many employers prefer to contact faculty in advance and arrange a dinner the evening before or after recruiting.

Office Evaluation. Placement offices desire feedback which can be used to evaluate the effectiveness of their services to employers. Many times forms are placed in recruiting schedules requesting employers to return a form or questionnaire anonymously to the service.

Recruiting Dates. Many placement offices enclose a request for new recruiting dates in the recruiter's interview schedule.

It is common for employers to establish recruiting dates for the next year while on campus.

Luncheon Plans. Because of the limited time available for lunch, a large number of placement offices make luncheon arrangements for recruiters. Usually special tables are set aside in a conveniently located facility for recruiters, faculty guests, and placement staff.

Group Meetings. Group meetings between students and employers are difficult to arrange during the campus interview time because of staff limitations and academic priority to classroom space. On many college campuses, student-employer programs may be most appropriately arranged during evening hours. If the group meeting relates to recruiting, it is often difficult to draw student attendance, particularly from the better candidates because they prefer individual interviews. Nonetheless, some employers insist on group meetings and many placement offices attempt to accommodate this type of recruiting.

Testing. A few employers still require job candidates to take a basic employment test and prefer that it be administered during the campus interview to those in whom they have a continuing interest. Most placement offices attempt to locate testing space when they have appropriate lead times. The trend, however, is to discontinue or shorten testing programs, particularly because of stringent new requirements that the criteria being tested are job related. Most employers still utilizing employment testing for college graduates prefer to do it under more controlled conditions at the employer's facilities during the time of the secondary interview visit.

Preselection. Preselection may become a major issue in the long-term future of college recruiting. Preselection is the obtaining of student resumes from the placement staff or names from faculty and then only opening campus interview schedules to candidates who are preidentified for consideration. The employer's motive is to reduce the number of campus interviews, thereby reducing overall recruiting costs. In theory, this method identifies all candidates with a realistic chance of obtaining further consideration from the employers.

Colleges are caught in two binds—one legal and one philosophical. The legal issue stems from the fact that an employer may be using a discriminatory variable (sex, race, creed, national origin) to select students, thereby making the placement service a party to an illegal practice.

The philosophical issue is that the placement interviewing service becomes a service only for a small percentage of the graduating class. If the scenario is carried forward, students in the lower part of their academic class and who otherwise might not be preselected will not be serviced in this manner. The theory is that the organization might hire candidates in the non-preselected group if applicants were given a chance to state their cases. There are large numbers of appropriate selection criteria that cannot be evaluated on paper or recommendations alone.

In this interim period, many placement services refuse to cooperate with employers requesting preselection. Some have reached a compromise stance that permits limited preselection by requiring at least as many open signups as closed signups. The issue is likely to be addressed on a national scale at some point in the future.

Follow-up. The relationship between employer and college does not stop when the employer leaves the campus. Employers continue the relationship with correspondence to students interviewed and followup visits by students to the employer's facilities. Most employers pay all of the student's expenses associated with the secondary visit, but there are some exceptions to this practice.

Placement services need to be informed of the continuing dialogue with students. Many employers send copies of all student correspondence to the placement service. It is especially important for the placement service to receive copies of all job offers and final acceptance letters.

Ethics. The College Placement Council has prepared a statement of ethical guidelines, the "Principles and Practices of College Career Planning, Placement, and Recruitment." Many of these relate to the campus interviewing process. Employers, students, and placement officials should be familiar with these guidelines.

Conclusion

The campus interviewing procedures which relate to the employer help make the lengthy process much smoother. On a national scale, when employers understand what to expect when recruiting on each college campus, the relationships between all parties involved can be best understood. Simple and standardized procedures allow a smooth operation which can satisfy the needs of all parties.

Student Interviewing Activities

The procedures that colleges adopt for dealing with employers vary little from campus to campus. It's also true that the procedures adopted for students who desire to participate in the campus interview process vary little from campus to campus. Usually all interview procedures may be found written in appropriate detail in a placement handbook, which is distributed to students wishing some information about the services. Some of the most common procedures are discussed below.

Registration. Placement services require that students who desire the service be officially registered. Registration involves completion of a standard resume form and, in some cases, developing a file which contains faculty references. The one-page resume is all that most offices request, but some want multiple copies of the form. Registration entitles students to interviewing, counseling, resume referral, and the other services offered. Because most employers prefer some type of resume before the campus interview, that form is nearly an absolute must on campuses with the campus interview program.

Publicity

Efforts to publicize the recruiting visits of potential employers normally go beyond posting on bulletin boards in the placement facilities. Announcements are often carried in the campus newspaper and posted on bulletin boards throughout campus, especially on appropriate departmental bulletin boards. Some colleges maintain "placement coordinators" in academic departments who can spread the word of an impending employer visit to many students. Many offices publicize employer visits by alerting appropriate faculty who often make announcements in class. A few employers also elect to advertise in the campus newspaper.

Signup Procedures. The employer signup arrangements vary from open posting of schedules to closed schedules. Open schedules are simple appointment sheets available for students to sign on a first-come basis. There is seldom any screening of candidates although there may be a system of monitoring the progress of the schedule. The schedules are self-policing in that students are expected to be qualified for the job opening and not erase other students' names. On campuses where signup numbers are small and honesty is no problem, this system is generally effective.

Many colleges prefer to screen candidates to insure that the individual's background matches the qualifications for a given job. The appointment sheets are kept behind a counter or at the desk of a staff member. Students must then request to sign up. After a few screening questions are properly answered, the candidates may sign the schedule. This process is much more time-consuming, but it provides a better service for employers and the screening assists students in putting their efforts where they are likely to be most productive.

Long Lines. The media continue to emphasize and even exaggerate the problem with long lines of students outside placement offices waiting to sign on employer interview schedules. In a few cases, the number of students wishing to sign on schedules may be much greater than the number of available appointment times, but in offices with a good management control system the lines can be greatly minimized. In instances where long lines are unavoidable, the effect is not always negative. Long lines motivate students to plan career strategies in advance and educate faculty and administrators to the real job market situation.

Many colleges with potential waiting lines solve the problems through use of signup priority systems other than first-come. Some colleges establish a limit to the number of employers any one student can interview. This forces the student to carefully map a strategy of interviews with employers with whom they have the best chance of finding employment. The less-than-blue-chip student will not waste precious interviews with blue chip organizations because of the lower probability of a job offer.

Lottery systems in assigning priority are common in some large institutions. Such a system gives each job aspirant an equal chance at obtaining a job interview. Only qualified candidates are permitted to participate in the lottery. The lottery may be used in conjunction with a limited interview system. Another approach is a point system which gives every student an equal number of points. Students bid on appointment times.

Without a computer, all of these systems, as well as other approaches, require much more administration time than a first-come or open sign-up system. These approaches are not recommended unless absolutely necessary.

Waiting Lists. The first-come system most frequently used by colleges forces preparation of waiting lists for the schedules of many employers. Students are called on a first-come basis as cancellations occur. Occasionally, when employers are called and informed that a waiting list exists, they find additional recruiters, opening the schedule to most students on the waiting list.

Even if the organization is unable to interview all students on the waiting list after they receive the resumes, many students are telephoned for interviews or the employer reschedules at a later date.

Tentative Schedules. Not all employers are as prompt in returning the campus recruiting information forms as they should be. This causes much consternation among students who may have waited in a long line to sign up only to discover that the requirements of the organization are unknown. Some colleges prepare a "tentative" schedule for the employer based on any previous job requests or telephone information. Opening a tentative schedule presumes that the organization intends to honor its recruiting commitment. The decision to open a tentative schedule is a tradeoff to avoid alienating a group of students or an employer.

Invitation Only. As noted earlier, a few employers request colleges to establish schedules only for a group of preselected students who meet job specifications. For those colleges that permit this practice, "by invitation only" schedules are arranged. Students are frequently told to bring a letter from the employer with them at the appropriate signup time. In essence, these schedules are "closed" to other students. Very few colleges permit "closed" schedules without an equal opportunity of non-invited students to sign on schedules. If "by invitation only" schedules are permitted on given campuses, negative publicity can result. Employers must weigh the animosity created within the student body, including toward the preselected group, against the positive benefits. Many professionals from both employer and the placement ranks see no easy way to bypass the interview process.

Student Followup Procedures

Obtaining interviews, whether on or off campus, is only the initial step in the job search process for students. A sequence of procedures faces students as they move to the point of obtaining job offers and making employment decisions. The placement service is not out of the picture either. Students must prepare for interviews by reading brochures, annual reports, periodicals, and other materials available in the placement service.

The employment process involves much correspondence with potential employers. To avoid misunderstandings, students usually are encouraged to file a copy of their correspondence with the placement service for inclusion in their placement file. This gives the placement office a good feel for the employment prospects of graduating students as well as a regular report on salary offers. The letter confirming an employment acceptance is an important placement record.

The placement staff should inform students of the ethical practices involved in the employment process, especially of the requirement to accept only one job offer after a thorough review of all job possibilities. The code of ethics adopted by the College Placement Council should be made available to all graduating students.

Summary

The campus interviewing activity fluctuates with changing economic conditions. The activity is also influenced by the willingness, even aggressiveness, of the college to foster a major campus interviewing program. The recruiting of employers is a new role for placement professionals but one which may be necessary to complete the educational process of graduating students.

This marketing viewpoint may not be popular among placement professionals of an early era, but that is no reason to abandon the concept. For the group of professionals who relate more to the counseling role, the solution may be to hire more management-oriented professionals in the future. The campus interviewing service—as it helps students and serves as an important educational mission—is a vital service that must be fostered in the future.

CHAPTER 8

MANAGEMENT OF CAREER SERVICES

MANAGING A CAREER planning and placement service requires a wide range of competencies. The management function involves organizing, planning, staffing, providing facilities, budgeting, and maintaining daily control. Regardless of the size and scope of an operation, certain basic tasks must be accomplished.

The final section of this chapter deals with the issues and plans for operating a successful placement program. The focal point of a successful operation is a successful manager.

Organizational Structure

The placement function gradually evolved over the years from faculty efforts to place their own graduates to a centralized student service. Recent surveys show that over 8o percent of career planning and placement services are centralized. The trend continues to favor a centralized organization.

Most decentralized operations evolved as a consequence of

historical development by specific academic departments. The placement function often began in schools of engineering, business, and education where a special demand existed for graduates by an identifiable employer group. The close relationship between faculty in these schools and practitioners created a need for an office to coordinate the process of getting students and potential employers together. As the schools grew in size, placement responsibilities gradually shifted from the faculty to the professional coordinator.

Once a successful decentralized service develops to a smooth and efficiently running operation, moving to a centralized function becomes difficult. Few faculty are willing to release control, especially the close ties with practitioners, including many alumni who have risen to levels of prominence. Close personal relationships with both employers and students can rarely be severed easily, nor should they.

Many decentralized placement offices are highly effective in the placement of graduates from both a quality and quantity viewpoint. Many offices get very involved in experiential programs that give students an advance view of the career field and greatly aid the student's career decision-making. Through highly organized procedures over years of successful experience, graduating classes are easily merged into the system despite the growing number of students. Employers respond positively to the system because it permits and aids selectivity by discipline, which often correlates with the job specifications for a high percentage of their job openings.

Several possible outcomes emerged from the decentralized operations in academic departments and professional schools. As the college observed a need in other departments, other placement services were started, proliferating the number of decentralized placement services. Efforts were begun to offer placement service to students not being served.

Many of the decentralized offices often open their services, particularly their on-campus recruiting, to non-majors. This accommodates other students and employers who may have personnel needs in addition to those in the given discipline. It is not uncommon to see decentralized offices in engineering, business, and education serving non-majors.

Another system that often results is one in which multiple offices on a given campus join in offering coordinated services to students and employers. Coordinated offices frequently adopt common procedures and forms which greatly lessen the problems for students and employers. This system still allows close involvement of faculty in the student-employer relationship as well as the maintenance of department loyalties. The trend to centralizing services results from efforts to reduce expenditures, eliminate duplication, and serve a broader base of students on a fair and consistent basis. Centralized services often bring several student services together in a central, convenient campus location.

Although the trend is toward centralization, no one way appears to be ideal for all colleges or employers. Each approach has its advantages and disadvantages. The organizational structure is an individual college decision based upon philosophy, cost, personnel available, faculty, and even the unique campus political environment. What works best at one institution may not be feasible at another.

Reporting Relationships

The administrative responsibility for the career planning and placement function varies considerably. In decentralized operations, the chief placement officer most frequently reports to the dean of the academic unit serviced. In some instances, the decentralized placement director reports on a dotted line basis to a central coordinator.

The majority of the centralized placement service directors report to either a dean of students, vice president of student services, or someone with a similar responsibility. In a smaller institution, the placement director may report directly to the president. A clear majority, however, report to an administrative officer in student affairs in contrast to academic affairs.

Although the frequency is small, a few placement directors report to vice presidents of public affairs, the development office, or alumni relations.

A few placement officers report to the chief academic officer such as the dean of the faculty, provost, or vice president for academic programs. The rationale is based on the premise that the career planning and placement service is an integral part of the student's educational program. This approach incorporates some of the advantages of decentralized career services that report to academic units, since the full support of the faculty as well as the administration is brought to the function.

Although there are a number of viable reporting relationships that can be reasonably justified and supported, the current trend is toward having the career service function report to the chief student service officer.

Staff

An important indicator of administrative support and the importance that a college attaches to the career planning and placement service is the willingness to provide adequate and highly competent professional and clerical staff. The quality of the services provided to students and employers depends upon the number of staff, capabilities, and attitudes toward the function.

Size. Staff size ranges from a single professional with a secretary to over ten professionals and related clerical support. The main determining factor is the size of the constituency served. As the enrollment grows, the need for staff assistance increases. Other factors that may influence the need for staff include the scope and diversity of academic programs, the size of the on-campus interviewing programs, and the number of job listings normally received.

Titles. The most frequently used job titles for professionals include director, associate director, assistant director, placement officer, career counselor, and office manager. Most offices have a clerical staff in charge of specific functions, such as campus arrangements, student files, alumni placement, employer files, etc. The *Career Planning and Placement Handbook* published by the College Placement Council details many of the specific duties and responsibilities of both the clerical and professional staff.

A paraprofessional staff of graduate assistants is common in a few placement offices that have large campus recruiting activities and career counseling programs. Graduate students normally work 10 to 15 hours per week and have often had prior work experience before returning to school. Depending upon the type of program, graduate assistants, often serving as interns, are involved in career counseling, schedule screening and signup, recruiter hosting, report analysis and preparation, etc. Assistants most often are paid a cash stipend plus tuition, but may be working to fulfill a practicum requirement where they also earn academic credit, usually in student personnel areas.

In many offices, assistant directors are in charge of a given area of placement such as business, education, engineering, cooperative education, liberal arts, etc. Another common arrangement is to place assistant directors in charge of functional operations including campus recruiting, alumni placement, career counseling, summer-part-time internships, office operations, etc.

No one best way to organize and staff a placement service has ever been recommended. The specific duties, responsibilities, and organizational patterns need to be determined by factors specific to a given campus. The important point is to have good, competent, well-trained staff members.

Staff Qualifications

For assistant directors and placement counselors, nearly all institutions now require a master's degree. It is not uncommon for some large institutions to require the equivalent of the doctorate. The major field of study is not nearly so definitive. In decentralized placement functions and in centralized services that organize around academic fields of study, the trend is often to look for candidates with a master's, or at least a bachelor's degree, in the subject area for which the individual will be responsible for counseling students.

The behavioral-oriented subject areas seem to be popular training disciplines for many new entrants. Individuals with training in counseling, guidance, psychology, personnel management, industrial relations, student personnel administration, and organizational behavior are often the most frequently selected applicants.

Although work experience is seldom required for entry-level positions in career planning and placement, preference is often given to candidates with prior experience in business or government positions somewhat related to the areas of interest of graduating students. For example, in an engineering placement service, the individual with a bachelor or master's degree in engineering with some limited years of work experience as an engineer would be a preferred applicant, if everything else is equal.

A few placement positions specify that preference may be given to individuals with a degree from the college. This is particularly apropos in operations where there is a close relationship between the alumni association and fund raising.

The increasing frequency of the doctorate degree in the profession is understandable. In some ways the interlock with faculty is a natural and important development. It is not unusual for a faculty member who has an administrative (versus research) orientation to want to move into the placement responsibility because, in many cases, some teaching duties can be retained. This arrangement also expands the counseling and service roles which most faculty enjoy. In smaller institutions, the teaching duties may be sorely needed.

In colleges and universities with enrollments above 5,000 students, some prior experience as an assistant is almost always a part of the qualifications for the director position. As a rule, larger institutions pay higher salaries. The assistant directors in large institutions and directors at smaller colleges frequently serve as the pool of applicants for top placement positions at large universities and prestigious institutions.

The profession has developed a moderate growth rate of about 5 percent per year, but turnover among individuals in the under 40 age range is very high. College membership directories frequently change by 25 percent per year. One hypothesis for explaining the turnover is that the lower-than-average salary and the low turnover of placement directors in prominent institutions force new entrants to "look around." Being able to review several hundred job opportunities annually plus interaction with employers places individuals in an attractive, high-exposure position. Persons leaving the profession usually increase their current salary by a large percentage.

Remaining in the profession requires commitment to the profession and often loyalty to an academic institution. Higher paying alternatives are always available for competent individuals. There are very few good placement directors who have not been tempted to leave with very attractive job offers.

Each spring, one of the issues of the *Chronicle of Higher Education* presents a listing of average annual salaries of college and university administrators. This is an excellent source of current salary information of college placement directors.

As a rule, starting salary rates for inexperienced personnel vary little from that of other recent college graduates with equivalent degrees and academic majors. For terminal-degree applicants, starting salaries approximate those of an assistant professor adjusted to a twelve-month appointment. The number one assistant (often associate director) typically earns 75–85 percent of the director's salary.

Because colleges frequently hire alumni, breaking into the placement profession for the non-alumnus may be difficult. As the academic standards become better defined over the next few years, entry may become somewhat easier.

Facilities

The physical facilities of a career planning and placement service correlate closely with an efficient and productive operation. As institutions become more aware of the public image that the placement service leaves with business, industry, government, education, and other external publics, the quality and quantity of space improve.

After World War II and Sputnik, the demand for college students caught many colleges unprepared. Many makeshift quarters like quonset huts, old houses, and boiler room space housed the placement facility. Most of that vintage space has now been replaced with new or remodeled quarters more in keeping with the significance of the office.

The amount of space allocated to placement depends primarily upon the type of services provided, the number of students using the space, and the number of full-time personnel. A given, fixed amount of space appears to be needed for essential operations (about 1,000 square feet) which increases with services, enrollment, and staff additions. Most institutions with enrollments of less than 1,000 rarely have more than 1,000 square feet. It is not uncommon for institutions with enrollments above 20,000 students to have well over 5,000 square feet. Since there are no recommended norms, great disparities in space exist among colleges with equivalent enrollments and staff.

Although there are few standards on the amount of adequate space, a consensus exists in the type of space needed in a career center. Once again, the type of space needed relates to the services offered and number of staff personnel. Given a basic set of services and the fact that staff size tends to grow slowly, the main variable is the number of interview rooms required. Where recruiting is on a central basis, obviously the number of rooms needed will be much greater. The accompanying box gives an estimate of the amount of space typically needed.

SPACE REQUIREMENTS

Type of Space	Estimate
Offices for professionals	120–150 sq. ft./person
Clerical staff	100–110 sq. ft./person
Clerical work areas	500–700 sq. ft.
Career library	300–400 sq. ft.
Reception/waiting	300–400 sq. ft.
Interview rooms	80–100 sq. ft./room

Budget

The range in total budget expenditures of career planning and placement services varies widely but is most directly related to the scope of the services offered and the number of students served. The quantity and quality of the myriad of services that may be offered to each constituency influences the initial size of the operating budget. Other sections of this book discuss the various services that may be considered. Which services to offer and to what extent they are funded is an individual college decision based upon the institution's philosophy and commitment to this type of student service.

Each service has a basic fixed cost as well as a variable cost most closely related to the number of students, employers, alumni, or faculty making use of the given service. No service offered is free. There may be substitutions of one service for another and tradeoffs in the quality, but each service has a definable expenditure level.

The basic fixed cost of every service needs to be established. Expanding the basic service to more users is calculated with a basic cost per unit. For example, in alumni placement, the hiring of a secretary to edit and type a job bulletin and respond to alumni inquiries is a basic fixed cost. The amount and frequency of correspondence with employers for job development and the number of alumni receiving the bulletins and referrals are costs that increase as the number of users increases. It would be a long time before a second secretary and basic planning costs would need to be increased.

If the total sum of funds available to placement is a fixed amount, compromises must be made between which service to offer. Some colleges prefer to place extreme importance on the campus recruiting program and job listing activity with little budgetary consideration (other than perhaps a token acknowledgement) to alumni placement or student and company file maintenance. Other colleges deemphasize campus recruiting and external relations while promoting career counseling.

The dollar is often an overriding consideration. Honest differences of opinion exist on which services offer the greatest assistance to appropriate constituencies. The decision must be made in consideration of each college's unique and special circumstances. On the other hand, presenting a strong and convincing case for budget increases is a never ending role of the placement director. New funds that exceed inflation rates may go to support new services and improve existing ones.

Expenditures

A few basic components comprise the typical placement office budget. A sample budget format is shown on pages 228–229. These expenditures must be supported and justified in an annual budget proposal.

Professional Staff. The largest items in the budget are the salary and fringe benefits of the director, associate director, assistant directors, counselors, and office manager. In any college these items may represent over half of the total budget and in small colleges they represent the major expenditure. Staff salaries should be equivalent to faculty salaries with comparable years of experience and levels of responsibility.

Clerical Staff. The paperwork in every placement office is tremendous. The larger the size of the clerical staff, the more time the professional staff can devote to the major responsibilities for which they are paid. Using a professional staff member to carry out clerical duties (not an infrequent occurrence) is a waste of talent and unwise use of scarce college resources. Clerical staff tends to be paid much less than professional staff and, to optimize use of funds, clerical staff should assume as many non-professional duties as possible. It is common to see one secretary handling files (resumes, recommendations, etc.) and activities (procedures, signups, etc.) which are student related and another clerical person responsible for employer-related activities, such as filing, correspondence, recruiting visits, and job listings. Clerical salaries must be competitive with the local market conditions for employment.

Part-time Staff. The workload in the typical placement office runs in cycles which means that during the especially busy times like registration, signups, campus recruiting, etc., extra help is needed. Graduate assistants or professional interns may be used for counseling students and extra assistance may also be used for general clerical duties, such as filing, answering student questions, reproducing resumes, or signing students on interview schedules. Few placement offices operate without a heavy reliance on some type of part-time assistance.

Postage. Postage is rapidly becoming the largest single non-personnel expenditure. With the telephone, mail is the basic communication mode with employers, students, alumni, and occasionally even with the faculty and administration. Although the expenditures can be greatly reduced with bulk rates and non-first class mailing, the item still looms as an important expenditure.

The major expense is first class letters to employers and alumni regarding job listings or campus recruitment. The mail solicitation of job leads and campus recruiting dates is significant and almost unavoidable for a successful operation. Newsletters and materials with less critical time value should be sent

ANNUAL BUDGET

Career Planning and Placement Service
July 1, 19xx through June 30, 19xx
Prepared on March 30, 19xx

Classification	Amount
Personnel Expenditures:	
Professional Staff	
Director	
Associate Director(s)	
Assistant Director(s)	
Career Counselor(s)	
Office Manager	
Career Librarian	
Clerical Staff	
Student Secretary(s)	
Career Literature Librarian	
Company Secretary(s)	
Corresponding Secretary(s)	

Classification	Amount
Non-Personnel Expenditures:	
Postage	
Telephone	
Printing	
Copying	
Office Supplies	
Publications	
Conference Fees	
Professional Memberships	
Professional Development	
Travel	
Equipment Purchase	
Equipment Maintenance	

Part-time Employment
  Secretary(s)
  Alumni Secretary(s)
  Co-op Secretary(s)
  Receptionist(s)
  Clerk Typist(s)

Part-Time Staff
  Graduate Assistants
  Professional Interns
  Placement Assistants
  Filing Clerks
  Work-Study Students
  Receptionists

Fringe Benefits
  Social Security
  Retirement
  Life Insurance
  Health Insurance
  Other

Facility Repairs and
  Improvements
Computer Time
Entertainment
Miscellaneous

by bulk rates. Advising students of opportunities and soliciting salary and placement information by mail represent largely non-postponable and unavoidable costs.

Telephone. The placement office telephone system should be one of the busiest systems on any campus. The telephone is the best friend and most useful office tool available to any placement officer. Contacting students by telephone is a daily necessity. Calls from employers also come daily. In metropolitan areas, job solicitation by telephone is possible. Even without special devices such as intercoms, the basic telephone charges represent a major part of the budget.

Long-distance calls add significantly to the total telephone charges. This is especially true in offices with a large clientele of national or regional employers. If feasible, one way to reduce these charges is to switch to a WATS line service, to call employers via an enterprise number, or to work out agreements to call potential employers on a collect basis. Collect calls were most common during the Sixties, but as employers faced internal cost-cutting programs, more and more discouraged collect calls. Many employers, however, still do accept them.

Printing. In order to serve large numbers of students and employers with a minimum of expense, it is necessary to establish guidelines, procedures, and forms. Forms are used for placement registration, resumes, job listings, employer contact data, recruiting information, interview schedules, faculty recommendations, placement records, counseling notes, etc. The possible forms and potential uses go on and on.

Multiple copies of blank forms are needed. Although some forms are typewritten, many are printed in a specially designed type set and reproduced by less expensive, high-speed processes. In a year's time, the expense of the various forms adds up significantly. Design and type setting can be expensive, but the cost of reproducing later copies is much less than most copy methods.

Bulletins, job listings, manuals, employer guides, etc., must also be printed to distribute to appropriate parties. The number can be large. Some printing, such as forms and manuals, is done on an annual basis, but much work is also printed on a monthly, weekly, and daily basis. Since effective communication is the hallmark of a successful operation, attention must be given to writing, editing, and reproducing materials. The budget must consider both the quantity and the quality of the materials because the image portrayed impacts upon the overall success of the service.

Copying. A central activity of career planning and placement is sharing student information with employers and vice versa. The flow of paperwork between the various constituencies is sizable. Because of the rapid turnaround required, most career services maintain some type of high-quality reproduction process in their facilities. The types of documents copied include resumes, references, job listings, transcripts, employer information, newsletters, etc.

Copy equipment may be purchased or leased. This represents some type of fixed cost. In addition, there is a variable cost that is usually calculated on a per copy basis (2–6 cents per copy) depending upon the process and quality needed. The variable costs are closely related to the number of registrants and the number of employers requesting service. Copy costs represent a sizable portion of the placement office budget.

A growing percentage of career services charge users for some portion of the copy costs. This practice is designed to make requests more reasonable to assist in helping tight budgets.

Office Supplies. Office supplies include many small items which often add up to amounts that cannot be overlooked. The best estimate of office supply expenditures is the previous year adjusted for increasing rates of inflation. Office supplies include letterhead, envelopes, paper, pencils, typewriter ribbons, paper clips, etc.

Publications. Almost all placement services maintain some type of career library that includes books, pamphlets, brochures, directories, government publications, newspapers, periodicals, etc. Library startup costs may vary from $300 to $1,000. More important from a budgetary concern is the fact that the library must be kept current to provide a useful student service. Remaining current involves expenditures for subscriptions, new publications, and postage to solicit material from sources such as associations and organizations that provide career information.

Certain publications, such as the *College Placement Annual, Business World,* and the *Graduate,* are distributed free to students but cost the placement office a nominal amount for postage, handling, and/or membership fees. It is a rare placement service that spends less than $300 per year for publications and $1,000 is not an unlikely figure.

Conference Fees. Most placement professionals are members of two to four professional associations, all of which sponsor at least one professional meeting per year. Most colleges pay conference fees. For career services with several professional staff members, the total can become large. Most conference fees are in the $40–$70 range, and many associations hold more than one meeting per year.

Professional Memberships. Many colleges pay the annual dues or membership charge of professional associations for faculty and professional staff. Membership is in the best interest of the institution as well as the individual.

Professional Development. Closely related to memberships in professional associations is the area of professional development. Although conferences may be important contributors to professional development, workshops and programs outside and inside professional associations frequently contribute to the institution. Most development programs are designed to make professional personnel much more productive to their employer. Many colleges pay for attendance at one or more workshops and other development programs each year for each staff member. This is another item which must be built into the annual budget.

Travel. If a college supports the professional development and external relations concepts discussed throughout this book, travel becomes a very significant component of the annual budget. Travel costs include transportation, housing, meals, and related expenses. Career services located in major metropolitan areas and centrally located within their sphere of recruiting influence may find costs somewhat less in contacting constituencies (employers, students, alumni). Travel is always expensive so, regardless of the individual circumstances, travel cannot be a minor cost factor if certain services are offered or methods of contact utilized.

Equipment Purchase and Maintenance. Most established placement facilities are outfitted with the basic necessary office equipment, but needs change over time and old equipment requires replacement. Items such as file cabinets, chairs, desks, bulletin boards, typewriters, dictating equipment, calculators, key punch machines, copy machines, computer terminals, microfilm, beautification items, etc., all are part of a well-planned budget.

Many pieces of office equipment require service contracts, occasional repair, or general maintenance.

Facility Repairs and Improvements. The facilities of many placement functions are not part of the original design of the building. Space is often modified to fit the special needs of placement. Many of the buildings are old and need continual maintenance. Floor covering, ventilation, lighting, painting, remodeling, window decorating, etc. are all items that occasionally need to be included in the placement service budget.

Computer Time. Because of growing numbers of students and alumni using the career services, many placement offices turn to the computer to maintain a high percentage of employer and student files. Management reports are more easily prepared. In other offices, the computer is used as an interactive learning tool designed to assist students in career decision-making within an overall career planning framework.

Computer time is expensive and in most cases is charged directly to the placement budget. In addition to planning for actual time usage, attention must also be given to related functions, such as data keypunching, computer programming, systems design, documentation, and other duties which require significant expenditures. Many placement offices are finding computer usage to be far less expensive than staff in the long term, but short-term expenses may be greater than what it might cost to do the same job without the computer. Computer expenditures may be viewed as a long-term investment.

Entertainment. A few placement services maintain a small budget for hosting important constituents at special programs. This might include funds for coffee, cookies, refreshments, hors d'oeuvres before lecture programs, morning coffee for recruiters, dinners for high-level executives on campus, a reception for alumni or employers, or a number of programs where it might be inappropriate to charge invited guests a fee. These funds usually constitute only a small portion of the total budget, but without access to special funds like these, the image of a quality effort can be slightly tainted. In view of the relatively small amounts required, this is hardly worth the risk.

Miscellaneous. Throughout the year every office develops unexpected requirements which largely are unexpected or which do not fit any specific category. Many expenses are for one-time items that last for years or for items that occur very infrequently. A small portion of the budget should be set aside as a last-resort contingency or explained in a specific note as an unusual special requirement.

Budget preparation is not an overly complicated process. It does, however, take considerable time not for the actual preparation but for justifying each level of expenditure to an administration that is continually faced with limited resources and increasing requests from every other department.

The ability to obtain financial resources for placement is one of the foremost skills needed by the director. The effective utilization of given resources is something to which every staff member can offer significant contributions. Obtaining the resources, however, is the primary responsibility of the placement director. The request must be a document that has the input and total support of the staff, but only one person can carry it forward. Obtaining the resources requires extraordinary skills in presentation, convincing arguments, friendships, and other factors that will convince an administration faced with limited funds to shift money from other university functions to placement.

The career planning and placement office plays a central role in the university. How that role is perceived by the administration and other constituencies determines whether or not needed resources come to the function. This book attempts to show why the service is one of the most important offices on campus.

As in sports, it is difficult to take a team with a losing tradition and turn it into a winner, even when the physical ability to win is available. The winners continue to win, often with less talented players. Frequently the difference is attitude.

A few placement offices do have national reputations and continue to improve as more resources are pumped into the program. Unlike sports, there are no winners and losers because every placement office can win on its campus. Frequently a major change in administrative attitude toward placement is required to turn things around, but attitudes do change. In fact, the climate is ripe in placement for major changes on a national scale in the next decade. The direction of that change at each institution largely depends on the professional placement leadership. The abilities to promote the service and gain necessary resources will be key ingredients in future success.

Levels of Support

The College Placement Council periodically publishes a report that gives an operational profile of career planning and placement offices. The latest study is entitled "Career Planning and Placement in the Mid-70's." The study does not offer financial guidelines, but it does compare what various institutions spend on the function. After reviewing these studies the authors concluded that there are major economies of scale.

For colleges awarding under 200 degrees, the median cost is $110 per student with a range of $70–$150 per graduate. The median costs decline to $80, $60, and $50 per student for institutions awarding 500, 1,000, and over 1,000 degrees annually. In general, most U.S. colleges spend between $60 and $110 per graduate per year. It is to be noted that the number and quality of services provided by institutions are not equal. A reasonable guideline for estimating costs of a fully staffed and adequately servicing operation is about $100 per graduate per year. With the inflationary spiral, these costs go up each year.

Income

Many career planning and placement facilities generate some levels of income, although far less than the total budget. The bulk of the income is derived from the reproduction of student credentials. Most offices do this on a cost basis, but the income offsets costs that otherwise would have to be taken from the operating budget.

The basic philosophy of career planning and placement is that the service is offered without any charge to employers, students, or alumni. Traditionally, colleges do not charge users for student services. Few, if any, colleges charge salaries of faculty and administrators back to students on a direct basis. Faculty who teach large classes and counsel more students do not get paid on a per unit basis. Students are not charged directly for processing of admission applications, financial aid assistance, counseling, or any other of the many student services which colleges typically provide.

Of course, nothing is free. Someone pays. In private institutions, tuition, endowments, grants, and gifts pay the way. Add government to that when public institutions are involved. Career planning and placement services represent one of the areas that must be supported as part of the total higher education bill. Breaking this service out is tantamount to permitting faculty to assess a fee on each student enrolled in class in order to pay the faculty member's salary. No one would propose such a system!

The placement service is part of the total education of the student. The value received is not equal among all students, just as some students gain more from a class in English than others. The placement service, however, should be open and available to everyone.

Although there is no extensive study to prove or disprove this statement, the placement service is enormously helpful in generating funds for the institution. Taxpayers are willing to support an institution which offers assistance in career planning to sons and daughters. Alumni are more willing to give. Employers, directly and through taxes, are willing to contribute when there are positive relations with the college through the placement service.

In short, no user fees should be assessed! Placement represents a service. Charges would bring priority commitments that would make the service more accessible to some groups than others.

Placement is a bargain for everyone. Efficient operations cost taxpayers, employers, students, and others far less than any other possible arrangement that could be used to meet given goals.

The Annual Report

Annual reports provide an historical reference to the past year's activities. Reports tend to become nuisances and time-consuming projects for the staff when recruiting and counseling activities subside. Placement professionals who fall into that trap simply are not using information wisely. Annual reports provide the information that counselors and students need so desperately in assessing the realities of the career marketplace. Annual reports, when translated into current, real-time activities, provide an important management tool and give immediate feedback on a variety of topics. Frequently overlooked is the fact that the skillfully prepared annual report is one of the best instruments for promoting the career planning and placement office, its programs and objectives.

Automated Management Reports

The annual report has frequently been the starting point for output design for a computer programmer who has been asked by a placement officer to place records on the computer. Compiling management reports on a more frequent basis gives the placement officer a wealth of information which can be used to make management decisions and give students needed counseling information.

An increasing number of management reports are being produced on a monthly or weekly basis through a computer system. The various tables and listings printed as part of the final annual report, which is normally released in late summer, are all available each week. In addition to these tables, many offices save considerable clerical typing by printing the schedule of recruiting dates, the student interview schedules given to the recruiter, regular job opportunity bulletins, and various mailing labels directly from the computer.

Not everyone has access to a computer. Where the number of registrants and/or employers visiting campus are not large, it may be just as convenient to do the reports and activities on a regular basis by a manual process. Since the direction of the future appears to lean toward machine processing, this book approaches the topic from that viewpoint. Nonetheless, the types of reports and projects, described for machine process, are directly applicable to hand processing.

File Development and Maintenance. The most important aspect of preparing good reports is to have accurate input data and information stored in a file. This involves setting up some type of form to collect the information. From the input form, the data is keypunched into a computer record. An alternative to keypunching is an optical scanning form which requires a special machine to read the mark-sensed copy. For online systems, the information might be entered into the computer via a terminal.

A machine record may be stored on punched cards, paper tape, magnetic tape, disk, or in the computer core itself. Each medium has pluses and minuses, but the usual method is to enter data into the computer via punched cards or through online terminals. The most common storage medium is magnetic tape, but disk storage is most preferable because of the shorter access time for such operations as sorting and merging records.

Computer output is usually printed on continuous form paper or mailing labels. Some jobs, however, might be displayed on a cathode ray tube (CRT) if they are for information purposes only and a regular hard copy reference is not needed.

Listed below are some descriptions for the most common types of files (records) maintained by placement offices.

Student Records. These include certain identification numbers, name, major subject, degree level, graduation date, sex, age, race, grades, type of position(s) sought, and location(s) desired if specified. The student record frequently includes the parent's name and permanent address which can be used to contact students upon graduation. The file also contains the local address, city, state, and zip code. The input may be taken from the student resume or a specially designed coding sheet which registrants are asked to complete at registration.

Placement Record. The placement record is an extension of the student record. It contains identification number, name, placement status (business, government, teaching, military, graduate school, placed but unspecified, unknown, still seeking assistance, or unemployed), employer name, employer address, position title, location, and starting monthly salary. Most offices like to obtain both the employer's address and the student's local address. This information is usually taken via a returned form or telephone call requesting the data.

Offer Records. This is an additional extension of the student record which is generated throughout the year as the student interviews and obtains specific offers from employers. The file contains identification number, name, employer name, employer address, location code, type of position, type of industry code, and the monthly salary. This information comes from copies of letters received from employers and "salary offer records" which students voluntarily turn into the placement office. The data is normally keypunched from the offer records and letters and filed on a regular basis in the student computer file using the student's identification number.

Alumni Records. These records contain student identification number, name, permanent home address, and present address. Many offices like to also maintain the employer's name and address plus the position title of the alumnus. By keying the alumnus' identification number to the student number, substantially more data can be obtained from the file by reference to the original student file.

Employer Records. Included are employer identification number, employer name, main contact's title, address, city, state, and zip. Also, additional contacts' names and titles with related addresses, positions normally sought with requirements (major and degree level) by each position, current recruiting date(s), and future recruiting date(s).

This information comes primarily from the "Campus Recruiting Information" form and job opening listings. Once the information is available in the file, the major problem is simply to maintain it. A periodic (annual) mailing needs to be sent to employers asking that the data be checked for accuracy.

Some institutions actually print the recruiter's interview schedule directly from the computer. When this is done, there is a close tie-back to the student's interviewing status and the employer's number of interviews each year. A weekly and year-to-year comparison of interview activity is possible. This involves maintaining another computer file for each interview taken by a given student. Printouts are then possible by student interviewing frequency, which greatly assists in the counseling of students.

A few institutions print their job opening bulletin on the computer. The input is a letter received from the employer or a form on which the job opening is coded when the information is taken by telephone.

System Design. Student and employer records provide an enormous amount of information for processing purposes. Each variable cited above may be selected as an independent variable and the dependent variable may be cross-classified or listed in selected reports.

Once the input data are chosen and placed into the system, a computer programmer can manipulate the data in a variety of ways. Although programming and system design are relatively expensive, the actual processing is inexpensive and can be done on a frequent basis. The system design and programming are a one-time cost. Normally there is some maintenance expense for debugging and minor changes over time, but usually this is not costly.

The greatest cost after the design and programming is for clerical help in inputing raw data and maintaining the data in an up-to-date fashion. It is still less expensive to maintain the computer records because the clerical staff does not have to do the statistical calculations manually or type tables, listings, or mailing labels because the computer will handle those projects. Maintaining an input record system is more time-consuming and labor intensive than the manual system; but the time is more than compensated for at the output end, and the result can be printed on a much more frequent and timely basis.

Output Reports. The output of a well-designed computer system can be as simple or as complex as the placement director wants. Routine mailings, including labels and the communication to employers and students, can be quickly and more efficiently accomplished on the computer. Routine typing jobs such as employer directories, student directories and mini-resumes, recruiter interview schedules, the alphabetical and chronological lists of recruiting dates, the job opening bulletins, etc. lend themselves well to computer applications.

A weekly report on recruiting activity is also a simple task. This includes such items as the number of interviews, employer visits, interview schedules, recruiters, and a classification of interviews by different majors, degree levels, etc. Comparisons can be made to the previous year or week to easily provide percentage changes. This gives the office an idea of how current activity relates to previous periods, which can be very helpful counseling data to share with students.

Also possible is a weekly report on average monthly salary offers which can be very similar to the CPC *Salary Survey* report. Many placement offices keep salary averages from their school posted for students to review. These reports are frequently referenced by employers who want to make certain that their offers to the school's graduates will be competitive. The information is normally classified by major subject, degree level, and type of industry. For each category, it is helpful to have the computer print out the mean, median, number of offers, and 80 percent range (omit top and bottom 10 percent to avoid skewing).

A number of summary report tables can be helpful in identifying the types of candidates available for employment. The most frequently used table shows the number of registrants cross classified by major and degree level. Some schools add a third classification—graduation date. Many other cross tabulations are possible. These report tables are extremely simple for an experienced computer programmer to write since most are part of a statistical package of programs like SPSS or other report generators.

Listings are also popular. These can be alphabetical listings of students or employers by a number of different cross classifications. These one or two-line listings simply show data such as major subject, degree level, graduation date, positions sought or available, placement status of students, recruiting dates of employers, and industry classifications. Ways for classifying the listings are almost limitless. Each institution must decide what type of information would be most useful for its needs.

Summary

The future is likely to see many more placement offices utilizing automated machine processing for maintaining records of students, alumni, and employers. A properly designed system will save an institution considerable time and money. Some clerical operations can be eliminated, counseling can be greatly assisted, and much more information will be available for decision-making purposes.

CHAPTER 9

THE LEGAL AND FINANCIAL ENVIRONMENT

P RIOR TO THE MID-SIXTIES, the activities of placement officials rarely came under much legal scrutiny. Among other legislation and executive orders, passage of the Civil Rights Act of 1964 and the Family Rights and Privacy Act of 1974 forced placement professionals and employer representatives to become much more conscious of legal requirements. The encroachment of the law into the profession's traditional activities is likely to continue at an accelerated pace.

The law is ever changing. Comments about various laws may well become obsolete before this book is published. The College Placement Council regularly reports on current developments. The CPC tabloid *Spotlight* and the *Journal of College Placement* serve as the most current and up-to-date sources of information on the legal and financial environment for placement offices. Placement professionals should continue to keep abreast of legal developments through publications such as these and professional meetings.

THE CIVIL RIGHTS ACT OF 1964—TITLE VII

The past few years produced some very potent weapons against unjust, unfair, and indifferent employment practices. Congress and the courts brought forth a battery of laws. Court decisions and regulations appeared to protect the employment rights of all people, especially minorities, females, older citizens, and the handicapped.

Perhaps most important was passage of the Civil Rights Act of 1964, especially Title VII, which is frequently referred to as the Equal Employment Opportunity Act. This Act, which was designed to stem wide-scale abuse of individual rights, has had an immense impact. It gives administrative agencies broad powers to accomplish statutory goals.

EEOA has been described as the working person's bill of rights because it provides the individual with the right to equal treatment in the job market. The language of Title VII is deceptively simple since it merely prohibits discrimination in employment by either an employer or an employment agency based on race, color, religion, sex, or national origin. The Act created the Equal Employment Opportunity Commission, which can "prevent" such discrimination or unlawful employment practices as well as redress wrongs with stiff penalties.

Placement Offices as Employment Agencies

College placement offices are affected because employment agencies as well as employers are subject to the provisions of the Act. "Employment agency," like most of the Act's key phrases, is very broadly defined. It means "any person regularly undertaking, with or without compensation, to procure employees for an employer or to procure for employees opportunities to work for an employer." Obviously this includes college placement offices. Indeed, courts have specifically so held. For purposes of the Act, college placement offices are treated as employment agencies because they engage in employment-oriented activities.

As "employment agencies" under the Act, the college placement offices are prohibited from engaging in or abetting any
unlawful employment practice as defined by the Act and/or interpreted in EEOC's regulations. Specifically, employment
agencies are prohibited from failing or refusing to refer an individual for employment, or from classifying or referring an individual, on the basis of race, sex, color, religion or national origin.

Selection Procedures

The Equal Employment Opportunity Commission has pro-
mulgated a sweeping set of guidelines on selection procedures,
with emphasis on testing. Testing is a major area of legal concern since testing can become systematic discrimination.
EEOC contends that occupational testing is frequently unre-
lated to determining one's ability to perform a task and is a
widespread form of covert discrimination.

College placement offices are prohibited under EEOC regulations from appraising or referring applicants based on the
results of tests which have not been validated in a prescribed
manner, if those tests have an adverse impact on minorities or
women. To ensure compliance, agencies should refuse to administer a test where an employer has not supplied satisfactory
evidence of validation. Under the Uniform Guidelines on Employee Selection Procedures, a placement office is independently responsible for compliance with the Guidelines and cannot rely on an employer's representation of validation. The
placement office must obtain evidence of that validation and
review it to ensure compliance.

The Commission defines selection procedures in the
broadest possible manner. The career counselor must be wary
not only of ability examinations but also of any technique of assessing job suitability. This could include specific educational
or work history requirements, scored interviews, interviewer
rating scales, and scored application forms. In short, if an em-

ployer provides a form to be used in selecting candidates for interviews or referrals, the placement officer should know if the form has been properly validated and should obtain evidence of its validity.

Test validation involves determining whether a test is job related. The Guidelines identify various methods for making this determination. A test is valid if there is a statistical relationship between scores on it and performance on the job, if it representatively tests significant parts of the job (such as typing), or if it identifies and measures psychological traits which underly successful job performance.

The rules regarding testing cannot be taken lightly by the placement professional regardless of the test author or general reputation. Any placement officer administering a test for employment purposes must obtain evidence of the test's validity before distributing the test forms.

Affirmative Action

The concept of "affirmative action" is that employers deliberately seek out and make job opportunities available to persons in classes previously subjected to discrimination. Although affirmative action programs can be instituted on a voluntary basis, certain employers, such as federal contractors, are required by law to institute such plans. To meet affirmative action plans or goals, many employers have turned to the college placement officer for assistance.

Title VII would appear to require employers to take a neutral approach toward job applicants, at least on the basis of those traits on which discrimination is prohibited by the Act. However, the Act also gives EEOC broad power to "prevent" discrimination. The Commission maintains that certain discriminating employment practices are so ingrained in the system that mere neutrality is not enough. In order for the organization to eradicate prohibited types of discrimination from its occupational environment, some type of direct action to correct past abuses is required.

Literally, affirmative action is not easy to reconcile with the statutory mandate that nothing in the Act should be interpreted to require any employer to grant preferential treatment to any minority group merely because persons of that group do not represent an adequate portion of that employer's work force, based on their proportion of the community's working population. The Act contains a contradiction by prohibiting preferences and then embracing the concept of affirmative action.

This apparent conflict is rationalized by the interpretation of the word "require" in the no preference clause to mean that nothing in the Act shall require proportional employment but that nothing, on the other hand, shall prohibit preferences. Additionally, this conflict is likely to be resolved in the courts in the not too distant future.

Affirmative Action Referrals

College placement officers become involved in this issue when employers request that qualified applicants of a particular minority group (or women) be referred to them for job interviews. Some employers are under court-ordered affirmative action plans to do this. Other employers may feel that past policies may have resulted in discrimination which now requires them to take more than a neutral position regarding future hiring.

For example, an employer might ask for a list of all minority students. This would seem to be an effective means of assisting the employer in meeting affirmative action goals. Title VII, however, prohibits employment agencies, and therefore placement offices, from referring individuals for employment on the basis of race, color, religion, sex, or national origin. An exception is where the employer's request may be a result of a court-ordered affirmative action program. Even then EEOC suggests that a list of *all* qualified people should be provided regardless of the group status.

These and similar legal inconsistencies place the college in a tenuous situation. The risks of running afoul of Title VII are substantial, even for the best-intentioned employer or counselor. The legal boundaries are unclear. The ruling in the Alan Bakke case further muddies the water. It appears to make quotas unlawful but says that preferences can be given to a particular group if a series of factors are involved in an employment or admission decision. Placement officials need to read and understand the laws but act only with the advice of the college legal counsel, and then try to do the most prudent thing.

FAMILY EDUCATIONAL RIGHTS
AND PRIVACY ACT

The Family Educational Rights and Privacy Act of 1974 (FERPA) caused many hours of consternation in the career planning offices throughout the United States for several years in the mid-Seventies. FERPA was enacted as part of the "Education Amendment of 1974" (PL93-380) and was subsequently amended in 1975. FERPA is frequently referred to as the "Buckley Amendment" because it was Senator Buckley of New York who introduced this amendment on the Senate floor without any hearings and with a minimum of debate. The amendment passed with few modifications and was signed into law by President Ford on August 21, 1974.

Purpose

Originally the Act was intended to establish the rights of parents to have access to children's school records, to challenge the accuracy and relevance of information in those records, and to limit the disclosure of personally identifiable information from school records without parental consent. Subsequently its scope was broadened to include post-secondary education. A student of 18 years of age or one attending a post-secondary institution was allowed to exercise these rights in his or her own behalf. This most directly affects the letters of recommendation which college placement offices maintain on students. Also affected are a fair number of other types of records that many offices had been required to maintain. The Act emerged from a whole era of privacy legislation designed to protect the individual rights of private citizens. The basic purpose of FERPA is to allow a student or parent to see school records and to protect privacy by restricting third-party access to those records. For an outsider to see the records, permission from the student or parent must be granted in writing.

Problems

From the beginning the law was fraught with problems. It raised hundreds of questions and provided few answers. At first, universities were unsure whether traditional student directories were permitted. Parents were initially barred from seeing the records of dependent college children. Many of these and similar questions were resolved later with amendments and regulations but not without many hours of concern on the part of university officials.

One of the biggest of the problems continues. How are misleading and meaningless recommendations handled? Many professors are squeamish about writing candid letters. Some professors try to avoid extreme statements, and write bland, meaningless letters. Other professors now prefer to make appraisals of students orally rather than risk putting criticisms on paper. This has tended to create an old-boy network of discreet phone calls and has forced evaluators, such as graduate schools and employers, to read between the lines.

Libel and Slander

When disseminating information, placement officers should be familiar with the legal doctrines of libel and slander. Libel is a written communication; slander is oral. In order for there to be libel or slander, three elements must be present: (1) there must be a false communication to a third party which is damaging of the person discussed; (2) this must be done without the consent of the subject of the report; and (3) the communication must be such that it does not fall within a recognized privilege. Truth and consent are absolute defenses to libel and slander actions. Privilege is a qualified defense.

The first two defenses are obvious. Privilege is a more technical area. Good faith communications between individuals with an interest in the subject matter are privileged. This means, for example, that if a college gives the wrong grades to another college to which the student is applying, the college is not subject to a libel suit for the mistake unless it was deliberate. It is likely that a placement officer's communique to a prospective employer falls within the scope of this privilege.

Thus, neither libel nor slander laws nor the student's right to privacy pose a serious threat to a placement office which handles records and disseminates information in a careful, professional manner.

FERPA Guidelines

On Thursday, June 17, 1976, the U.S. Department of Health, Education and Welfare printed the final rules in the *Federal Register*, Volume 41, No. 118, pages 24662 through 24675. It would be appropriate for every placement professional to read through this. A summary of a few of the key provisions and rights follows.

Scope of Coverage. Section 99.1 of the regulations broadens their coverage to include institutions receiving federal funds directly as well as those with students receiving such funds. For example, even though the institution does not receive direct Office of Education funds, it will be covered by the regulations if its students receive federal funds through the Guaranteed Student Loan Program.

Attendance. Section 99.3 makes it clear that students to whom these regulations apply must be in attendance at the institution; however, attendance has been broadened to include both attendance in person and by correspondence courses.

Students—Employees. Education records which must be disclosed to the student or which cannot be disclosed to third parties without the student's permission do not include employment records of students who are also employed by the educational agency or institution. Thus, if students are also working at the university, their employment records are not covered by the act, only their education records.

Alumni Records. The regulations do not cover records of an educational agency or institution which contain only information relating to the person after that person is no longer a student. An example of this exception would be information collected by an educational agency or institution pertaining to the accomplishments of its alumni.

Annual Notification. Section 99.6 of the regulations, which requires each educational agency or institution to give eligible students annual notification of their rights under the act, has been interpreted to mean *constructive* rather than *actual* notice. Thus, the university may select any means of notice which is reasonably likely to inform students of their rights. It does not have to contact each person individually.

Waivers. Section 99.7 sets forth the limitations on waiver of rights of students to inspect and review their records, including confidential letters and confidential statements. Subsection 99.7 (b) allows the institution to *request* students to waive their rights under the section; however, it forbids the institution from *requiring* students to do so. The revocation must be in writing and *is only effective with respect to actions occurring after revocation and not before.* Also important is the fact that a waiver may be made with respect to specified *classes* of education records and persons or institutions (Section 99.7 (e)). Thus, the waiver does not have to be made with respect to each specific piece of information or originator thereof. (See the Appendix for a sample waiver developed by CPC.)

Prior Consent for Disclosure. From CPC's standpoint, the most significant change in the regulations was made in Section 99.30 regarding prior consent to disclosure of records. Under the regulations, no personally identifiable information from education records of students may be released without prior written consent. The regulations have been amended to allow prior written consent for disclosure to a *party or class of parties* of particular records for a particular purpose. This would allow for consent to release records to classes of employers, government agencies, etc. Thus the placement officer can secure consent to release information to a category of recipients without having to check with the student prior to each release. It should be stressed, however, that the consent must identify the records to be released (eg., recommendations and transcripts) and the purpose of the disclosure (eg., to assist potential employers in evaluating applications for employment). (See the Appendix for a sample of CPC's form for Consent to Disclosure to Third Parties of Information Contained in Records.)

Student Records Policy

The intricacies and details surrounding each area are something that every placement official must decide. There are no universal forms and succinctly written guidelines. As a result, it is important that the law be read in its entirety. Under Section 99.5 of the regulations, each educational agency must formulate a written statement of policy and procedures regarding student records.

Actual day-to-day practices vary rather widely among placement offices. Some institutions appear to be greater risktakers than others, or they simply interpret the regulations from a different perspective. The policy statement adopted by the Indiana University Faculty Council in 1977 is summarized in the next pages to give the flavor of one institution's interpretation of what the law requires. As noted, the interpretations of specific points by other institutions might differ. Any policy statement should be cleared by the institution's legal counsel before it is adopted.

In compliance with Section 438 of the "General Education Provisions Act" (as amended) entitled "Family Educational Rights and Privacy Act," the following constitutes the institution's policy which instructs the student in the procedures available to provide appropriate access to personal records, while protecting their confidentiality.

A. Certain definitions and principles contained in the law and proposed guidelines are specifically adopted in the policy:

    1. "Student" is defined as one who has attended or is attending Indiana University and whose records are in the files of the University.

    2. "Educational records" do not include files retained by individuals which are not accessible to any other person except a substitute faculty/staff member.

    3. "Public information" is limited to name; address; phone; major field of study; dates of attendance; admission or enrollment status; campus; school, college, or division; class standing (year); degrees and awards; activities; sports; and athletic information. Records of arrests and/or convictions and traffic accident information are public information and may be released to anyone making inquiry.

    4. "Record" means any information or date recorded in any medium, including but not limited to: handwriting, print, tapes, film, microfilm, and microfiche.

B. Public information shall be released freely unless the student files the appropriate form requesting that certain public information not be released. This form is available at: (Here each campus will list its offices and locations appropriate for that campus.) Public information which cannot be restricted includes name, enrollment status, degrees, and dates of attendance.

C. All students have records in one or more of the following offices and maintained by the administrative officer listed: (Here each campus will list its appropriate offices, locations, and officers.) (This section includes the permanent record, school or college files, etc.)

D. Some departments maintain records separate from the school or college. A list of departments which have separate records, their location, and person responsible for the record may be obtained from the office of the dean of the school or college in which the department is located.

E. Students may also have records in the following places: (Here each campus will list its appropriate offices.) (This section includes offices such as financial aids, bursar, placement, and police.)

F. The privacy of all records may be broken at a time of emergency defined in terms of the following considerations:
1. The seriousness of the threat to health or safety
2. The need for access to the record in meeting the emergency
3. Whether the person requesting the records is in a position to deal with the emergency
4. The extent to which time is of the essence in dealing with the emergency

G. A student's record is open to the student, with the following exceptions:
1. Confidential letters of recommendation placed in files prior to January 1, 1975
2. Records of parents' financial status
3. Employment records; see #H below
4. Medical and psychological records; see #1 below
5. Some items of academic record under certain conditions; see #3 below

H. The employment records excluded from accessibility are records kept in the normal course of business which relate exclusively to persons as employees and are not used for any other purposes.

I. Medical and psychological records are presently governed by State Statute, *Burns Indiana Statues,* 1971 Code Edition, 34-1-14-5 and 25-33-1-17, which rigidly protects their confidentiality. They are not available to anyone other than those providing treatment, but can be reviewed by a physician or appropriate professional of the student-patient's choice.

J. To ensure the validity and confidentiality of references prepared off-campus and on-campus, certain documents may carry waivers, signed by the student relinquishing the right of access to the document.
1. Waivers are subject to the following conditions:
   i. Waivers can be signed only for the specific purposes of application for admission, candidacy for honor or honorary

recognition (including financial aid based at least in part on merit), and candidacy for employment.

   ii.   Waivers cannot be required.

   iii.   The student shall be told, upon request, the names of those supplying references.

2. All items in the academic record not covered by waivers are open to the student. Material not covered by waivers may not be protected by keeping it out of the student's file.

K. Student records are open to members of the faculty and staff who have a legitimate need to know their contents, except where access is prohibited by special policies such as those governing medical and psychological records.

   1.   The determination of "a legitimate need to know" will be made by the person responsible for the maintenance of the record. This determination must be made scrupulously and with respect for the individual whose record is involved.

   2.   Academic documents inaccessible to students (because the documents have been filed before January 1, 1975 or are segregated by waivers) are to be used only for the purpose for which they were prepared.

L. The University has established the following procedures enabling the student to have access to his or her record and has provided for interpretation and challenge:

   1.   The student may see his or her record by filling out a request form at the office where the record of interest is maintained.

   2.   Access is to be granted promptly and no later than thirty days from the date of request.

   3.   The student may make the request in person or by mail.

   4.   The student may obtain copies upon request (for which the University may charge).

   5.   The student may request and receive interpretation of his or her record from the person (or designee) responsible for the maintenance of the record.

   6.   If the student considers the record faulty, he or she can request and receive an informal and/or formal hearing of the case to the end that the record will be corrected if judged faulty or in violation of privacy:

      i.   The informal hearing will be in conference with the person (or his or her designee) responsible for the maintenance of the record and—where appropriate—the party or parties authoring the record segment in question.

      ii.   The student may request a formal hearing by obtaining from the Dean for Student Services' Office a request form on which he or she must designate the location of the record in question and a brief explanation of the reason for faulting the record. A panel of not fewer than ten Hearing Officers will be appointed by the chief administrative officer for each campus. The Dean for Student Services will forward a copy of the request to the person responsible for the record and will provide the student and the keeper of the record with three names of Hearing Officers. The parties (student and keeper of the record in challenge) shall each strike one name; the remaining Hearing Officer shall conduct an administrative hearing with both parties present.

The hearing shall be held within a reasonable period of time; notice of the date, place, and time must be given reasonably in advance. The student shall be afforded a full and fair opportunity to present relevant evidence and may be assisted or represented by any person of his or her choosing (including an attorney at his or her own expense). A written decision based solely upon the evidence presented shall be prepared within a reasonable amount of time and shall include a summary of the evidence and the reasons for the decision. The judgment of the Hearing Officer shall be final, and the record shall be changed or retained as recommended.

If the institution decides the information is accurate, it shall inform the student of his or her right to place in his or her educational record a statement commenting upon the information, and/or noting any reasons for disagreeing with the decision. Any statement of this sort shall be maintained as long as the student's educational record or contested portion is maintained; if the student's educational record or contested portion is disclosed to any party, the student's statement shall also be disclosed.

M. Normally, records can be released—or access given—to third parties (i.e., anyone not a member of the faculty and staff) only at the written request of the student.

   1. Without the consent of the student releases to third parties may be given only as follows:

      i. To parents of students who are dependents as defined by IRS standards

      ii. To federal officers as prescribed by law

      iii. As required by state law

      iv. To research projects on behalf of educational agencies for test norms, improving instruction, etc. (provided that the agencies guarantee no personal identification of students)

    v. To accrediting agencies carrying out their functions

   vi. In response to a judicial order or lawfully issued subpoena (provided that the student is notified prior to compliance or provided that a reasonable attempt to notify the student has been made)

  vii. By IU Police to other law enforcement agencies in the investigation of a specific criminal case.

2. A student may secure from the Registrar's Office a "consent form" authorizing the release of specified records to specific individuals.

3. A notification of releases made to third parties must be kept in the student's record. This notification is open only to the student and the person in charge of the record.

4. The third party must be informed that no further release of personally identifiable data is authorized without the written consent of the student.

N. Nothing in this policy requires the continued maintenance of any student record. However, if under the terms of this policy a student has requested access to the record, no destruction of the record shall be made before access has been granted to the student. Persons in charge of records should ensure that only pertinent items are retained in student files.

Requests to View Files

The Appendix (beginning on page 355) includes a typical form that could be used by a placement office when requests are received from students wishing to view their file. In the majority of cases, students would be permitted to see their file immediately (rather than wait up to 45 days), but a record needs to be maintained of this request. Each institution must establish an appeal procedure to remove information if a student so requests.

Placement offices must obtain a waiver signed by the student before releasing a resume or other information such as recommendations to other parties (for example, employers or graduate schools). A sample developed by the College Placement Council is shown in the Appendix.

Waiver Statement

Because of FERPA regulations, the use of letters of recommendations and other forms of evaluations has become more complex. Many faculty members are reluctant to write a candid evaluation if it is not a confidential document that will not be seen by the student. Most employers say that recommendations that are not confidential are bland and of little value.

Many placement offices give students a specifically designed recommendation statement with a waiver clause clearly printed on it. The student's instructions are to give this to the faculty members who know them best. The faculty member returns the completed form directly to the placement office. Obviously, the student does not see the evaluation unless the evaluator sends the student a copy or the student sees it in the placement office file.

The faculty member (counselor, previous employer, or any other type of evaluator) has the option of submitting the form or not. As just noted, some will not return evaluations for a variety of reasons, ranging from being too busy to having personal biases against the system. If the waiver clause is not signed, some faculty will not bother to submit the form out of fear of being sued for slander or at least of being demeaned. Other faculty prefer that students read their candid evaluations.

FERPA permits placement office registrants to sign a waiver relinquishing their right to read a letter of recommendation. A College Placement Council sample waiver statement can be found in the Appendix. Any letter of recommendation received for inclusion in a student's placement file prior to the effective date of the amended law, January 1, 1975, is normally not available for student inspection. Letters added after that date are open for the student's inspection unless the student has signed the waiver. If the waiver is signed, the right to see that evaluation is waived forever.

When a waiver statement appears on the form, the evaluator and the student both have a clear idea of the action to follow.

Students are advised that evaluation statements can be advantageous in seeking employment and almost essential in gaining acceptance to respectable graduate schools. Students must be advised that these forms will be sent to employers and graduate schools upon request.

Some placement services require a specific number of evaluation statements but usually this is a voluntary activity on the part of students. In most cases, students must present the blank forms to faculty and others with the expectation that the evaluation will be sent to the placement service. Of course, students and the placement service have no control over whether the forms ever are returned. Fortunately, most forms are returned, but this explains why it is difficult to require the evaluations.

THE REHABILITATION ACT OF 1973

"Hire the handicapped—it's good business." This slogan did a remarkable job during the Fifties, Sixties, and Seventies in helping millions of handicapped people gain employment. Some strong teeth and power were added to the slogan with the passage of the Rehabilitation Act of 1973.

Although it is difficult to fix a date when the handicapped consumer movement began, it clearly took its cue from the civil rights movement of the Sixties. Its techniques are similar—demonstrating, lobbying efforts, public relations, adjudication, etc. Aside from being good business, employers who do business with the federal government were told that the law required them to take direct action to hire handicapped people, not unlike that required with regard to minorities and women.

Purpose

The new laws requiring employers to hire and promote handicapped people have employers assessing their past practices and procedures. The modifications that employers make in the employment process will impact upon the job of the college placement office, both in terms of the job placement and the career counseling aspects. These laws could affect over 10 percent of the clientele serviced by career planning and placement services.

In terms of counseling, the placement professional can easily get caught in the middle. Is the employer making a reasonable effort? Is the student being discriminated against? A few words of counsel with the handicapped student can easily be interpreted as encouragement and result in the student resorting to court action. Court awards can include reinstatement, fines, jail terms, and revocation of important contracts. Clearly the placement staff is in a tenuous situation and should thus be aware of the rights and limitations set forth in the law.

The Legal Sections Defined

The law is the Rehabilitation Act of 1973. Two of its sections, 503 and 504, removed the hiring of handicapped people for many employers from the realm of voluntary action into the arena of legal requirement. Section 503 states that any contractor (employer) doing business with the federal government in excess of $2,500 shall take affirmative action to employ and advance in employment qualified handicapped people.

This means that if any employer doing any federal business, such as selling of goods or construction, refuses to hire or advance a qualified handicapped employee, then federal contracts may be revoked and the employer declared ineligible for future contracts. This is rather a severe penalty for most major organizations. The Office of Federal Contract Compliance of the Department of Labor enforces Section 503. Many discrimination cases have been settled and retribution made including back pay awards. Clearly the full power of the law is being used to prevent discrimination.

Section 504 is the second part of the Rehabilitation Act of 1973 that impacts upon employment. This section is tantamount to a civil rights law for handicapped people. It states: "No otherwise qualified handicapped individual in the United States . . . shall, solely by reason of his handicap, be excluded from participation in, be denied benefits of, or be subjected to discrimination under any program or activity receiving federal financial assistance." A qualified handicapped person in an employment context is one who can perform the tasks of a particular job after a "reasonable accommodation" (barrier removal) has been made by the employers.

Enforcement

The Office of Civil Rights of the Department of Health, Education, and Welfare is the enforcing agency for Section 504. Regulations cover all programs administered by HEW. These regulations clearly affect universities and colleges and the college placement office. All other federal departments have published similar regulations for programs that they administer. Despite these regulations, there is still a need for information on the mechanics of employing handicapped people. For example, where are they? What training programs are available to them? How are reasonable accommodations made?

The law does not guarantee jobs for handicapped people. If handicapped people do not have the ability to do the essential functions of the job with reasonable accommodation, the employer is not obligated to hire or promote them. If the cost of making architectural changes is unreasonable and causes "undue hardship," it is the employer's prerogative to refuse to make the accommodations. The great change is that the employer must justify any refusal to hire or promote if challenged. This legalistic, time absorbing, and detailed task is not something employers particularly appreciate. Thus, the pressure to make reasonable accommodations is significant.

Reasonable Accommodations

The subject of "reasonable accommodations" is not a simple matter. Nonetheless it will impact upon the placement officer and the employer visiting the campus. It involves job modifications such as alteration of equipment, seating arrangements, and use of adaptive devices. Reasonable accommodations include some restructuring of specific jobs which might mean giving the impossible job tasks to others in exchange for accomplishable ones. The most noticeable "reasonable accommodation" has been the change in physical architectural barriers, such as ramps, wider doorways, restroom modifications, and special parking. Guidance in all of these areas is best obtained from professionals working in vocational rehabilitation and employment security.

Summary

The laws and regulations continually change. Many federal laws relating to handicapped peoples' rights are passed each year. Many changes have been amended to Title VII of the Civil Rights Act of 1964. State laws vary considerably and over two-thirds of the states have amended their fair employment policies to include the handicapped.

The definition of "handicapped person" is so broad in some laws that almost anyone can qualify. The best source of information at any one point in time is the publications which are usually available free-of-charge from "The President's Committee on Employment of the Handicapped," Washington, D. C., 20210.

As important changes revelant to any of the laws are made, the College Placement Council will communicate changes directly to the membership. Although this section focused on only three major laws, several more pieces of legislation are pending which will impact on both placement professionals and employers. The profession appears to be on the threshold of a much more legalistic approach to how various activities are handled within the institution.

THE FINANCIAL ENVIRONMENT

The traditional source of funding for career planning and placement services is the institution's general budget. Private and public colleges tend to make the service part of the overall responsibility of an academic department or the student services function, and the placement budget is built into the normal operating funds.

Different colleges place different priorities and importance on the placement function. Some consolidate the function with other functions. The quality of service offered varies greatly from institution to institution.

Few offices receive funds to conduct research or support programs beyond their schools. Innovative programs on a given campus frequently do not receive support because the institution is pressed to barely support ongoing activities. As a result, resources beyond the typical university budgets are sorely needed.

If the College Placement Council had sufficient resources, a number of things could be better and more efficiently accomplished on a national scale rather than on a local basis. Like most associations, the regional and national placement groups cannot afford extensive programs beyond a minimum operating budget. The sources of income are simply not available. If some of the needed projects are to be accomplished, funds must come from outside sources. This section discusses some of the potential outside sources of funds that have been suggested.

Charging Fees to Students

The majority of career planning and placement services charge no fees to any of their constituents. In the few places where fees do exist, there appear to be three kinds of charges: registration fees, credential fees, and publication charges for bulletins or newsletters carrying job information.

Registration fees are nominal, usually running in the $3 to $10 range, with larger amounts covering service for a number of years ($25 for five years' service). These fees appear to involve the creation of credential files, especially for teacher placement. In most instances, where there is a small registration fee, there is no credential fee.

Credential fees are charged by a few placement offices, usually those having teacher placement responsibilities. Usually a certain number of sets of credentials (ranging from 3 to 25) are sent out free-of-charge, with charges after that ranging from $1 to $5 per set. Teacher education credentials are often multi-page documents in contrast to the one-page resume that business and public agencies usually request. Collection of credential fees is frequently a nuisance when one considers the limited income generated and the cost in time for processing the paperwork.

Placement offices which publish newsletters or job bulletins for distribution seem most likely to charge for this service, especially when they are sent to alumni. Most of the charges are nominal—in the 25–50 cents per issue range, which often does not cover postage and rarely covers writing and printing.

An increasing number of placement offices are charging employers a small fee per resume (or resume book) when these are requested for prescreening of candidates. Charges usually range from 10–30 cents per resume.

A large number of colleges do have a special student or activity fee in addition to the normal tuition. These fees range from $10–$300, with the median about $50. Few, if any, allocate any portion of the "Student Activity Fee" for specific use by placement. The activities most frequently are in the extracurricular, student organization, athletic, or recreation areas. A few are in the health services or library areas.

A fee tied to a visible and measurable transaction, such as the duplication and mailing of a set of credentials, creates no particularly harmful hurdle to the use of the other available services. Indeed, the fees may on occasion serve a useful negative effect in discouraging the indiscriminant flooding of employers' offices with unsolicited confidential papers.

Registration fees, when they become substantial enough to be more than a token, are seen by many educators and placement professionals as having a strongly limiting effect on the essential role of the career planning and placement service. Separate registration fees can limit the role of placement and are not in the best interests of students. Some of the reasons placement services are not in favor of general charges are:

Career Exploration. If the emphasis on assistance to students in career exploration and planning is to be maintained and further developed, any fee would tend to discourage use of the office by individual students. The perennial problem in career counseling is to reach and motivate students to start this exploration process as early in their college career as possible. The last thing needed is a barrier between the career counselor and the student.

Employment Agency Connotation. A substantial fee emphasizes the role of the office as an employment agency. It suggests that the staff should focus its efforts on "getting students a job" rather than on sound career counseling and planning which may not have an immediate payoff.

Financial Burden on Students. A fee injects a solvency standard into the placement process. Students who might best benefit by the service might be unable to pay the fees without a severe financial hardship.

Support From Tuition. If it is accepted that career planning and placement is indeed part of the educational process, then this service should be supported in the tuition and fees required of all students.

Charging Fees to Employers

Following a membership position taken in 1969 by the Midwest College Placement Association and a subsequent survey of employers by the College Placement Council, CPC went on record in 1971 as opposed to charging employers a fee to use college placement services. This CPC policy statement was succinctly stated in an "Information Memo." A number of valid reasons for the policy came from the MCPA group and the CPC employer survey. These reasons appear to be as valid today as they were then.

University Contributions. Contributions from private industry to public and private colleges are no small factor. Although rarely explicitly stated, these contributions frequently result from a close working relationship with the recipient college. A close working relationship, among many other things, often means placement assistance. If an institution does not produce the caliber and type of candidates that the employer normally hires, the amount of financial contribution to the institution is likely to be small.

If employers were charged a fee for placement services, the motive for making contributions to the institution could conceivably be lessened. One of the reasons for supporting higher education would be weakened.

Assuming that there is a limited sum of money in each private organization that can be given to colleges, requiring a fee would certainly decrease the allocation. This would have the effect of reducing scholarship funds, unrestricted grants, and donations for various services and equipment. The decision by any one college or university to institute a fee must be weighed against its potential to increase its share of the corporate allocation.

Image. A fee is likely to change the existing image of the placement office and its role in the educational process. A fee to employers would make the placement office very similar to an employment agency, a concept that many professionals have long been fighting.

The placement office often creates the first impression that employers have about the institution. The connotation of a weak placement program can be quickly translated into a weak academic program. The concept is analogous to that of the universities with outstanding football and basketball programs. The external image helps produce large sums of money that can be pumped into the institution.

Market Fluctuations. Placement office budgets need some stability. Unlike private enterprise, there is seldom a cushion called "retained earnings" and "dividends" which tends to take up the slack during poor sales years. Colleges do not tend to hire and fire people as fluctuations occur. They do not lease a large amount of space one year and then cancel the contract the next year. In other words, the expense items tend to remain constant over time, with a small increase annually for inflation and growth of services.

Charging a fee would tie the operation much closer to the marketplace and the national and local economy. Income would be great during boom periods and terrible during recessions. Colleges tend to have the same number of students graduating each year with only minor variations. The supply cannot be turned on and off like a production line in a big factory. During lean years, the focus is more on teaching students how to face a difficult market and still find employment. During good times, the market, in the form of recruiters, comes to students on campus. A prorating fee structure would play internal havoc with a professional career planning and placement function.

Supply/Demand Implications. Fees could limit the student's career alternatives. Large organizations would be more able to afford the added cost of recruitment while smaller organizations might feel that it is too costly to recruit on campus. This would have the undesirable effect of limiting the number of employers coming to campus. Employer fees might also eliminate many social service, government, and nonprofit organizations from campus recruiting because of their inability to pay employment agency type of fees. There is no budget allocation for such a "purchase."

A fee could also reduce the opportunities of students in liberal arts and other areas where the demand is not strong. It would not be prudent for a firm to visit a campus to see a group of students who would most likely be walking in their offices later.

Many employers might well use the fee as the excuse for cancelling recruiting visits at some of the less productive schools. Other reasons might be given for the cancellation, but the fee would be the item that moved the decision off of dead center to the negative side.

A significant amount of career counseling is currently done in the campus interview. A fee could change the nature of the on-campus interview. Many interviews which previously turned into guidance sessions would revert to purely recruitment sessions with lesser concern for career development of students. There would be a tendency for employers to cut nonproductive interviews short so that more time would be available to spend on recruiting and selling those candidates who have a closer match with the firm.

Employer Demands. If employers were to begin paying for services, they rightfully could demand a fair amount of service for their fee. In essence, career service professionals would soon become the equivalent of "employees" for the corporations using the service. Career counseling and other services to other constituencies might well suffer. Employers would begin to have a stronger voice in the administration of the function.

One of the most important services that employers would immediately demand is some type of prescreening of potential candidates. Placement functions could quickly become organizations that place the best graduates and forget the rest. This concept runs counter to the philosophy of working with all graduates and assuming the responsibility to help everyone, not just the best.

No one likes to begin paying for something which previously has been free or cost very little. Resentment can build, even if the cost is justified and reasonable for the service received.

Some employers argue that their firm already "pays" for the placement service through the regular tax arrangements. Corporations are large taxpayers, and both private and public schools usually receive tax-related funds in one form or another.

Administration Problems. A system to charge employers would require establishment of some equitable basis. The fee structure could be based upon the number of interviews, the number of actual placements, space rental, a flat recruiting fee, a fee for various services, or a combination of these and other approaches. Any fee structure would invariably be a problem to enforce. It is not uncommon for a student to interview on campus and through private employment agencies. Who would actually get credit for a placement that a private and public agency shared in arranging? Another question is whether large employers should pay more or less than smaller employers?

The administration of a fee schedule would obviously be extremely costly but probably not impossible. Few universities are in a position to really "cost-out" their various services to constituencies and then charge a fee plus a marginal overhead factor. A fee system would create great confusion as different campuses adopted different approaches. Rather than hassle with administrative red tape, many employers would find other sources of tapping the college market where their exact costs could be better predicted.

This book has identified dozens of different services offered by placement offices to various constituencies. Every service has a cost. Someone must pay for it. There are also substantial overhead costs. Should the cost be prorated to the constituency using it? How about things like faculty newsletters, student counseling, promotional materials? Should one constituency pay the cost for another constituency if one cannot afford the expense? Are expenses with internships a charge to students, employers, or part of the educational and academic cost of the program?

Placement is part of the basic educational mission of the institution. One could argue that the knowledge gained by students is equivalent to that realized in mathematics, English, history, or any other academic discipline. Students are required to enroll in these disciplines in order to meet the requirements for a college degree. Is career planning and counseling any less important? Income for most universities comes from taxes, student fees, government and private grants, and gifts to the university. Should not the placement function share equally in the distribution of these funds?

Whatever fee structure to charge employers might eventually be agreed upon, competition and cost-cutting would inevitably enter the picture. Can I cut my cost of recruiting at ABC University by renting a hotel room nearby and running an ad in the student newspaper? Can I hire one of the better students to screen out the poor candidates so I would not waste so much time. Can I hire a local agency at less cost to preselect a few candidates for me?

There are and always will be differences in the quality of the placement service offered by various colleges to employers. The real point is that employers might not be willing to pay a fee for the quality of service offered, and thus a large number of students would be deprived of some excellent opportunities.

Given the administrative problems, it is questionable that charging a fee would produce a net increase in funds for the institution. The savings would likely be minimal compared to the cost in time, money, and goodwill.

Summary

Colleges and universities, public and private, frequently find themselves in a state of fiscal crisis. Inevitably there must be a careful scrutiny of every department and every service offered by the institution, as well as an avid search for new sources of revenues.

It is understandable that career counseling and placement services, along with everything else, must come under this scrutiny. Because some of the activities differ in a formal sense from the teaching and research functions, placement may be viewed as less "educational" and thus may be considered more susceptible to the paring knife.

If the goal of higher education is to help individuals find a fulfilling and satisfying position in society, occupational as well as social, then the placement service must remain an integral part of the educational process. Basic support of the service must be included in the main institutional budget.

The professional resources of a career planning and placement program, including counseling and career information services, should be available to all students at all levels without the imposition of special fees to either the student or the employer. However, fees charged for the setting up and duplication of credentials/resumes or for the mailing of newsletters or job-listing bulletins are in the category of tangential expenses. They may be considered quite apart from the educational services of the placement service. Such fees seem acceptable as long as they reasonably relate to the cost of reproduction and mailing.

A separate "placement office fee" charged to students will have a repressive influence on the career counseling mission of the career service and will appear to deny its broad educational role in higher education.

Fees charged to employers for the "privilege" of visiting campuses to interview students are deleterious to the educational institution. Such fees run the risk of endangering the many cooperative relationships and programs jointly developed over many years.

Fees charged to employers would also be a disservice to students, for the range of on-campus contacts with employers would certainly be limited, if not eliminated. These contacts contribute substantially to the career exploration and career orientation education of students. The educational benefits gained from the employer relationships would be difficult to replace without great expense.

GOVERNMENT FUNDING

Federal government funding of projects supported and administered by career planning and placement services has not been extensive. Although a few projects were funded under the Comprehensive Education and Training Act (CETA), the funding has not been significant on a national level.

The rationale for such lack of federal funding probably relates to the image that college graduates are not a class of "disadvantaged" people. The past few decades have suggested that getting a college degree almost assured one of a job in an attractive career field. When the supply-demand balance started changing in the early Seventies, many people began to question that thesis.

Shift in Concept

Things are changing. One of the factors altering the supply situation is the shift from an elitest concept of education to a mass education approach for higher education. The job market has traditionally followed a cyclical pattern, influenced by the demand for college graduates.

The large, taxpaying middle class of America sends its children to college and then sees them unemployed or underemployed upon graduation. Pressure is being exerted on Congress to support programs that might help remedy the situation.

Until the late Seventies, most of the federal funds for career education went to primary and secondary educational institutions. The Educational Amendments of 1976 did permit some resources to be expended for post-secondary education, but the money was channelled back to the states for administration by the state's department of education. As a result, little money actually found its way to career education at the post-secondary education level. State departments of education have traditionally been vocational education oriented and most of the resources were allocated to these areas.

The Career Education and Incentive Act, Section 11, may be the stimulus needed to obtain federal resources for use by college placement offices. This Act authorizes funding specifically for career education at the post-secondary level. Unlike the Education Amendments of 1976, grants under the Career Education Incentive Act are made directly to institutions for demonstration projects.

The College Placement Council and placement and recruitment personnel throughout the U.S. spent many hours encouraging passage of the Career Education Incentive Act. Numerous obstacles were overcome but, just when money seemed assured, another setback was encountered. Funds for fiscal 1979 were rescinded at the last minute. But CPC has not given up the fight. At this writing, the Council was starting another all-out effort to assure funding for fiscal 1980.

Summary

The legal arena is likely to become a much more potent problem for the placement professional of the future. The College Placement Council must continue to monitor legislation impacting upon the profession, and professionals in the field must continue to feed information to CPC for review and analysis. As a group, placement and recruitment professionals must begin to take an active role in seeking needed legislation and opposing federal encroachment into the field.

On the other hand, federal legislation can also be a source of much-needed funding. Here, too, efforts must be mounted to gain the support required for passage and funding of legislation that will help post-secondary institutions provide better career services programs.

CHAPTER 10

PROFESSIONAL DEVELOPMENT

THE COMPLEXITIES OF career planning and placement demand highly qualified personnel and a commitment to excellence. If higher education is to fulfill its declared mission to educate for life, logically there must be some commitment to counsel students regarding their career interests and employment eventualities. This commitment increases the importance of professional assistance.

The rationale for including a section on professional development in this book relates to the need to draw into a coherent form a wide spectrum of philosophies, concepts, principles, and accepted practices. All of these elements have been in operation in many offices, but until recently few attempts have been made to establish basic standards of excellence for practitioners to follow. Quantifying all of the elements in a qualitative manner should help strengthen the case for viewing career planning and placement as a profession.

Historical Perspective

Over the years, non-classroom programs for students tended to develop in response to directly expressed needs. Thus, in the early 1900s, many colleges started "employment offices," "bureaus of occupations," etc., which were set up by college administrators, alumni leaders, or individual faculty members. The activities and functions of these offices dealt with part-time employment of students while in college and full-time employment upon graduation. Many departments of education established teacher placement bureaus, and a few other departments, such as engineering and the sciences, started placement programs for their students.

During the Fifties, in order to accommodate employers' needs for job candidates, placement officers were appointed to coordinate this activity. Many placement officers functioned as traffic mangers who worked primarily in arranging appointment schedules for employers and graduates. This type of operation still lingers today. However, in the late Sixties and early Seventies, supply and demand conditions in the labor market changed markedly. No longer was a college degree per se a guaranteed entree to the professional, technical, and administrative job market. As a result, career counseling assumed an increasingly important role. The quality of the job placement was given a new and different perspective.

As the lifestyle and role of the placement officer changed from traffic cop to that of a counselor, new programs began to emerge. Concepts and ideas were borrowed from a variety of disciplines such as economics, psychology, sociology, and education. A number of pioneers had been studying occupational structures and the factors which contribute to career choice. In addition to collecting occupational information, many of the early researchers took a close look at qualities of the person as they related to career selection and career success.

The career planning and placement profession began to assume a separate and unique position in the scheme of life in colleges. Leaders drew upon a diverse set of disciplines and ordered the related components of these disciplines into a different, yet highly meaningful, field of inquiry. The most interesting component was the intertwining of theory and actual practice. The theory materialized into an applied behavior which could be directly observed. The study and practice brought results for both students and employers.

As the profession nears the end of the Seventies, no formal statement of standards or universally accepted body of knowledge has been agreed upon. The standards are present and the body of knowledge is defined, but they need to be stated. The necessity for stating and proving that career planning and placement practitioners are part of a profession is at hand. A united front on this issue promises to raise the stature of the profession on the college campus.

If the membership of the College Placement Council and the affiliated regional associations do not take the lead in calling for greater professional development, the profession may not survive the next decade. The field is ripe for free enterprising marketers to move the "employment agency" concept onto the campus. Another alternative is for the U.S. Employment Service to assume the placement role. In budget-tight colleges and universities, the promise of a "freebee" is enticing to faculty, administrators, and legislators. The real losers are likely to be students and employers. Creating a loose federation of professional career planning and placement practioners is a better alternative.

Professional Development Defined

The first chapter laid the groundwork and spelled out many of the elements present in the current body of knowledge. The next step in the profession's evolution is to devise means of teaching the theory, principles, and practices to new generations and to foster the continuing education of current practitioners.

Professional development means growing in the profession.

Growth comes from learning, which implies a planned system of study. The main purpose of this book is to lay out in detail what has been learned to date in order for this knowledge to be shared with others. This sharing of ideas and practices is professional development.

Career planning is a developmental process in the lives of college students. As part of the educational experience, career services must be available during the entire period of the student's academic involvement. These career services include career courses, individual counseling, group counseling, development of decision-making skills, career libraries, career information programs, and initial job placement.

Optimal placement of the student in employment (or further professional preparation) is the prime objective of the career planning process.

Training of Professionals

People learn by reading. With this in mind, over the years, the College Placement Council and the regional associations have prepared hundreds of publications. Several books have been written on various parts of the profession. The *Journal of College Placement* keeps professionals aware of current thinking and new techniques, and the CPC newspaper, *Spotlight*, and the regional association newsletters keep practitioners informed. Hundreds of practioners have written publications and articles designed to share knowledge gained through experience.

Learning also comes from attendance at conferences, seminars, workshops, and other programs where material is provided in both formal and informal settings. CPC, the regional placement groups, and various other organizations sponsor programs throughout the year.

Learning need not come from a text or from attendance at special programs. Experience may well be the best teacher of all. Educational institutions have long acknowledged the educational value of cooperative work-study arrangements, professional internships, and on-the-job training.

Readings, programs, and personal experience form the basis of what is learned over time. Each approach has advantages and limitations. A good professional development program would thus utilize all three modes of sharing information with colleagues and potential colleagues in the profession.

Establishing Levels of Competence

Establishing high initial levels of competence guarantees a higher level of performance by professionals who want to be proud of the type of work they do. Taking pride in one's work and striving for continued excellence are important components of a respected profession. The career planning and placement profession must, therefore, set the highest possible ideals consistent with what is realistically achievable by the practitioners.

Setting standards at a point low enough to appease and accept the largest portion of those desiring membership in a respected profession is absurd. Such a practice guarantees a strong membership base, but it invites mediocrity. It is counter to any profession's claim of excellence.

The primary method of producing quality is to set standards above the average level of the membership's competency and then to invite and challenge everyone to aspire to attain the peak level of performance. Inviting and encouraging everyone to strive for excellence and to achieve professional recognition is the most realistic way of generating acceptance by external, yet very important, university colleagues and other constituencies with which the profession must relate.

In order to evaluate potential entrants into the profession, an evaluation scheme needs to be developed. This must either involve evaluation in courses, seminars, and similar programs, or testing aspirants on the body of knowledge, or both. As is done in earning units of credit to attain an academic degree, the same concept could be applied in earning units to attain competency in the profession. Units could be assigned for various years of experience in various types of work common to the profession. Some "Professional Standards Board" might well be the mechanism to use in setting the levels of accomplishment.

PROFESSIONAL STANDARDS FOR COLLEGE PERSONNEL

In the past few years, two very important publications have been published as a result of the work of the College Placement Council's Professional Standards Committee: "Professional Standards for Career Counseling and Placement Personnel" and "Professional Standards for College Recruitment Personnel and Programs."

For a number of years the Committee focused its attention on the area of certification. A basic assumption underlying its efforts was that one of the distinguishing criteria of fields of professional practice is the availability of programs through which the capability of practitioners can be certified. Traditionally, such certification follows the establishment of professional standards for the field and of a substantial body of literature.

In recent years, certification has become one of the most discussed issues in college placement and recruitment. The concept was reviewed by all seven regional placement associations and analyzed in surveys of members of various associations. And the CPC Board of Regional Governors on several occasions approved the concept developed by the Committee on Professional Standards.

However, just as the certification program was nearing the implementation stage, some snags were encountered. Potential legal problems and tax ramifications became apparent. At its June 1979 meeting, the Board of Regional Governors concluded that the potential legal risks were significant enough to cancel further efforts to introduce a certification program.

In place of certification, the Board decided to expand CPC professional development activities, increasing the number of programs as well as the substantive content. This new approach, the Board felt, will enable CPC to still achieve the goals of the proposed certification program, which centered on improving the professionalism and competence of individuals in career planning and placement.

The Board instructed the Committee on Professional Standards to develop alternatives to replace certification. The objective was to develop a means for recognizing those completing established professional development goals.

All of this happened as this book was about to be printed so further details were unavailable at press time. One point still seemed clear, however. Although the Council had to abandon its plans for certification, the Board of Regional Governors will press with renewed vigor for a program that will provide career planning and placement personnel with the opportunity to upgrade themselves professionally and to receive suitable recognition for successfully completing programs that meet prescribed standards.

Summary

Setting professional standards and guidelines for placement professionals is not always a popular move. The activity is analogous to the professional manager who operates on the principle of management by objectives. What we think we know is occasionally different from what we do know. It seems desirable for the profession to establish and enforce some fair and equitable manner of identifying individuals wishing to practice in the field and use the profession as a mark of excellence.

Accepting national standards and guidelines would not be easy to take for hundreds of competent individuals who have been doing a good job for many years. New approaches invariably generate disagreements. But even disagreements help create a healthy climate because they force the organizations that must develop professional criteria to do a superior task. Mistakes will continue to be made, but gentle and firm pressure helps insure that appropriate guidelines will be set fairly, accurately, and with prudent care and deliberation.

Becoming a recognized professional is a goal to which nearly everyone subscribes. The concept of growing in the profession through continued learning and leadership is also nearly universally accepted. As Theodore Roosevelt once said, "Every man owes some of his time to the upbuilding of the profession in which he belongs."

Accreditation of Career Services

Accreditation of career services implies an evaluation of a given office by a team of peers with a set of acceptable criteria. The concept of accreditation is not unlike that of a regional college accreditation association or the professional school accrediting bodies, such as the American Assembly of Collegiate Schools of Business (AACSB).

When CPC was considering certification, there were some who suggested that the Council undertake accreditation rather than certification. Their contention was that an individual could be certified but still have a poor career planning and placement program because of lack of support from the institution.

The Council, however, believes that a CPC accreditation program would be infeasible for a number of reasons. The most compelling is that college presidents would not be receptive to the idea since the college has to pay for accreditation visits. So many accrediting bodies have been established that the trend is for college administrations to push for a reduction in the number rather than encourage establishment of others for evaluation of specific programs.

A new development occurred at the June 1979 meeting of the CPC Board of Regional Presidents, just before this book went to press. The Board voted to have CPC become actively involved in the development of a Consortium for Accreditation and to have CPC join the Consortium if the final design is consistent with CPC objectives.

The Council was one of eleven student-oriented organizations involved in the initial conceptualization of the Consortium. The Consortium's goal is to develop a program which would provide for training of individuals with expertise in student services to serve on the visitation teams of the regional accrediting organizations. These individuals would concentrate on the evaluation of a campus's student service functions, such as the career planning and placement office.

The motive in evaluating an individual career service is the same as in accrediting academic programs in specific colleges. The goal is to raise and/or maintain quality standards on a consistent and equitable basis across institutions. An accredited career service would meet a universally accepted minimum level of service.

As any recruiter who visits many career service offices knows, there is a wide variation in the quality of the services offered to employers and students. The accrediting team would point out all deviations from an accepted norm. The ensuing report would likely have the impact of encouraging the central administration to garner the finances, people, or other types of resources needed to meet the minimum level of acceptance for accreditation.

If accreditation were to become a reality, the criteria would likely involve staffing, operations, facilities, and budget. A number of appropriate ratios and standards could be produced that relate to these four areas. Throughout this book a wide variety of activities are suggested that should be an integral part of any sound career service. Many of these areas would undoubtedly be used in the evaluation of career services.

PROFESSIONAL STANDARDS FOR EMPLOYERS

Professional development and the setting of guidelines and standards are not limited solely to college personnel. The employer community has always been interested in the continuing education of college relations and recruiting personnel. The need for the background enhancement and training of employer personnel has always been present. As more and more employers developed structured college recruiting programs, it became apparent that some guidelines for recruiters were needed. This led to the development of the "Professional Standards for College Recruitment Personnel and Programs" by the CPC Professional Standards Committee in 1976.

The professional development theme is consistent with the concept of creating an effective college relations program. This brief section attempts to summarize and update what has been written in publications and covered in seminars and workshops. It is designed to give the college placement professional, as well as employers, an overview of the components of college relations from an employer perspective.

Rationale

Finding the right person for the right job has been the goal of employers from time immemorial. The means, techniques, and sources have changed over the years. The type of people being sought has significant impact on the techniques and sources. Since World War II, colleges and universities, via their career planning and placement services, have increasingly become the prime source of talent for professional, technical, and managerial positions.

As more employers developed structured college recruiting programs, some ethical guidelines for recruiting needed to be established. The need became particularly acute when employers found themselves using a variety of approaches in dealing with students, faculty, alumni, and placement staff. Some approaches became contradictory, confusing, and occasionally counter productive. Structure was needed. This led to the development by CPC of a document known as "The Principles and Practices of College Career Planning, Placement, and Recruitment."

The subsequent growth of college recruiting mandated that management develop guidelines for effective organization of college relations and recruitment programs and for effective performance by representatives visiting the campus. The following paragraphs should offer some basic standards for college relations and recruitment which will help employers maximize their recruiting efforts.

Responsibilities of Management

An employing organization first needs to take an overview perspective of the goals and objectives it wishes to achieve with and through the colleges to which it relates. This assumes that the employer is then willing to take responsibility for planning and organizing a system that will most effectively help meet the overall goals.

The development of a short- and long-range human resources program is coordinated with the planned intake and development of college-trained personnel. This planning cycle, complete with numerical objectives by type of position, is reviewed with top management. Provision is then made for the adequate funding of the college recruiting program. To insure a realistic recruiting program, the impact of the economy and the changing needs of the organization need to be assessed on a continuing basis to help minimize fluctuations in the hiring of college graduates.

It is management's responsibility to make adequate provision for the staffing and administration of recruiting programs. The selection of well-qualified and trained personnel to produce continuity in the program helps maintain a smooth working relationship with college personnel. A well-managed recruiting program makes provisions for efficient in-house procedures involving personnel selection, assignment, and development.

Crucial to the total process are the supporting resources used in the recruitment activity, such as recruiting literature, educational support, seminars, faculty and student internships, and other experiential education programs. This might well involve the participation of employers in career education activity. One method of developing the needed relationships with colleges is to actively join and participate, including taking leadership roles, in CPC, the regional associations, and other professional organizations.

Desired Qualifications

Three major qualifications seem especially important for recruiting personnel. They include personal qualities, knowledge of the employing organization, and professional qualifications.

The personal traits and qualities which are desirable for the college recruiting professional include integrity, maturity, poise, decision-making ability, enthusiasm, good interpersonal relations, objectivity, intellectual capacity, empathy, and the ability to communicate freely with individuals and groups from a wide variety of backgrounds.

To be effective, the college recruiting professional must have a thorough knowledge of the employing organization, its industry group, and factors relating to the specific employer as they impact on employment decisions of graduating students. It is imperative that the employer have an industry-wide orientation and an understanding of the organization's competitive environment. The types of information required include a history of the organization, objectives, hiring procedures and policies, employee benefit programs, affirmative action plans, specifics of positions advertised, selection criteria by type of position, and advancement possibilities.

As in any function, several levels of responsibility are likely, including the recruiting manager, school coordinator, field recruiter, and clerical support staff. Most firms require a minimum of one year of personnel-related (management) experience before sending a recruiter to the campus. It is rare for the recruiting manager to have less than three years of personnel related/management experience. Most organizations are committed to professional development and urge attendance at the various professional conferences, institutes, and workshops for personnel directly involved in the recruitment function.

Training of Recruiters

Frequently it is not the recruiting personnel who do the actual interviewing on campus. Line and staff managers often do the campus screening, with the recruiting staff serving as coordinators and trainers. Regardless of who is actually visiting campus, it is important that a certain amount of training be provided.

Every college recruiter should be afforded the opportunity to develop skills and acquire knowledge in a number of critical areas: interviewing skills, evaluative techniques, relating candidate qualifications to job requirements, legal factors, and knowledge of the college placement function. For each specific campus, the recruiter should be aware of recruiting date policies, academic programs, procedures on dissemination of recruiting literature, daily operational procedures, names of key faculty and placement people, EEOC rules on campus, follow-up procedures with students, job offer plans, etc.

Each recruiter should be made aware of the formal and informal programs that the employer has developed over time with the college. The factors that help strengthen the employer-college working relationship cannot be effective if they are not known and followed in the recruitment visit.

College Relations Programs

Another section of this book focuses on the importance of developing a total college relations program from the viewpoint of the employer. This is in direct contrast to visiting a given campus once or twice each year for the sole purpose of recruitment only. A program-oriented approach insures that all of the important details involved in college-employer relations are properly handled.

In setting up a college relations program, provision should be made for campus contacts with faculty and students, local exposure to many audiences, participation in experiential education programs, sharing trend-setting ideas with faculty and placement staff, developing recruitment literature, and evaluating the entire relations program.

Employers have a major role to play in professional development. Learning and growth are not confined solely to college personnel. In addition, there is much to be learned from each other. The learning curve increases much faster when the flow of information passes through a variety of different parties. The communication flow must be represented by employer/faculty/placement/student if true professional development is to occur.

Summary

The subject of professional development must involve nearly every topic covered in this book. This section was intended to bring the reader up-to-date on the general meaning of professional development for both employers and college personnel. Through the literature and through formal and informal meetings, individuals will continue to grow strong in the profession.

PROFESSIONAL PRINCIPLES

Philosophies and principles state the highest ideals and objectives and create the environment in which all professions must act. They form the precepts under which actions by professionals must be made and evaluated.

Guidelines for operation and working practices represent a level below philosophy and principles. Guidelines and practices are accepted modes of operation which the profession believes are most consistent with stated philosophies and principles. The three major participants in the career planning and placement process are employers, college personnel, and career candidates. Each party should be committed to responsible conduct, as outlined in the following material which is adapted from the *Principles and Practices of College Career Planning, Placement, and Recruitment.*

Career Planning

The parties believe that the consideration of careers and the selection of employment opportunities by college students and graduates should be based on an understanding of all relevant facts. The consideration of alternatives by graduating students should be made in an atmosphere conducive to objective thought.

Recruitment

The parties believe that the recruiting of college students and graduates for employment should be carried out by employers, career candidates, and college authorities in a manner that best serves the following principles:

1. *Free Selection.* Candidates should be provided the opportunity for open and free selection of employment alternatives that will provide candidates with the optimum, long-term utilization of their talents, consistent with their personal objectives.

2. *Personal Choice.* Of primary concern is the promotion of intelligent and responsible choices of careers by the candidates for their greatest satisfaction and the most fruitful long-range investment of their talents for themselves, employers, and society.

3. *High Standards.* Of highest priority is the development of the placement function as an integral part of the educational system so that it, as well as the total recruiting process, may be oriented toward the establishment of high standards of integrity and conduct among all parties.

Guidelines

Guidelines need to be established for employees, colleges, and candidates. Guidelines may be differentiated from practices. Guidelines are good faith standards which may be used to evaluate contemplated actions. Practices are accepted operational actions which experience has shown greatly facilitate a smooth working relationship between the interacting groups.

Guidelines for Employers

1. *Direct Representation.* In direct on-campus recruiting an employing organization is best represented by its own personnel. In all other recruiting activities, the employing organization is expected to assume responsibility for all representations made in its name and in accordance with the *Principles and Practices of College Career Planning, Placement and Recruitment.*

2. *Job Information.* The presentation of career job information should be made in a knowledgeable, ethical, and responsible fashion.

3. *Salary Ethics.* Ethical salary administration principles are expected to be followed.

4. *Special Inducements.* Special payments, gifts, bonuses, or other inducements should not be offered.

5. *Employment Conditions.* All conditions of employment, including starting salaries, should be explained clearly to candidates prior to or at the time of the offer of employment.

6. *Reasonable Time.* Reasonable time to consider an offer should be given candidates. In no case should candidates be subjected to undue pressure to make a decision concerning employment.

7. *Honoring Commitments.* An employment offer should be made in good faith with sincere intention to honor the commitment.

8. *Preferential Service.* Preferential service should not be requested of any college placement office.

9. *Offer Confidentiality.* Individual salary offers made by other employers should not be solicited by an employer.

Guidelines for Colleges

1. *Freedom of Choice.* The candidate's freedom of choice in the selection of a career or a position should be protected from undue influence by faculty and placement staff.

2. *Pertinent Information.* Pertinent information should be made available to employers by the placement office.

3. *Offer Confidentiality.* Salary offers made to an individual by an employer should not be divulged to other employers.

4. *Referral.* Referral of an employed graduate must be preceded by that person's request for active status.

5. *Preferential Service.* Preferential service should not be extended to employers.

6. *Communication.* Communication and exchange of information among employers, students, faculty members, and administrators should be fostered. However, an employer should not be required to present and defend a corporate position before college and university groups as a condition for recruiting on campus.

Guidelines for Candidates

1. *Honesty.* Both written and oral material presented by a candidate should be an honest statement of relevant data.

2. *Expense Reimbursement.* Reimbursement for visits at an employer's expense should be only for those expenditures pertinent to the trip. If other employers are visited on the same trip, the cost should be prorated.

3. *Employer Deadlines.* The employer's deadline for acceptance of offers of employment should be met unless an extension has been obtained from the employer.

4. *Honoring Commitments.* Acceptance of an employment offer should be made in good faith and with sincere intention to honor the commitment.

Sanctions for Violations

Colleges and Employers. In cases referred to the regional association committee, and after due notice and opportunity to be heard in accordance with the procedures set forth in the Bylaws of the College Placement Council, any necessary reprimand may include:

1. A warning.

2. Forfeiture or denial of membership in the regional association.

3. Notification to the College Placement Council.

Job Candidates. A complaint against a candidate involving a breach of ethical conduct in these matters should be made directly to the placement officer concerned. Sanctions, if required, should be as prescribed by that candidate's college or university. The placement officer should advise the employer registering the complaint of the disposition of the case.

Procedures

Breach of accepted guidelines constitutes a major deviation from standards set by the profession. Failure to adhere to guidelines demands remedial action and imposition of strict sanctions upon violators. Recommended operational procedures represent quality standards to which all parties should aspire or attempt to follow. In some instances, because of constraints imposed upon the parties and over which they have little or no control, little can be done to adhere strictly to recommend procedures. These constraints may relate to financial, facility, or staff limitations or to internal organizational policies.

Procedures for Employers

1. *Early Recruiting Dates.* Desired interview dates, broad categories of employment expected to be available, college degrees, and other pertinent information should be given to the placement office well in advance. Any change in the original request should be communicated promptly.

2. *Interview Schedules.* Interview schedules must be arranged with the placement office. Every effort should be made to avoid changes that require prior notification of all for whom appointments have been made.

3. *Parent/Subsidiary.* When both the parent organization and subsidiary or affiliated organization conduct interviews at the same college, an explanation of their missions and exact affiliation should be made both to career planning and placement staff and to candidates.

4. *Schedule Adherence.* Interview time schedules agreed upon should be adhered to.

5. *Number of Interviewers.* The number of interviewers brought on campus by an employer should be adequate to cover the pre-arranged schedule.

6. *Selected Candidates.* If an interview is desired with a particular candidate, the employer should request the candidate to sign up on the placement office interview schedule.

7. *Class Schedules.* Candidates' visits to employers' premises should be arranged to interfere as little as possible with class schedules. Details of such visits should be carefully explained to the candidate.

8. *Communications.* Following an interview, employers

should communicate with both candidates and career planning and placement offices concerning the outcome of interviews and subsequent negotiations.

9. *Excessive Demands.* Representatives of an employer, including graduates of the college, should not make excessive demands on the time of faculty, administration, or candidates.

10. *Principles.* Employers and their recruitment representatives should be acquainted with and abide by the *Principles and Practices of College Career Planning, Placement and Recruitment.*

Procedures for Colleges

1. *Career Counseling.* Competent career counseling and other assistance to aid candidates in reaching career decisions should be available.

2. *Employment Literature.* Career literature and employment material should be made available to candidates and faculty members.

3. *Informing Employers.* As soon as information is available, employers should be informed about graduation dates, the number of students who are candidates for degrees in the various curricula of the college, and other pertinent information.

4. *Employer Visit Announcement.* As early as practicable, the names of employers and the dates on which they will be recruiting on campus should be announced. Announcements should be made later to incorporate subsequent changes.

5. *Unrestricted Interviews.* The number of interviews per candidate should not be restricted.

6. *Adequate Facilities.* Adequate space and facilities for quiet and private interviews should be provided.

7. *Candidate Files.* Candidates should be urged to file resumes and/or related placement material in the career planning and placement office. Such materials shall be maintained in accordance with the rules and regulations concerning confidentiality of records and shall be released in accordance with the directions of the candidate.

8. *Faculty Arrangements.* Arrangements for an employer to meet with faculty and staff should be made at the employer's request.

9. *Specific Qualifications.* Specific qualifications requested by the employer should be observed in the scheduling of interviews.

10. *Schedule Feedback.* Information concerning the schedule of interviews should be given the employer as soon as practicable.

11. *Principles.* Career planning and placement staff and any college personnel involved in career planning and placement of candidates should be acquainted with and abide by the *Principles and Practices of College Career Planning, Placement, and Recruitment.*

Procedures for Candidates

1. *Interview Preparation.* In preparation for interviews with prospective employers, candidates should analyze their interests and abilities, consider their career objectives, seek information about the fields of their interest through published materials and counseling, and organize their thoughts so that they may ask and answer questions intelligently.

2. *Procedures.* Before an interview, candidates should read the employer's materials and fill out such forms as may be required. The candidate should observe recommended procedures as to interviews.

3. *Interview Appointments.* Interview appointments should be arranged as early as practicable and in accordance with the career planning and placement office's procedures. Necessary cancellations should be made in keeping with that office's procedures.

4. *Employer Visits.* An invitation to visit an employer's premises should be acknowledged promptly and should be accepted only when there is a sincere interest in a position with that employer. Arrangements should be made sufficiently in advance to permit mutual confirmation of dates.

5. *Employment Decisions.* Decisions concerning employment and terms of employment where practicable should be communicated to the career planning and placement office.

Summary

The philosophy and principles of career planning and placement remain the controlling factors that influence decisions by employers, candidates, and college personnel. They form the basis upon which moral and ethical questions can be resolved. Specific practices, techniques, and methods serve to guide practitioners in the profession but do not limit the scope of operation.

Professional organizations succeed only if members agree on some basic common bonds. Principles represent uniting forces. Principles define rules of conduct based on universally accepted truths which serve as motivating forces designed to provide adherence and integrity. Principles emerge after establishment of a sound philosophy base. Principles are basic agreements among professionals that serve as a guide to ethical practice. Principles are a step beyond any outside constraints imposed by legal or social regulations.

CHAPTER 11

ROLE OF EMPLOYERS IN PLACEMENT

EMPLOYERS PLAY a significant role in the career planning process, and the involvement generates enormously positive relationships between employers and colleges which serve the interests of all parties. The placement function bridges what could be (and is in some countries) a major gap in effective communications between several influential groups in society. Placement's role in creating a mutually satisfying working relationship is of no minor consequence nor is it an accident.

Most major employers of college graduates recognize and accept an obligation and responsibility to colleges and universities. Interconnected motives encourage the groups to work together in a partnership arrangement. As in any partnership, the binding glue is mutual trust, respect, and understanding. Common concerns come naturally, but building a strong relationship takes work by everyone involved.

Creating and developing a working arrangement that will serve all parties involves selling. The marketing function requires competition and satisfaction of needs and goals by all participants. Compromise mediates disputes and misunderstanding, but compromise is possible only if communication is present. Communication opens the door that permits the parties to hear each other's position and point of view. Placement is the facilitator that keeps the channels of communication open.

Selling is based on communication. Effective communication spins a web of information that tends to interrelate common motives and binds together mutual interests. The information from effective and efficient communications creates a desire to serve each other.

Who are the principal actors involved in this free flow of information? What motivates the parties? What benefits accrue? How do the participants get involved? What forces moderate excessive zeal? The answers form the basis of this presentation.

Interchange of Information

The three principal groups of participants are colleges, students, and employers. The top chart on page 301 illustrates the complicated flow of information among the participants. Common sense suggests that these channels face the possibility of interference that impedes and perhaps destroys the intelligent comprehension of the transmission. The bottom chart shows how the placement office can serve as the hub for facilitating the interchange of information.

The picture is not as simple as the illustration suggests. Complications set in as more and more broadcasters enter the picture, as depicted in the chart on page 302. On each college campus, the broadcasters include faculty, administrators, academic counselors, career counselors, organized activity leaders, institute heads, auxiliary enterprise directors, alumni, fund raisers, etc. Each campus may have several hundred people throwing information at students, employers, and each other.

Employers offer the same type of communications explosion. The employer broadcasters include college relations staff, per-

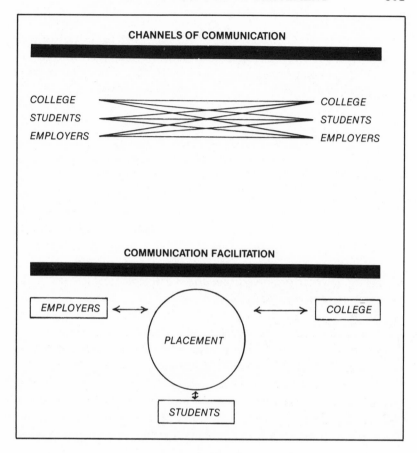

sonnel managers, employees in various professions, positions, or plants, alumni of a given college, sales representatives, foundation administrators, top management, etc. Employers may be represented by hundreds of industries, government agencies, educational institutions, and non-profit organizations. Each of these employment sectors may have over a hundred different employers attempting to pass information.

Students also get into the act. A thirst for career-related information and a desire for career employment exist on campus. Often scores of student groups and approved academic, profes-

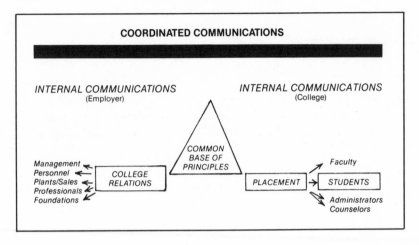

sional, and social organizations enter into the business of communicators utilizing various programs. The magnitude of the communication problems staggers the imagination when one considers that there are over seven million college students.

Obviously, room exists for false information, half truths, incomplete facts, garbled information, etc. An array of problems faces the profession if some help is not offered to organize the communication networks. No attempt to take over or control the channels by any one professional group can or should succeed. But, there is room for considerable improvement that would benefit all parties involved.

The college placement profession, including employers and colleges, must assume some responsibility for moderating the information explosion. Although the basic function of the college placement office may remain career planning oriented and the employer college relations staff may remain recruitment oriented, both groups need to recognize the importance of expanding their horizons beyond the immediacy of the hour. The long-term results of broader horizons will impact and influence the short-term goals of both colleges and employers.

Planning, organization, and management form the basis of effective communication. The audience is clear. The need is real. The college-employer role as partners translates into reality only if each participant understands the goals, organization, and hopes of each other. The bridge is built on the commonly accepted principles and practices of the professional organization which serves as the foundation.

College Benefits

Career Planning. The major benefit of the interchange of ideas between employers and colleges is the realistic element it brings to the career planning function. The career information available to students greatly aids in the career decision process as the information expands alternatives and refines tentative choices. Career information permits a real-world appraisal of the self-concept which, when combined with further career choice specification in the career search activity, produces optimal career decisions.

A definitive statement of short- and long-term career goals leads to successful placement and starts the graduate on the road to a productive, fruitful career. The career information aids the career planning learning process that allows for periodic review, reevaluation, and later redefinition of aspirations, if desired. A major goal of the college career planning and placement function is to provide the maximum amount of realistic career information possible and to assist in guiding the career planning process in a direction that best satisfies the needs of students and graduates. Employer participation greatly assists in career planning.

Academic Reputation. Academic institutions in higher education gain reputations from a variety of sources and through different methods. Important variables include a quality faculty, superior facilities, excellent financial resources, an intelligent student body, well designed curriculums and programs, a supportive alumni base, etc. Clearly, these variables are interrelated, for it is difficult to have one variable without the others. One measure of success is short-and-long-term employment of graduates. As a rule, unemployed, non-productive graduates do not enhance an institution's reputation. Graduates who consistently fail to function successfully in our society probably detract from an institution's reputation as a trainer of responsible people.

Institutions want to see graduates gaining rapidly in upward mobility, which is usually correlated with higher earnings, the traditional measure of success in our society. An equally important yardstick of success is job satisfaction even though it is much more difficult to measure.

Successful alumni enhance the reputation of institutions of higher learning. University leaders often point to examples of prominent alumni when citing the merits of their institution. University leaders also call attention to the fact that a high percentage of the graduating class found employment quickly upon graduation. Universities want and need a strong cadre of successful alumni.

Colleges have a major stake in placement. Often, the initial position greatly influences upward mobility. The college that effectively educates graduates and then hopes that the candidate will find the right niche without help is analogous to the graduate who goes to college taking all the right courses but fails to incorporate realistic career planning into the academic program. Colleges that rely on happenstance for graduates to find the proper initial job abdicate important educational responsibilities.

There is a considerable merit in teaching students how to help themselves in finding rewarding, career-related assignments after college. Halting career planning at that stage, however, is a cop-out. Every experienced placement professional knows that the most successful entry-level assignments are obtained through the use of "contacts." A job candidate may obtain employment through use of a personal contact, public contact (third party), or a college-related contact. College-related contacts include faculty, administrators, alumni, or the placement service. Candidates finding employment through the use of a college-related contact have a much higher probability of loyalty, be it service or financial, to the institution.

Developing college-related contacts is time-consuming, expensive, and hard work by dedicated faculty and staff. Attempts to evaluate the costs versus the returns seem impossible; but the universities with the highest national, even international, reputations have consistently supported the activity. Who is to say that the results relate to the initial placement efforts? The decision to move into this arena must be made on a gut-feel or non-cost/benefit analysis.

Institutional reputation correlates with success of alumni. A prudent course of action demands some direct assistance for students in the employment process. The level or extent of that assistance is judgmental by institutions. From the point of view of the career planning and placement professional, career planning is an integral part of the educational program. Participation in a professionally guided career search is an important element of the total learning process.

Successful initial placement of graduating students requires contacts with potential employers. If one assumes that the reputation of an institution as a trainer of productive citizens is related to the success of past graduates, colleges have much to gain in creating, developing, and maintaining positive working relationships with employers.

Revenue Source. Colleges recognize that much financial support, directly and indirectly, comes from employers of their graduates. Many of the funds received by colleges are provided without strings attached, and seemingly for altruistic reasons, by foundations, business firms, and governmental programs. These gifts signify an interest in producing a generation of talented employees for business, government, education, and the professions.

Regardless of the employment sector, employers serve as a primary or secondary source of financial resources. In an age of tighter and tighter budgets, education needs these resources. It seems logical that colleges should strive for development of joint working relationships.

External revenue sources provide funds for scholarships, fellowships, research efforts, buildings, salaries, and many other budgetary items. Without these sources, many of the items would be impossible or would have to be funded at a greatly reduced level. Private resources often provide the margin of excellence that moves a public institution to a position of prominence.

A major revenue source is alumni. Not only are prominent alumni important for large personal contributions but the influence alumni can have on a major organization often is significant. A high-ranking alumnus in an organization may have the clout to direct a substantial portion of the organization's resources to a college. Many employers offer a major benefit program to salaried personnel in which the employer will match the contributions made by employees to their alma maters.

Almost no institution operates on a set of fee charges to students that pays the entire cost of education. Tuition receipts make up only a portion of the total educational budget. Gifts, grants, church donations, and tax monies provide the remainder. The development effort for additional support grows annually at most institutions of higher education.

Colleges need the financial resources from outside gifts. Since the primary product of colleges is trained personnel, it is in a college's best interest to develop a close working relationship with employers, even if this sounds somewhat crass to many college faculty members. The placement function offers the college a source of external contacts. Placement is the interface for two groups of people that can and should be working together.

Cooperative Research. One criticism of research conducted by colleges is that it is done in a sterile environment devoid of real environmental limitations and constraints. To be sure, some research which is not related to a product must be handled in such an environment simply to satisfy thirst for expansion of knowledge. Government and education are willing to fund such experiments. Other research, physical and social, may be undertaken in a cooperative spirit between college faculty and professionals in business and government.

Joint support is possible and perhaps preferable. University goals may well be furthered by fostering cooperative research efforts. Precedent exists. One of the forces that could be influential in bringing interested parties—colleges and employers—together is the college placement operation.

Consulting. Keeping faculty current requires a constant training process, particularly in the technical disciplines. Faculty members are a highly motivated group of individuals who continually desire to remain on the thresholds of knowledge within their discipline. One significant means used by faculty members is consulting. Consulting with outside organizations creates a high level of practical, application knowledge and reinforces the motivation to excel.

Consulting is a two-way street. Faculty and outside organizations learn from each other. Sabbatical leaves and time off for consulting permit this flexibility. Consulting is a rather inexpensive method for faculty to receive training and retraining in their specialities. Consulting also serves as a source of revenue for talented scholars who might otherwise leave the institution for greater monetary opportunities.

Consulting can be facilitated by a forward-thinking placement operation. Placement officers who know the faculty members, are in a position to assist employers who inquire about a given expertise. Placement can and should act as a referral and coordinating function.

Summary

The college gains significant benefits by offering a placement program that serves as an important interface with employers.

The benefits to the institution include assistance in career planning, nurturing a strong institutional reputation, fostering cooperative joint research projects, and encouraging consulting. Although there are several other related benefits, these alone should motivate colleges to desire a working relationship with employers. There are many entrees into the non-college environment, but the placement function is one of the most strategically centered.

Student Benefits

Employment. The greatest beneficiary in a close employer-college working relationship is the student. Appropriate contacts play an influential role in finding the initial job after college that most closely matches current career interests. Employer presence in the campus scene offers the most effective communication possible—the one-on-one relationship. The employer-on-campus concept extends well past the on-campus interview situation and involves off-campus interfaces as part of an educational experience.

One of the strongest loyalty-creating activities that a college can render is to take part in the successful career search process of a graduating student. The first job after college often influences work attitudes more than anything else. Alumni seldom forget the first experience at finding a career assignment and the learning that takes place in the initial entry-level assignment. A strong impression remains throughout life.

The placement office traditionally gets the recognition for bringing the employer together with the student, but frequently a faculty member, counselor, or administrator really deserves the credit. Sometimes it is the design of a curriculum or class project that brings the employer and student together. Regardless of the source, the important thing is the result which materialized because of a close tie between college and employer. Permitting the college to earn credit for the contact is most important. Student employment is the outcome of good college-employer relations.

Realistic Career Planning. Students may not accept employment through a college-employer contact and yet the experiences gained in the cooperative work-study environment may impact greatly on the student's career planning. Relationships with employers fostered by the college provide a needed realism in the decision on career choice. Conversations, lectures, and work activities add significantly to career information. This information is a major variable that alters or reinforces career plans. Students gain this information when they work and study in a climate that generates open communication between employers and colleges.

Upward Mobility. Another benefit gained by students studying in a mutually receptive college-employer relationship is that it may enhance upward mobility. A program designed with employer-college arrangements in mind shows students various career alternatives. Deadend jobs abound. People do get locked into career niches. College-employer interaction engenders a high level of career awareness that enables observance of career pitfalls and shows ways to avoid such obstacles.

Upward mobility results from performance on the job. Higher levels of performance are possible if people understand the what, why, and how of each assignment. The answer to these inquiries often stems from career awareness which is fostered by close working relationships. The placement function can pave the way for these needed relationships.

One side benefit to good college-employer relations not often recognized by students is an equitable starting salary. Many factors go into determining appropriate salary offers and, without an open market, the tendency would be for employers to pay less than they currently do. Widely published averages by degree and curriculum become the base for the salary offer. Starting salaries fall into a much narrower range and, hence, realistic expectations are developed for the first job after college.

Summary

A strong placement function that effectively interfaces with potential employers brings important benefits to graduating students. The unemployment rate among college graduates would probably be much higher without a strong placement profession that links academia and the job market. An understanding between colleges and employers impacts positively upon realistic career planning, upward mobility, and fair compensation packages. Students can only gain from a free-functioning career planning program that builds strong ties between colleges and employers.

Employer Benefits

Private and public employers gain many advantages not otherwise available when they join in a cooperative and open flow of communication with colleges. Positive working relationships lead to significantly lower costs for employers in many areas of their organizations and impact upon their image and long-term personnel resources. It is in the best interest of business and government organizations to develop, build, and maintain close ties with the nation's college campuses.

Employment. Without question, the greatest benefit is the employment of college graduates. Every organization requires employees to work in professional, technical, or managerial assignments. Managers, engineers, scientists, health professionals, etc. come from colleges, and few organizations can survive long without highly qualified and trained personnel. Organizations can be no stronger than the people that make up the work force at the managerial and technical levels. This one factor alone—employment—could well be the sole reason for employers to develop close ties with colleges, but there are many other reasons as well.

Hiring graduating students for full-time professional positions is not the only type of employment that employers typically seek from the campus, although that may be the prime motivating force. Many employers hire cooperative education and professional-practice interns as paraprofessionals who are able to make contributions to the organization's goals and who may likely return to the employer for full-time employment upon graduation. Employers find the maturity and intelligence of college students and their desire to work hard to be of great value in part-time jobs and as extra help in the summer months.

Placement directors occasionally are asked by potential employers why they should recruit on college campuses and what advantages they will realize from developing strong ties to the college. Some of the more common replies include:

1. *Superior Quality.* The goal of every employer should be to have the highest quality employees as possible, given the constraints under which they operate. Accepting that premise, most employers recognize that most of the top-ranked high school students go on to attend college. Strong colleges with sound academic programs turn the top talent into superior trained individuals in a wide range of career interests. The superior college graduate who is in the top of the graduating class, based on whatever variables (grades, leadership, personality, etc.), does not normally contact employers. Even in periods of slack economic activity, the top graduates are recruited. Competition for superior graduates can be keen.

This competition for talent is a healthy phenomenon, and it moves employers to strive for a higher level of meaningful relations with college personnel. Good things happen when people begin to talk to each other and develop mutual understandings.

Fortunately, from the college's perspective, the qualities that go into creating the superior college graduate vary greatly. Hundreds of variables and qualities form the unique background of graduating students, making the combinations almost limitless. Few employers place emphasis on the same factors or on only one or two factors such as grades or activities. In the end, hundreds of employers walk away from campus with the feeling that they recruited the best qualified candidates available for the jobs available.

If the colleges meet their responsibilities, all graduates will possess the ability to successfully handle employment assignments. The colleges have a monopoly in a sense because their is no other source offering the level of superior talent to which employers can turn.

2. *Reasonable Quantity.* The number of college students receiving degrees each year increased annually from the Fifties through the Seventies. The two principal factors were the baby boom after World War II and the fact that a higher percentage of college-age youths elected to attend college. Although enrollments may reach a plateau in the next decade, the number of college graduates available for employment will remain over one million per year.

There is no other source to which employers can turn to find potential employees in such numbers. The Department of Labor estimates that over one million new, college-trained individuals will be needed annually in the work force. If that estimate is correct, employers have few other major alternatives. They can promote and upgrade a few employees within and pirate experienced personnel from others, but these are very temporary solutions.

Some might argue that the colleges fail to turn out graduates with the proper academic mix. To be sure, there will be years when there is a shortage of engineers and business majors and an oversupply of history majors. The point is that employers need the best talent available and, if special skills are not available, employers will still hire the best available and develop the special skills where possible.

As long as society remains free, students have a choice of academic fields to study. Colleges cannot pigeonhole students into fields for which they have little inclination. The career planning specialist may lay out the alternatives, but the final choice remains free. As discussed later, employers can influence choice and, therefore, alter the mix with the help of the placement professional. Employers, however, must turn to the colleges to produce the talent needed in reasonable quantities because employers do not have the resources or the expertise to venture into the business of education.

A few employers will wait for students to walk in to apply for jobs, but because of competition the top half of the class will not use this employment approach. No employer likes to think about hiring only someone else's castoffs. Pirating experienced employees only creates musical chairs as it does not bring new personnel into the needed professions. The employer's logical solution is to turn to the college campus for talent and there the employer will discover that success really means a commitment to a sound college-employer relations program rather than a one-shot gamble at recruiting.

3. *Reliable Supply.* The lifeblood of an organization is people. People make organizations successful, not raw materials or other natural resources. The supply line for materials, natural resources, energy, and capital occasionally runs dry. Recent history suggests that the supply of college graduates is a stable resource, one that is consistently available. Even the mix is reliable and readily predictable within a reasonable planning cycle.

Other sources of candidates seldom offer the same stability. Write-ins, walk-ins, advertisements, referrals, agencies, etc. just are not reliable on a consistent basis. In the short run, other sources of job candidates may produce results, but few employers want to gamble with a resource that has such a major impact upon the results of their efforts.

Counting on a reliable supply of college graduates requires a commitment from employers, often at high levels. Effective college relations is not a sometimes thing. More often than not, reliance on college graduates means the institution of internal human resource development programs which are designed to train personnel and guide their career progressions as part of an internal career planning program. Major reliance on a promote-from-within concept becomes an integral part of the development program.

The more successful organizations tend to be those who rely on time-tested approaches supplemented with an environment conducive to innovation. College-employer relations are built on a sound, reliable base but occasionally require some new wrinkles.

4. *Moderate Cost.* College recruiting, whether on campus or by referral, is a free service to employers. Obviously, there are expenses associated with a college relations program. However, a number of studies have shown that college relations is the most economical approach to personnel acquisition. Employers must develop a personalized estimate of their current college relations and recruiting costs based upon their unique requirements. A program need not be centralized but frequently it is. Most employers use line managers or local personnel for recruiting and coordinate activities centrally. The campus contact tends to remain constant year after year as strong relations develop. Often the additional out-of-pocket costs are extremely low in comparison to all other forms of recruitment.

5. *Salary Stability.* A major advantage to employers in developing strong college ties is the entry-level salary stability that it builds into compensation schedules. Salary ranges and averages are available by degree level, academic major, and industry, and the spread rarely varies significantly. The salary stability that has matured over the years has almost removed the variable of salary as a factor for consideration by graduates when evaluating two or more career possibilities.

Recent salary increases for college graduates have been increasing at about the rate of inflation with only minor exceptions. Obtaining human resources, particularly experienced personnel through other means often produces compression in the compensation plan and creates dissension among current employees.

This salary stability results from a close working relationship between colleges and employers. Salary information is open and shared between students and employers, although individual offers still remain confidential. Publication of ranges produces a more realistic appraisal of career advancement and salary expectations by students. It has also eliminated much of the bargaining and jockeying for position that often accompanies the hiring of a new employee. Joint understandings between college and employer personnel represent another of the benefits available to employers.

6. *Consistent Practices.* Colleges, students, and employers benefit from an approach to employment built upon a system that calls for relatively uniform practices and procedures on all campuses based upon a set of mutually acceptable principles. This type of system offers structure, organization, and lower costs to all parties.

Individual differences in procedures among employers pose few problems to college personnel or students. This was not always true. The common denominator is the professional organization that monitors and encourages cooperation. This consistency and reliability is not always available in other sources of employment.

7. *Sanctions.* The reason that the system of college-employer relations works is because each party has accepted the responsibility to be disciplined for inappropriate actions. A censoring letter to a chief executive officer of a college or employer from a professional organization carries clout. As a result, the need to use the club is rare, but it produces a strong motive for everyone in the process to insure fairness, equality, honesty, and adherence to an accepted code of principles and standards.

The rationale for employers to participate in a program of college-employer relations for employment reasons is formidable. The benefits accruing to employing organizations far outweigh the disadvantages and costs. It makes good economic and social sense to join together with colleges in working relationships.

The employer who views employment as the sole reason for cooperating with universities overlooks an enormous set of returns for a minor investment in time and money. The dividends cannot always be measured in the number of people hired, but the results nonetheless can be extremely positive for the employing organization. Throughout this book, and particularly in the following sections, a number of the benefits are discussed.

Decision-Making Input. Employers can and should have some input into the various decisions on a college campus that influence the attitude and talents of the graduates. This is not to suggest that employers should make decisions for faculty and administrators who happen to be much closer to the scene. Employers may, however, voice opinions on certain topics that may be one of the variables that educators will consider before making decisions.

Everyone complains that colleges do not listen to their ideas. Faculty, department heads, librarians, counselors, employers, etc. feel that no means exist for entering their opinions into the system. Mechanisms need to be created to permit a free flow of communication. Leaders can solicit ideas, but rarely do more than a handful of constructive suggestions emerge.

Employers occasionally complain about poorly designed curriculums and students with unrealistic attitudes. The only way the problem can be resolved is to quit complaining and take action. The action can take several forms, but changes come slowly until the employer gains the respect and friendship of educational leaders. Respect is gained only after dialogues and an understanding of mutual concerns. Communication cannot start until someone takes the initiative to bring the parties together.

Bringing people together is an involved process that takes time to develop. Effective college and employer working arrangements rarely occur in a one- or two-year period of time. Basic changes in education often take several years. A later part of this chapter discusses many of the specific methods used in developing and nurturing a relationship. The process obviously must involve methods that bring employer representatives at various levels into the academic environment and encourage educators to move into the employer's environment. Effective communications emerge when the parties involved understand the problems and concerns of each other.

Employer input into the decision-making process results from a planned and well-managed program of college relations. The interface on the campus is often the placement office, but the placement function serves as a facilitator rather than the orchestra conductor.

Image Development. Few employers overlook the importance of a sound public relations program. Employers of college graduates, whether public or private concerns, want customers, clients, and others to feel that the organization is interested in the direction of society. The future leaders of society are college students. Employers must influence that group of potential leaders if their organization is to succeed in the long run.

To an educated student body, a good public relations program is not a lot of words. It is action. It is contribution. It is deeds. It is visibility. It is concern. During the recession of the Seventies, a few employers, for public relations purposes, sent college recruiters to recruit students for jobs that did not exist. As the reject letters flowed into students' hands, the employer's black eye kept getting bigger. College relations are not only college recruiting. College relations rest on a foundation much stronger than a function that comes and goes with the economic winds.

From an employer's perspective, college relations and public relations may be bed partners. From a student and college perspective, college relations translates into an action program designed to assist the college in satisfying its educational mission. There is a happy medium where both points of view can be tolerated as long as the goals of all parties have a decent chance for being satisfied. A joint program, worked out in an atmosphere of harmony and mutual concern, is possible and in the best interest of all parties.

Research and Consulting Assistance. Employers benefit from programs that bring students, faculty, administrators, and employer personnel together in cooperative arrangements. Working with each other increases mutual understanding among all parties, especially if the efforts are directed toward a realistic, productive goal.

Consulting arrangements bring faculty into public and private organizations for the central purpose of helping solve a given problem. Often the ramifications become more important than the expressed goal. The educator takes back to campus an experience that may be shared with other faculty members and students many times over. Students involved in the consulting effort learn more about their career plans and share this information with others on the campus. The employer's personnel directly associated with the project gain fresh ideas which, in turn, get passed throughout their sphere of influence.

Research and consulting activities may influence the direction of both organizations, and the impact from cooperative arrangements may be felt for several years. To gain this type of experience, employers must foster working relationships with college leaders.

Aid to Education. Corporations, foundations, and government organizations give large sums of financial resources to education to assist in the teaching, research, and service missions of the educational process. This support—whether in the form of grants, scholarships, equipment, personnel—appears to be headed into directions where the outcome produces benefits for both society and the donor, directly or indirectly. The potential resources at the disposal of educational institutions are huge and may represent a significant part of operating budgets.

Some organizations question the use of these often unrestricted grants. The future may see funds moving into directions that relate closer to the goals of the donating organization. The gift cannot and must not be *quid pro quo*, but funds can be directed to programs that increase the quality and quantity of selected academic curriculums or address special social goals, including sound career planning.

The career planning and placement profession may be the

intermediary between donors and recipients. An employer's college relations program may have significant input into the dispositions of corporate contributions or those of a related foundation, and the interfacing placement function may well play a leading role in the development and receipt of financial contributions. An effective college-employer communications effort permits the parties to understand each other's wishes and desires.

Because a student should not be influenced to accept employment with contributing organizations, special arrangements need to be worked out on each campus. The placement officer cannot become the principal fund raiser of an educational organization. Nonetheless, the service provided by the placement function may well influence receipt of outside contributions. As such, it is imperative that the placement professional exhibit an attitude of supportive and yet reserved involvement.

Organizations Involved

The creation of partnership arrangements between employers and colleges is not the sole domain of the large universities or business and technical colleges. All colleges share in the concept although there may be individual differences among colleges. The employer may not be the large corporate organization or the federal government agency. City colleges, community colleges, state universities, private universities, liberal arts institutions, teachers colleges, technical institutions—regardless of size—have an important stake in good college-employer relations. The employer may be a small local business, state and local government agencies, nonprofit organizations, subsidiaries or divisions of large corporations, retail establishments, professional groups, or financial institutions. Regardless of the size or type of organization, a college relations function is essential. After all, people make organizations and institutions. People must communicate.

What constitutes a good college-employer relationship?

What are the components of a program? How do the parties organize? What does involvement mean? The first point to recognize is that one college cannot serve all employers and one employer cannot serve all colleges. The clientele must be narrowed to manageable proportions. One university may interface with 700 employers while another concentrates on 25. One employer may work with over 300 colleges while another may narrow the scope to only 10. Each college and employer needs to define its objectives and develop an appropriately sized clientele.

No quick and dirty answers exist to the questions posed. Some methods that colleges and employers have used in the past might serve as ideas for creation of a program uniquely suited for a given organization. Either party may take the initiative in implementing any of the activities.

College Recruiting

College recruiting is one of the most important activities because of its ability to get all of the interested parties communicating. College recruiting is visible, positive, and productive for everyone. Even students who do not receive job offers learn from the process, particularly if feedback is given by a placement professional. Students learn from both the interview and counseling sessions which add importantly to the student's education. An initial contact is reached by the college and the employer and this may be used as a starting point for other interactions.

College recruiting is not a substitute for college relations, and recruiting is not an extremely useful method on every college campus. College recruiting is not effective in obtaining the best job candidates on some campuses for a variety of reasons, including a desire for students to stay in the area, student interest in graduate study, limited number of applicants in a given field, or even a lack of emphasis by faculty and counselors on the on-campus interview method of obtaining employment. On the other hand, recruiting can be extremely effective. In either event, the college relations function needs a much deeper root than does college recruiting.

Referrals

A high percentage of college graduates find employment by being referred to a given employer by faculty, counselors, placement staff, or other college personnel. Referrals result from previous contact between college and employer personnel. The referral could be from an employee or department, not necessarily from a college relations staff member.

Referrals are most effective if the two parties know each other well. Creating the environment for college personnel and employer personnel to get to know each other often falls on the college placement staff and the personnel staff of the employer. Because of the large number of people involved on both sides, no one person or department should have total or sole responsibility for referrals, but control and coordination aid the referral process greatly.

Cooperative Education

Career planning and placement is part of the total education process. One of the most important ways to carry this concept forward is to involve the employer in the educational process. Cooperative education alternates study with work. The work gives the student an opportunity to test the career choice with reality before making the final career choice. The study phase allows the student to bring realism into the classroom and begin to integrate the two environments. The realism permits other students not in the work-study program to share in some of the benefits of the arrangement.

Cooperative education offers financial aid to the student. Often this may be the only way some students can obtain a college degree. The students usually earn their keep within the organization by providing a productive skill to the employer. The arrangement gives the employer a look at what is happening on campus, a chance to evaluate the student for long-term potential, and a competitive recruiting edge on the best qualified students.

Internships

An internship provides experience for a student at the facilities of an employer in the profession for which the student is being trained. Internships normally last for a complete term and may be taken any time during the year. Most colleges encourage internship during the junior or senior years of college. College credit is often awarded.

Many educational experts believe that internships should be taken by all college students. In the career planning process, internships provide the needed exposure to the world of work, something which can only be talked about in the classroom. The work experience provides testing of the career choice and permits a re-evaluation of that test before final commitments are made.

Internships place employers in the educational process and facilitate the development of communication with college personnel.

Extern Programs

Externships represent another type of experiential learning in which employers play a major role. The concept is to allow a student to gain exposure to a given career by observing and discussing the role with people currently employed in the field. Alumni of colleges frequently participate in these programs although many employers take an active role in offering the services of managers, technical personnel, and professionals to various colleges. Students contact the employees and arrange to spend one to five days with the employee interviewing, working, and observing.

Classroom Lectures

Many employers sponsor a speakers bureau, which contacts various employees to determine availability and interest in speaking about their area of expertise on the college campus. The availability of this service is communicated to colleges, and the speakers' services are offered free of charge. The placement office then canvasses student organizations and appropriate faculty to ascertain interest in the various programs.

When it works, this is an excellent way to open channels between various groups on campus and employers. Students learn from a firsthand experience, and the employer makes important contacts on the campus. The challenge is to find an appropriate point in a faculty member's course outline that fits neatly with the material that the guests plan to present.

Class Projects

Some employers offer meaningful, topical-related projects that a faculty member may wish to use as a class assignment. This might include preparing a marketing plan for a given product in a marketing class, costing and pricing a new product in an accounting class, designing a product or process in an engineering class, or solving a major social problem in a social science class. The project or case is complete with data, products, tools, and other facts that make the project a real world problem in the classroom.

Career Planning Seminars

The placement office frequently offers students an opportunity to participate in career planning seminars or courses. Man-

agers, professionals, engineers, personnel representatives, etc.,
frequently are invited to participate. These sessions may revolve around a presentation on a given career field or a part of
the career search process. The presentations vary from a single
guest to panels and last from one hour to several days.

These presentations offer students a chance to get answers to
many of their questions. The credibility of the outside expert
aids in raising the level of career awareness for students. Employers appreciate the invitation to assist because it opens the
door for increased involvement in the career planning and
placement process.

Group Meetings

Sometimes more students express interest in an employer
than the employer is able to interview, and the employer is
frequently willing to set up a large group meeting. Although
such meetings are not interviews, they serve a similar function
in that students may screen themselves out of consideration for
a given assignment. The information provided in group meetings is designed to adequately describe the various career
openings available.

Group meetings may be called by an employer the day before the campus interviews for all of the job candidates on the
schedule. Much time in the interview process can be saved for
evaluative purposes if basic questions and descriptions can be
discussed in a group setting. This process makes the actual interview much more productive for both parties, but it con-
sumes a larger time commitment by candidates and recruiters.

Facility Visits

An excellent way to introduce students to the world of work
is to take them to the work setting in groups. Spending a day
with a group of five to ten students involves the employer in

the educational process and gives students a realistic under-standing of what to expect upon entering a selected career field. Field trips and plant visits are not as effective as a longer term co-op or internship experience, but they do offer many of the same benefits to students and employers.

As in a classroom lecture, the important point is that the trip be organized and structured as a learning experience. Ideally, the visit is preceded by a study plan and succeeded by a review of the experience. The type of program depends largely on the type of employer and common interests of the students. The program creates some positive interrelations between the col-lege and employer and continues to benefit both parties as the experience is shared by the students with other students.

Career Conferences

The career conference is more of a learning experience than a job placement program. Through a coordinated effort, often through the career planning and placement function, a large group of students, counselors, faculty, and employers are brought together for a program with multiple goals. Students are counselled, employers hire a few people, college and em-ployer personnel communicate concerns, and most participants walk away feeling that the activity produced something for them.

Career conferences demand tremendous amounts of work as many diverse populations must be reached. In addition to bringing together the participants, a program needs to be pre-pared. Rarely does the "mill around" approach produce the maximum amount of information sharing. Given that each group is willing to invest the time, money, and creative thought, a successful conference can produce lasting results for improved college-employer relations.

Executives in the Classroom

Students can learn about the world of work by meeting with executives. Bringing the high-level executive into the classroom for a presentation and follow-up discussion materially adds new career information that could not be obtained in any other way. Even on the job, few employees get to interact in this manner with a chief executive officer.

Many executives want the opportunity to gain this interactive experience and find it a two-way learning process. Happenings on campus occasionally may be screened out of the everyday life of executives, and an exposure to the campus scene opens new vistas. Students learn that the top is not as isolated as often imagined. This type of program is best coordinated by top university administrators and faculty, but frequently the driving forces are the college placement staff and the employer's college relations staff. The long-term effects of this activity may be shared for months as students and employer personnel discuss it in various settings.

Show-and-Tell Programs

Some joint programs between employers and colleges have little lasting impact because the participants leave the organization. Students graduate; faculty and employer personnel leave or are promoted. Colleges and employers should, therefore, look especially close at programs that have longer term effects. Usually this is best accomplished by programs that encourage contacts at mid-level management points in both organizations. Good examples are senior placement personnel, faculty and administrators about the assistant professor level, top-level personnel managers, and middle management and department heads.

An effective way to get these people together is for employers (or college personnel) to prepare an in-house, show-and-tell-program and invite the other group to it. Employers often invite placement and faculty from several colleges to attend such a program, most frequently during the summer months. These programs offer an excellent interchange of ideas.

Summary

Employers of college graduates have much to gain from getting involved in the educational process. Becoming involved means developing a close working relationship with a reasonable number of academic institutions. Although employment of college graduates may be the principal dividend, many other benefits accrue to the conscientious employer. Because of its strategic location within the educational institution, the career planning and placement program is a logical unit to serve as a facilitator of communications.

CHAPTER 12

EXTERNAL RELATIONS

COMMUNICATION WITH POTENTIAL employers is a planned program that utilizes all forms of media. The career planning and placement function is responsible for initiating contacts that utilize personal methods, publications, or the news media. Use of the news media must become part of an overall strategy to bring public awareness to placement and enhance the employer's desire to use the career services.

The printed and spoken word represents one of the most powerful forces utilized in the career planning and placement function. The entire career planning process rests upon the communications foundation. Dissemination of information sparks the cycle to an active mode and impacts upon all involved parties: students, faculty, administrators, managers, personnel staffs, and the general public. Because of the long-term societal implications, the public must hold a basic awareness of actions and circumstances occurring in institutions of higher education.

As a convenience, the arena of effective communications is labeled external relations. This goal-directed effort is aimed at providing information designed to raise the level of career awareness of carefully chosen publics. External relations represent a collection of efforts to educate and inform, using various forms of communication tools. The thrust is to reach out to the various groups that rely upon the placement profession for information.

Successful external relations bring together people who hold common concerns. Resulting from the mutual concerns, a variety of courses of action often emerge. External relations attempt to organize a sharing of information that impacts upon the lives of the constituencies involved.

Development of Contacts

The heart of every successful career planning and placement office beats to the tune of two important drummers: students and employers. Failure comes when either one of the ventricles stops pumping. Although the student population is given, use of the service by students who pass by daily is not a natural occurrence. Students use the service only when they know about it, know what it provides, and respect its past success record. The flow of information to students is not a simple or inexpensive process, but the traditional channels of communications, especially the grapevine, work reasonably well.

The channels of communication to employers pose far more complex problems. Employers do not represent a homogeneous group that lends itself to concrete definitions. Employers represent an amorphous group of people who have an interest in developing working relationships (often related more to employment than college relations) with a selected group of colleges. The employer may not realize the college service is needed until approached by either a personal contact or mail solicitation. Complex considerations arise as colleges ascertain the most appropriate method of contact and the frequency of contacts.

As in most professions, the placement professional must develop a given clientele. The clientele seldom use the service on an exclusive basis, but a major characteristic is frequent use. The once or twice a year, out-of-town visitor deserves the same service as steady customers. Rarely, however, is that client the bread and butter of the career service. The most valued employer client uses most of the services offered, not just on-campus recruiting.

Development of contact lists is an important activity and might initially consume the energies of a great many people. Without well-defined clientele lists, placement professionals stumble over each other, and much money is spent on useless mailings and non-productive personal contacts. Colleges cannot afford to squander resources on uncooperative employers any more than employers can continue to work with colleges that do not produce results consistent with defined goals. One classification of contacts might appear as follows.

Directory of Employers. A directory of employers prepared by the placement office lists all of the employers who have hired students or reported job openings within the past two years. A directory that contains contacts over two years old is likely to be out-of-date and disruptive in some job searches. Directories contain the organization's name, unit (division, agency, or department), address, city, state, zip code, and central telephone. Frequently more than one person (or location) represents the organization. Each personal contact's name, title, unit, address, and telephone number is required because this is the contact needed by all college personnel and students in order to reach the organization.

The directory of employers serves as the primary contact tool and description of the employer clientele. The directory often includes names submitted by faculty, administrators, students, and others. Sources are not limited to placement staff, but it is the responsibility of the placement staff to cull and evaluate the quality of potential contacts.

The employment directory published by the placement office is not a rehash of directories available in public libraries. Well-trained students know how to take the initiative and locate other names and addresses. The directory of employers published by the placement office is a source of names who hold a special interest in graduates from the college and maintain continuous contacts and an excellent rapport and working arrangement.

In some organizations, the recruiting function is centralized or coordinated by a single unit. The directory of employers should contain some notation of those specific instances to avoid unnecessary contacts with organization personnel who must simply forward inquiries about employment to a key person. Other personnel within the organization should still be included because these contacts often are the people that most frequently interface with college personnel. Since the directory is often a source of mailing labels to send materials, individual names are important as these contacts must continue to learn and grow in knowledge about the college in an effort to strengthen ties.

Prospect Lists. The prospect list is an internal working document of the placement office used by the staff in developing a relationship with potential employers. Just as no placement office can afford to maintain contact sources that represent the universe, placement offices cannot afford to sit back and rest on laurels. A continuous effort to expand the directory of employers is needed. The prospect list represents a realistic missionary and outreach activity to broaden the sphere of influence of the college.

Prospect lists should be no larger than the directory of employers as a general rule because the ability to serve employer clientele might be greatly impaired if such an effort materialized. It is wiser to serve a limited clientele extremely well than to provide poor service for everyone.

The potential for employer prospects to turn into meaningful contacts varies by employer. Employers with an employment interest in the type of graduate from a given college are much more likely to become positive contacts and working partners with the college. The potential of a liberal arts college wooing an engineering consultant contact, even if located next door, is not high nor likely productive from either party's perspective. Organizations on the prospect list might, therefore, be classified as excellent, good, doubtful, etc. Efforts to expand contact sources must be approached on a realistic basis in order to avoid expensive and time-consuming, non-productive results.

Alumni Contacts. For many colleges, alumni employed in organizations that frequently hire college students represent an important source of external relations contacts. This special list may not include information on every alumnus but it should zero in on alumni who can influence employment of graduates or have an impact upon the college relations functions for their organization.

Alumni contact lists may be shared with students for temporary experiential employment or career employment upon graduation. Most frequently, however, these lists are used by the placement staff. Alumni may be used in a wide variety of ways, including career panels, job search workshops, classroom lecturers, etc. Loyal alumni frequently are influential in the career employment decisions. Once the cadre of alumni have been identified as potential helpers, they should be placed on the alumni contact mailing list to receive college information and job request forms.

VIP Lists. Most colleges maintain lists of very important people who continually befriend the institution. The VIPs may be alumni, educators, executives, agency heads, professionals, politicians, business leaders, etc. The tie to the college may be through children, friends, alumni, civic concern, or for a number of often personal reasons. Influential people care about being kept informed but do not want to be badgered by petty activities. Such contacts need to be nurtured in a special way and in a manner that goes beyond general administration. VIP lists are not designed to be widely shared but become extremely valuable when unusual circumstances warrant.

Contact Summary

These four lists of college-related contacts serve as a clientele base for most career planning and placement offices. These contacts form the population that is likely to be most cooperative with the college constituencies. The external relations program is directed at these contacts in order to provide employment leads and work environment exposures to students, graduating students, faculty, and staff. The contacts bring personal realism into the process of career planing.

Publications

In an external relations program, it is not always necessary to create all of the data to be shared. Some times it is possible to distribute information already available. Colleges traditionally prepare information about the institution which is sent to prospective students, current students, faculty, news media, and alumni. Some of this information is useful to potential employers, even without a reformat or editing process. The additional bulk rate postage, brief handling required, and marginal cost for printing copies represent insignificant additional expense.

Placing college publications in the hands of employers accomplishes more than just providing information. It also shows that the college is concerned about and interested in the employer. Receipt of college publications reminds the employer about the services offered.

Every contact with an employer, whether personally or through a publication, is not designed to drive the employer to a high state of activity. Contacts gently nudge employers to consider establishing or re-establishing closer working relationships with the institution. If every employer in the nation suddenly were inundated with mail, a problem would exist. Employers traditionally have a circle of colleges with whom they work. There is a limit to each party's span and scope of control, and this is why development of key contact sources is extremely important. If the placement office maintains a reasonable population horizon, the situation is not likely to fly out of control.

Placement Handbooks. Placement handbooks are directed to students and contain the guidelines, procedures, and regulations for using the services of the career planning and placement office. These handbooks describe the range of services offered and define who is eligible to use them. Most contain a list of the organizations planning to recruit on campus.

Some colleges prepare handbook-type publications and finance them through advertising. The majority of colleges prepare and publish the handbook using college-budgeted funding. In most cases, the publication is a rather extensive, attractive document that contains a wealth of valuable career information.

Although the publication is not designed to serve employers, it can play a role in helping the employer understand the plight and concern of students. Empathy goes a long way in opening communications.

Recruiting Packets. Whether the on-campus recruiting volume at a college is large or small, instructions need to be provided to visiting employers. In non-recruiting employer visits, instructions similar to those in a recruiting packet need to be provided in advance of the visit. An attractive, informative, and complete recruiting packet is an essential ingredient in the publications program of a career planning and placement office. No college can afford to risk alienating contacts regardless of the purpose of the visit. Positive external relations begin with the impression left by the materials received from the school.

The contents of a recruiting packet may vary by campus and by the purpose of the employer visit. Most packets include the following information:

1. Campus map
2. Parking instructions (permits)
3. Finding the university and office
4. Itinerary (times and activities)
5. College information
6. Career services offered
7. Specific curriculums and programs
8. Accommodations (if necessary)
9. Special instructions

These items are not simply nice amenities, but essential. Updated recruiting packets must be sent to employers prior to every planned visit. In addition, they can be sent to employer prospects in an effort to establish working relationships.

Placement Brochures. The placement brochure is analogous to the placement handbook except that its message is directed to the employer. The placement brochure is designed to explain and promote the various services offered by the college placement office to potential employer users of the services. In a sense, the brochure advertises the services but frequently omits much of the detailed procedures involved in an employer's use of the services. The brochure strives to induce the potential employer to want to become involved in joint working arrangements or to expand existing relationships.

The brochures tend to be expensive to prepare because they are often professionally designed and printed. Many brochures are just one page, both sides in color print, and folded to insert in a No. 10 envelope with a personal or form letter. Some large schools with publications staffs may prepare multi-page brochures not unlike those sent by large employers to campuses.

Placement brochures need to be sent at least every two years to all key contacts as part of a strategically planned communications program. All requests from employers for information should be answered with the placement brochure and an individually typed letter introducing the college and inviting the employer to participate in the various activities. Correspondence to all new employer prospects should be accompanied by the placement brochure. In addition to being a mail piece, the brochure should be versatile enough to serve as a source of information to be distributed in person or as part of displays of various types. The brochure, with complete return mailing information, should accompany all job solicitation requests.

Placement brochures should briefly discuss each of the services offered to employers, including on-campus recruitment, job listings, candidate referrals, resume availability, speaking arrangements, and other nonrecruiting services. As design and financial resources permit, a brief description of how to utilize the services is appropriate. By using photographs, illustrative forms, and unique graphics and design, the facts can be presented in an interesting format, enabling the reader to quickly scan the material and review it later as time and circumstances permit.

Many placement brochures offer a short history of the college, location, size, organization structure, and list important administrative and faculty personnel. Brochures often give a brief description of some of the various academic programs.

Whether simple or extensive, placement brochures leave an accurate picture of the institutions in the hands of constituencies outside of the immediate university community. From a function and cost perspective, placement brochures represent an essential communication tool and are an important element of the external relations of every career planning and placement office.

College Bulletins. Requests for college bulletins and catalogs frequently come to the career planning and placement office. Bulletins are used by employers to evaluate various academic programs in order to determine compatibility with specific career openings in their organizations. In some instances, employers simply wish to investigate the availability of specific programs, to learn more detailed information about the institution, or to share the information with current employees who may be considering continuing education on a full- or part-time basis.

Placement offices should arrange a system for sharing bulletins with employers. The bulletins should always contain a section on placement services that might be adequate for both students and employers. Bulletins and other college-related publications should be included in the publications arsenal of well-managed career planning and placement services.

Employer Newsletters. Employers want to know what is happening on campus. Most employers do not subscribe to campus newspapers or have the time to rummage through all of the campus news to spot items of special interest. The placement office offers a unique service by summarizing information and feeding it to employer contacts on a consistent, periodic basis through a newsletter.

Few colleges currently offer a newsletter service. By using bulk postage and simple printing, the newsletter is inexpensive and may take less than ten hours per month to prepare. The mailing can be limited to key employment contacts, rather than the list of all contacts.

Another related idea is to send any material to employers that leaves the university from other sources, such as the news bureau, development or foundation office, and alumni office. The medium is not as important as getting college news in abbreviated form into the hands of employers. The sharing of internal information can only strengthen the bonds that tie colleges and employers together.

Publications Summary

The list of potential informational items that may be shared with outside constituencies extends beyond placement handbooks, recruiting packets, placement brochures, bulletins, and newsletters. Colleges print a wide variety of publications that may be very helpful in keeping employers apprised of the campus scene.

However, sending everything available to employers is worse than sending nothing. Information must be screened and limits must be placed on the timing and frequency to help insure that the employer is not inundated with campus materials which would be impossible to review. The list of employers should also be screened and limited to individuals who are responsible for developing close working ties with the institution. Creation of the mailing list is as important as screening the material and planning the distribution.

A planned program of sharing campus news and placement information with employers can greatly enhance the perceived image of the career planning and placement service. An organized and well-managed external relations effort helps foster an environment that encourages strong relationships between colleges and outside organizations that need a role in the educational process. Such a role greatly aids the career planning of individual students.

Personal Contacts

A career planning and placement service that relies primarily on the printed word to reach students or employers cannot succeed any more than a service that relies solely on word of mouth. Effective communication means the difference between success and failure. The personal contact with students, employers, and other constituencies is an essential ingredient of communication success. A personal approach, combined with printed materials, makes for a successful placement service.

Effectiveness in personal contact depends upon personality and sincerity. A predominately introverted person finds success difficult in both counseling and external relations because success is frequently measured by the ability to get diverse population groups talking with each other. Creating this environment requires a person who feels comfortable in various work settings and who has the ability to spot common areas of concern and interest and bring the parties together. Frequently years of experience are required to develop the maturity and finesse needed.

Even the old pro faces frustration, pain, disappointment, and challenge in the personal contact arena. Failure to break through cliques, defeats in democratic and political selection processes, putdowns, reprimands, and occasional blunders become part of the game. Status and personal gains rise and fall. Dealing with a variety of constituencies with diverse goals means occasional failure. Given the wide range of activities of the career planning and placement service, leaders invariably find themselves in politically sensitive arenas. Unique abilities are needed to function successfully in work settings involving academia, business pressures, and government procedures. Walking a tightrope is frequently necessary.

With that admonishment and warning, let us look at the specific settings in which personal contacts must be initiated and conducted. The constituencies involved include faculty, administrators, counselors, and students on the college side and executives, managers, technical personnel, personnel staffs, etc. on the employer side. Another important interface is the professional in other placement offices. Frequently this contact is through professional associations, but it may be on a more personal basis. Personal contacts tend to bring the various parties together in a manner that fosters harmonious relationships and joint working arrangements.

Campus Relations

The first and foremost external responsibility of the placement director is to get to know the campus community. Respect, rapport, and support from the campus community must precede any efforts to develop contacts outside the institution. The commitment means gaining concurrence from the various groups regarding the stated goals, structure, and proposed plans of action of the career service. Obtaining this support requires an initial and continuing strategy to establish lines of campus communication and to keep the channels clear. Placement impacts upon many facets of the campus, but five areas tend to be key support elements.

Faculty. An unsupportive faculty can kill the best laid plans for offering career services to students and external organizations. A supportive faculty forms one of the most influential bases needed to insure success in a career service. Faculty traditionally have become involved in the career planning process, even on campuses where the number of students far surpasses the ability of the faculty to individually counsel them. In most institutions, the faculty initially planned the program that is now known as student services and only in recent years have they relinquished part of the responsibility to student personnel specialists.

Even young faculty come from a background where they studied under several key mentors on a doctoral program. The mentors handled much of their professionally related career planning. Young or old, most faculty members view themselves as career consultants, especially as this relates to their disciplines.

Career service professionals can never hope to have enough staff to adequately counsel and teach all of the students who seek help. For a variety of reasons, many students turn to faculty for counsel and advice rather than the placement staff. The faculty needs to be able to answer career-related questions. The career planning and placement service must be prepared to teach faculty, answer questions, provide information, and get faculty involved in the external relations programs to the same degree as the placement staff.

Counselors. Colleges and universities employ large numbers of personnel who interact with students on a continuing basis.

Counselors are involved in psychological counseling, career counseling, advising, and academic program planning. Even clerical staffs and librarians are called upon to answer career-related inquiries of students. Some counselors are able to offer accurate advice while others are not well informed. It is the responsibility of the career planning and placement service to train all university personnel involved in the career counseling of students. Although some of this training may be accomplished with publications, gaining acceptance often requires a personal touch.

Administration. Career counseling cannot stop with faculty and counselors who must interact with students. Administrators (president, vice presidents, provosts, deans, chancellors, etc.) set policy in both academic and financial areas. These policies impact upon placement. Policies conducive to a productive career services environment can be established only if support of the service comes from top levels. It behooves every placement service to keep the administration informed.

Another important reason for keeping top college management informed is that they frequently interact with top management in organizations outside the college. Just as a college relations staff in industry informs top management on personnel policies and practices, the career planning and placement function must keep college administrators informed. Personal contact on a regular basis is one of the best ways to keep administrators aware of current conditions.

Admissions. Career counseling clearly is not the sole domain of the career services staff. Admissions officers interact daily with students contemplating attending a college. Invariably the students ask questions about job prospects. Unfortunately, some admissions officers are overlooked in the process of sharing career information and, at best, can give only a hedged reply. Admissions recruiters are often on the road meeting with high school groups and must respond to inquiries from prospective students and parents on career possibilities. Although admissions officers should seek the most accurate information, the career services should offer the information without the prod.

Some legislation may soon require that admissions and financial aid staff give prospective students definitive placement results of past graduates. Legislation is not required; professional, service-oriented career planning and placement personnel are required. Admissions staffs and placement staffs need to develop a closer working atmosphere.

Development Staff. The most logical donors to a college are alumni and employers of a college's graduates. Both groups have a stake in the future and well-being of the institution. The placement service offers one of the best sources of information on the names of employers hiring graduates in recent years. A communications channel must be established between development staff and placement staff if the right hand is to know what the left hand is doing. Without coordinated efforts between development and placement, the external relations impact looks shabby to outside contacts. A personal understanding and appreciation of mutual problems and concerns between placement and development is essential in achieving maximum results from each group's work with organizations outside the college.

Campus Relations Summary

Personal contacts include people in the campus community who are in roles that impact upon the career planning and placement service. The career service must train, utilize, and get these individuals involved in the external relations of the program. No career service can stand alone in the counseling of students. It must reach out to the community for assistance in this function. Personal contacts need to be established and used in bringing together career information from outside the campus that can be used to serve the career planning needs of the student body.

Employer Relations

Government agencies, business firms, industrial organizations, and other employers of college graduates want to provide an interactive input into the career decisions made by college students. Often, organizations not in the immediate campus structure do not know how they can offer service that can be readily communicated, directly or indirectly, to students, faculty, and counselors. One of the roles of the career services office is to bring external organizations together with the campus community.

Before parties can be brought together in a meaningful dialog, the career services facility must have the respect of and a rapport with all parties on a rather personal basis. Requests from strangers to an employer seeking participation in a campus program probably will receive less consideration than requests that emanate from someone the employer knows well and trusts. The personal touch has a positive influence on decisions.

The placement office is not the only campus source for personal contacts with external organizations and important people in them. But given a regular working relationship, the likelihood of a placement professional knowing individuals in outside organizations is much stronger than for almost any other unit on campus.

Developing personal contacts with a select external constituency does not occur naturally. A concerted effort is required; but nurturing external contacts is important in the career planning function because these contacts are the key people most likely to provide career information that is based on a work situation.

The college community looks to the placement function for leadership in providing resource people as needed. Placement services that consistently fail to provide meaningful external contacts quickly lose some influence on the campus. Nothing can replace the personal one-on-one relationship between placement leaders and external contacts.

Professional Meetings. Professional meetings provide one of the greatest opportunities for creating and nurturing personal friendships. The major purpose for attending such meetings is to renew knowledge about the profession and return to the campus with fresh ideas and challenging plans for the future. In addition to the spiritual revitalization, building close relationships with colleagues at other institutions and with employer representatives is an important secondary objective. Attendance at professional meetings can have multiple goals.

The socialization process between college and employer representatives is a far stronger positive benefit to both organizations than most people realize. Each person is unique in interests, personality, and ability. Two people who understand each other's position are far more likely to work well together. The social bonds have a way of becoming professionally active ties, particularly over long time frames.

Jam-packed recruiting schedules often preclude the placement staff from really getting to know employer representatives as they come to campus. Professional meetings let one get away from the daily pressures and into a situation where new learning can occur in an environment that is conducive to establishing new friendships and renewing others.

In many ways, the development of new contacts at professional meetings, whether in small workshops or large conferences, is not a natural byproduct. College representatives must go out of their way to meet and interact with a wide variety of people. Professional programs are not college sales conventions, but such programs do present an opportunity to share information. In addition to the learning-oriented program and the socialization, much institutional business is accomplished, but that should be an extra benefit rather than a major concern.

The career planning and placement professional who overlooks the importance of local, regional, and national professional meetings and workshops is missing an opportunity to grow professionally, make contacts, and promote efforts that bring important results to their campuses.

Professional Committees. The work of most large professional groups is rarely completed in large meetings or by a small cadre of elected officers. Elected officers usually set policy and pass on the work to various committees. Participation in committees means commitment to the profession. Most committees represent an even distribution of college and employer representation, and close ties between college and employer representatives can result from committee work. Committee work has far more meaning than the initial outcome of the problem or project being addressed.

Committee participation by both placement and employer groups keeps the profession alive. That fact is rarely evident in any one meeting, but the collective impact of many members and different committees working with each other generates the combined force that turns drudgery into action. The smaller group offers a more cohesive effect, and the results almost always relate to the total membership's wishes. Involvement in committee work is a sound investment in money and time that pays long-term dividends.

Campus Programs. With a goal of obtaining and sharing career information, career planning and placement offices serve as catalysts in bringing campus groups together with employer representatives. Career services staff assist student leaders by offering suggestions for various activities that relate to professional development. Student groups frequently solicit opinions and help from cooperative career services officials. The staff, however, must do more than wait for student requests; it must plan a student outreach program.

Employer representatives rarely turn down responsible opportunities to involve themselves in the daily life of student activities. The motive may not necessarily be employment of students or even professional development. The motive may simply be fun and social interest. Fireside chats, brown bag luncheons, fraternal dinners, etc. are positive elements in strengthening relationships between campus and outside orga-

nizations. Academic-oriented student groups can play a similar role.

Academic Programs. One of the strongest student-motivating educational activities is involving the professionals, managers, engineers, etc. from an external organization in the classroom. Many faculty members find that integrating academic material with real case projects increases the comprehension of the course content. Although many faculty have contacts outside of the college, others, especially young faculty who began teaching immediately upon earning a terminal degree, do not have contacts. The placement staff needs to establish an outreach program to assist faculty who may need such assistance.

Involving employers in the classroom setting is not limited to engineering, research, or business fields. A great many social science problems and circumstances germane to the humanities exist in these organizations. The career service must encourage and offer assistance to both employers and faculty in integrating work experiences with academic subjects. Such a posture aids in the overall career planning process of each student.

Campus Committees. Many colleges make it a policy to invite individuals from outside the campus to sit on committees. A high percentage of decisions made by administrators in higher education result from committee recommendations. Nearly every academic department and student organization regularly has committee meetings. Input from the non-campus community is extremely valuable because of the slightly different point of view taken. Decisions based on committee recommendations that have had input from a variety of viewpoints frequently help narrow the perceived gap between the "real world" and academia's ivory tower.

The true beneficiary of such arrangements is the student body. Even if the ivory tower image is completely unjustified, the concept of accepting differing opinions strengthens the educational process. The career planning and placement service has an important role to play in suggesting appropriate individuals to include in these decision-making capacities.

Advisory Boards. For years, many of the professional schools of law, medicine, business, engineering, etc. had a policy of inviting high-level, experienced leaders in the profession to sit on policy determination boards. Advisory boards consult with college leaders, such as presidents, chancellors, deans, alumni secretaries, development and placement office heads, and offer recommendations on the general direction of a specific program.

Few placement services have traditionally played much of a role in the recommending of top executives to college administrators to serve on advisory boards. The trend may change. If external relations are effectively carried out in the future by placement directors, the placement director may be the first person to be asked for suggestions. The importance of personal contacts in external organizations cannot be overemphasized if the career services office is to gain and maintain a high-level posture within the academic community. This posture is directly tied to the ability to gain the resources required to create the type of career planning service needed by students.

Study Commissions. Study commissions are not unlike advisory boards except that they are not normally standing bodies. Their lifespan is usually limited to making recommendations on a specific, campus-related problem or investigation. Because of public relations considerations, most college leaders desire to appoint individuals with important influence to these commissions. As with advisory boards, the chief placement officer may well play an important role in the selection of candidates to be considered for appointment.

Employer Relations Summary

The placement function rests in a communications bridge between academia and outside organizations. Individuals in ex-

success is frequently measured by the ability to get diverse population groups talking with each other. Creating this environment requires a person who feels comfortable in various work settings and who has the ability to spot common areas of concern and interest and bring the parties together. Frequently years of experience are required to develop the maturity and finesse needed.

Even the old pro faces frustration, pain, disappointment, and challenge in the personal contact arena. Failure to break through cliques, defeats in democratic and political selection processes, putdowns, reprimands, and occasional blunders become part of the game. Status and personal gains rise and fall. Dealing with a variety of constituencies with diverse goals means occasional failure. Given the wide range of activities of the career planning and placement service, leaders invariably find themselves in politically sensitive arenas. Unique abilities are needed to function successfully in work settings involving academia, business pressures, and government procedures. Walking a tightrope is frequently necessary.

With that admonishment and warning, let us look at the specific settings in which personal contacts must be initiated and conducted. The constituencies involved include faculty, administrators, counselors, and students on the college side and executives, managers, technical personnel, personnel staffs, etc. on the employer side. Another important interface is the professional in other placement offices. Frequently this contact is through professional associations, but it may be on a more personal basis. Personal contacts tend to bring the various parties together in a manner that fosters harmonious relationships and joint working arrangements.

Campus Relations

The first and foremost external responsibility of the placement director is to get to know the campus community. Respect, rapport, and support from the campus community must

books, recruiting packets, placement brochures, bulletins, and newsletters. Colleges print a wide variety of publications that may be very helpful in keeping employers apprised of the campus scene.

However, sending everything available to employers is worse than sending nothing. Information must be screened and limits must be placed on the timing and frequency to help insure that the employer is not inundated with campus materials which would be impossible to review. The list of employers should also be screened and limited to individuals who are responsible for developing close working ties with the institution. Creation of the mailing list is as important as screening the material and planning the distribution.

A planned program of sharing campus news and placement information with employers can greatly enhance the perceived image of the career planning and placement service. An organized and well-managed external relations effort helps foster an environment that encourages strong relationships between colleges and outside organizations that need a role in the educational process. Such a role greatly aids the career planning of individual students.

Personal Contacts

A career planning and placement service that relies primarily on the printed word to reach students or employers cannot succeed any more than a service that relies solely on word of mouth. Effective communication means the difference between success and failure. The personal contact with students, employers, and other constituencies is an essential ingredient of communication success. A personal approach, combined with printed materials, makes for a successful placement service.

Effectiveness in personal contact depends upon personality and sincerity. A predominately introverted person finds success difficult in both counseling and external relations because

ternal organizations often want to contribute to the education of students but have no mechanism for making their wishes known to institutions of higher education. Colleges need the advice, knowledge, and input of these individuals, especially as it aids students in the self-analysis, career exploration, and career search aspects of career planning. Involvement of outsiders in the educational process requires the opening of channels of communication.

If the placement service is successful in developing personal contacts, it can serve as a catalyst in this communications process. The specific methods for involving non-campus personnel in the educational process are too numerous to mention, but none of the methods can even be started unless career services personnel take the initiative to establish and nurture personal contacts. This requires placement office policies and procedures that support external relations. Such policies must begin at high leadership levels.

Alumni Relations

Alumni relations represent an important part of external relations because, unlike employers, alumni already hold a loyalty commitment to the college. Obviously, overlap exists between employer relations and alumni relations because many alumni move into managerial, technical, and professional assignments in a variety of organizations. In some ways, alumni relations are somewhat easier to maintain than employer relations, for the motivation to work with the college is already present.

Most of the points about interactions with the campus community discussed in the section on employer relations apply equally to alumni relations. However, in alumni relations the career services staff has a head start because the population is readily identifiable and willing to assist. For the same investment in time, money, and effort, a sound alumni relations program can be much more productive.

The career planning and placement office is not the center of alumni relations, but liaison with the alumni secretary or association assists in building important personal contacts for the placement service. The alumni contacts provide yet another avenue for expanding personal relationships to constituencies outside of the career service.

Effective alumni relations involve two primary sources: (1) interaction through alumni activities (group or individual), and (2) publications. Getting involved in activities or publications is consistent with satisfying the long-term goals of a career planning and placement service.

Activities. The motivation to help is usually present in alumni, but transferring the desire into action requires organizational leadership. Alumni must be asked to help; few volunteer. The results are worth the initial planning efforts because, once started, a snowballing parade of volunteers soliciting other volunteers often follows. Placement needs to light the fire, but a well conceived program may have lasting impact.

Many alumni activities center around major events that occur on a regular basis on campus, such as homecomings, founder's days, sporting events, or other traditional activities. Placement leaders may want to piggyback on these campus activities to involve the alumni in the classroom or meetings with current student groups or individuals. Alumni tend to serve as role models for students, particularly if the alumni have been highly successful.

The placement service may wish to create the on-campus activity and make the theme career centered. Building an educational experience into the social-centered atmosphere of returning alumni often gives students a less formal learning environment but one that is equally as fruitful. Communicating with students, faculty, and alumni can only generate positive results in the career planning process.

All alumni activities need not be on the campus. It may be necessary to take part of the campus community to the major alumni population centers. Where there are large concentrations of alumni, it makes good sense to take a limited number of faculty and administrators to the site to insure greater alumni participation. This may be in the form of evening reception, dinners, luncheons, local club events, and may involve a small group of alumni leaders, alumni with influence, or large open events to which everyone is invited. Regardless of the type and scope of the activity, the goal remains the same: development of personal contacts which can be used in a variety of ways to assist current students in career planning.

Alumni can be used in programs that advance the overall mission of the college. Some of these programs leave more of an exhilarating feeling for alumni when they see that their efforts significantly influenced the college's goals. Three examples of such programs are described below.

1. *Student Recruiting.* Recruiting high-quality students for the college is not an easy task, for competition for the top students is keen. Other colleges are also seeking the best. Alumni can assist admissions officers by calling on principals, counselors, and other personnel in their area to explain the college's program. Another approach is for the college to send names of specific potential students to alumni with the request that the students be contacted and given some personal first-hand information about the college.

2. *Employment Networks.* Many alumni may know of career openings or they may even be in a position to do the hiring. Regular solicitation of career openings is often effective in providing the college with a wealth of job information to be shared with students.

3. *Fund Raising.* The solicitation of funds to expand and operate institutions of higher education may appear to be crass, but the necessity is a reality for both public and private institutions. Alumni may be effective in contacting other alumni and organizations likely to support the college.

Alumni Activities Summary

Promotion of alumni activities is helpful to both the college and the career services function. Alumni represent a cadre of dedicated volunteers who often are eager to offer their time and effort to assist. To be especially helpful in the career planning and placement service, organization and management cannot be left to chance. Alumni get involved only if asked. An effective career service needs assistance from a variety of sources, and one means that often is productive is alumni activities. The contacts made through participation in such activities over the years provide important returns that enhance the career planning organization on campus.

Alumni Publications

The best sources of contacts remain those which are developed personally, but that luxury is not always possible. People become known because their name remains in the limelight. Alumni publications represent one way in which news about the career planning and placement service can be kept in the forefront of the alumnus' memory. Alumni contribute to many facets of a successful career service, and support can bring a much improved service to students.

Most alumni associations publish newsletters and/or magazines that provide news about the campus community. Every-one is interested in placement because it frequently impacts upon their personal lives or that of a friend or relative. Regular and frequent news about placement status, salary averages, new programs, etc. reminds alumni of the importance of the service and provides them with career-related information that is useful in their lifelong career planning. Placement news says the college cares about students and alumni.

Alumni offer their services upon request only if they feel that participation is a worthwhile venture. News reinforces the positive attitudes and, through personal contact, alumni will be more likely to contribute when asked.

External Relations Summary

The career planning and placement office serves many masters even though the primary audience is students. In order to successfully serve students, channels of communication must be opened between the campus community and the work environment. Realistic career planning never takes place in a sterile, isolated environment. Attention to external relations opens the appropriate channels that permit a free flow of career information.

Successful external relations requires commitment of time, money, and people. Developing contacts demands a supportive policy from high-level administration and a strategy for maximizing use of various types of relevant contacts. Populations need to be defined and efforts need to be made to reach the people involved on a systematic basis. The contacts may be developed and nurtured by mail solicitation, but a key element remains the one-on-one approach.

The central role of placement in external relations is to serve as a catalyst in bringing all parties together for a common purpose. The purpose is to assist in the various phases of career planning: self-assessment, career exploration, and career search. The result is an optimal career choice by students after compromises which are based on "real world" considerations.